SPURGEON ON THE PSALMS

BOOK THREE

Psalm 51 through Psalm 79

CHARLES H. SPURGEON

Compiled and Edited by Beverlee J. Chadwick

BRIDGE LOGOS

Alachua, Florida 32615

Bridge-Logos
Alachua, FL 32615 USA

Spurgeon on the Psalms: Book Three
Charles H. Spurgeon
Compiled and Edited by Beverlee J. Chadwick

Copyright ©2015 Bridge-Logos, Inc.

All rights reserved. Under International Copyright Law, no part of this publication may be reproduced, stored, or transmitted by any means—electronic, mechanical, photographic (photocopy), recording, or otherwise—without written permission from the Publisher.

Printed in the United States of America.

Library of Congress Catalog Card Number: 2015946337
International Standard Book Number 978-1-61036-145-3

Scripture quotations are from the *King James Version* of the Bible.

CH 08-27-15

SPURGEON ON THE PSALMS

Book Three

Psalm 51 through Psalm 79

Table of Contents

Foreword	1
Preface	3
Psalm 51	7
Psalm 52	23
Psalm 53	29
Psalm 54	35
Psalm 55	41
Psalm 56	59
Psalm 57	69
Psalm 58	77
Psalm 59	85
Psalm 60	97
Psalm 61	109
Psalm 62	117
Psalm 63	125
Psalm 64	133
Psalm 65	139
Psalm 66	151
Psalm 67	165
Psalm 68	171
Psalm 69	197
Psalm 70	223
Psalm 71	225
Psalm 72	240
Psalm 73	255
Psalm 74	269
Psalm 75	283
Psalm 76	289
Psalm 77	295
Psalm 78	307
Psalm 79	355
Study Guide	365

Foreword

PSALMS FIFTY-ONE through seventy-nine in Volume Three reveal the great psalmist David's heartfelt guilt and loneliness of personal penitence but are equally well adapted for a gathering of those poor in spirit. We know that David wrote seventy-two psalms and, it is most likely, at least fifty more. Some writers have denied that David authored all of them, including Psalm 51; however this psalm reflects David's style without question and is not likely to have been imitated. Indeed, it would be far easier to imitate Milton, Shakespeare, or Tennyson than David. His style is sui generis.[1] David's penitent spirit was due to his sin with Bathsheba, and when the prophet Nathan delivered his divine message, it pricked David's conscience and made David see the greatness of his guilt, which resulted in his writing this psalm. He had set aside his psalmody while indulging his flesh, but returned to his harp when his spiritual nature awakened, and he poured out his song with sighs and tears to his God, who forgave His erring King of Israel.

These inspired psalms are an excellent example to both the redeemed and the unredeemed of the forgiveness and love of God.

Charles H. Spurgeon's expositions throughout Volume Three are timeless and will motivate, inspire, and bring all who read them spiritual growth and a new dimension in their relationship with our triune God.

Always and ever to His glory and praise,
Beverlee J. Chadwick, Senior Editor
Bridge-Logos Inc.

---

1. not like any other

Preface

THIS VOLUME completes one half of the labor upon this priceless book, and my humble prayer is that I may be spared to conclude the other portions. So uncertain is human life and so often have men's best designs remained unfinished, that I will press on with all diligence, lest, perhaps, the lamp of life may go out before the writer has seen by its light the word FINIS at the conclusion of the last verse.

This volume has cost more labor than any other, because upon the larger proportion of the psalms contained in it no great writers have expatiated at length. Some six or seven of them are specially notable, and long, and have, therefore, been expounded and preached upon on all hands, but the rest remain untrodden ground in sacred literature, hence the gathering of extracts has required a wider range of reading and far more laborious research. Where one author writes on a portion of Scripture, all write, while other passages remain almost untouched.

This has driven me much more to the Latin authors and in them to a vein of exposition very little worked in these days. The neglect of these voluminous expositors is, however, not very censurable[2], for as a rule the authors are rather heavy than weighty, "Art is long and life is short;"[3] hence I found myself unequal to the unaided accompaniment of my task, and I have had to call in the aid of my excellent friend Mr. Gracey, the accomplished classical tutor of "the Pastor's College," to assist me in the work of winnowing the enormous heaps of Latin comments. Huge folios full of word spinning yield here and there a few goodly grains, and these, I trust,

---

2. deserving of blame
3. aphorism by the ancient Greek physician Hippocrates

will be valuable enough to my readers to repay my coadjutor[4] and myself for our pains. For the selection of extracts I alone am responsible, for the accuracy of the translations we are jointly accountable. The reader will note that not without much expense of money, as well as toil, he has here furnished to his hand the pith[5] of Venema, LeBlanc, Lorinus, Gerhohus, Musculus, Martin Geier, Mollerus, and Simon de Muis, with occasional notes from Vitringa, Jansenius, Turrecrematta, Marloratus, Palanterius, Savonarola, Vatablus Theodoret, and others as they were judged worthy of insertion. I can truly say that I have never flinched from a difficulty, or spared exertion to make the work as complete as it lay in my power to render it, either by my own endeavors or the help of others. My faithful amanuensis,[6] Mr. Keys, has been spared to me, and has been a continual visitor at the British Museum, Lamberth Palace, Dr. Williams' Museum and Sion College, and many have been the courtesies which, despite difference of creed, I have received in his person from those who are in authority in these treasuries of literature; all for which I now would record my hearty thanks.

No object has been before me but that of serving the Church and glorifying God by doing this work right thoroughly. I cannot hope to be remunerated pecuniarily; if only the bare outlay be met I shall we well content, the rest is an offering to the best of Masters, whose word is meat and drink to those who study it. The enjoyment of the work is more than sufficient reward, and the hope of helping my brethren in their biblical studies is very sweet to me.

The late increase of wages of printers, and the rise both of paper and binding may compel an advance in the very

---
4. assistant
5. the choicest or most essential or most vital part of the works of the sixteen men listed
6. literary or artistic assistant or stenographer

Preface

low price charged for these volumes hitherto, but this shall not be made unless it becomes absolutely necessary to screen me from loss. As a larger sale will secure the return of my outlay, the matter is mainly in the hands of the public. Volume One, now being in the third edition, and the Second edition of Volume Two, being upon the press, I am led to hope that the present volume will also meet with a large and rapid sale; and if so, the old price will suffice to cover the outlay.

There is no need to multiply words in the preface, but it is incumbent upon me to bless the Lord for help given, help daily and hourly sought while I have been occupied in this service; and it is also on my heart to ask a favorable mention of my volumes among their friends from those who kindly appreciate them.

— C. H. Spurgeon

Psalm 51

Psalm 51:1–Psalm 51:19

Psalm 51:1 *Have mercy upon me, O God, according to thy lovingkindness: according unto the multitude of thy tender mercies blot out my transgressions.*

EXPOSITION: Verse 1. *Have mercy upon me, O God.* He appeals at once to the mercy of God, even before he mentions his sin. The sight of mercy is good for eyes that are sore with penitential weeping. Pardon of sin must ever be an act of pure mercy, and therefore to that attribute the awakened sinner flies. *According to thy lovingkindness.* Act, O Lord, like yourself; give mercy like your mercy. Show mercy such as is congruous[7] with your grace.

> Great God, thy nature hath no bound:[8]
> So let thy pardoning love be found.

What a choice word is that of our English version, a rare compound of precious things: love and kindness sweetly

---

7. compatible
8. hymn: *Show Pity, Lord! O Lord Forgive* by Isaac Watts, 1710

blended in one—lovingkindness. *According unto the multitude of thy tender mercies.* Let your most loving compassions come to me, and make your pardons such as these would suggest. Reveal all your gentlest attributes in my case, not only in their essence but in their abundance. Numberless have been your acts of goodness, and vast is your grace; let me be the object of your infinite mercy, and repeat it all in me. By every deed of grace to others I feel encouraged, and I pray you let me add another and a yet greater one, in my own person, to the long list of your compassions.

Blot out my transgressions. Draw your pen through the register. Obliterate the record, though now it seems graven in the rock forever; many strokes of your mercy may be needed, to cut out the deep inscription, but then you have a multitude of mercies, and therefore, I beseech you, erase my sins.

Psalm 51:2 *Wash me thoroughly from mine iniquity, and cleanse me from my sin.*

EXPOSITION: Verse 2. *Wash me thoroughly.* It is not enough to blot out the sin; his person is defiled, and he fain[9] would be purified. He would have God himself cleanse him, for none but He could do it effectually. The washing must be thorough, it must be repeated, and therefore he cries, "Multiply to wash me." The dye is in itself immovable, and I, the sinner, have lain long in it, until the crimson is ingrained; but, Lord, wash, and wash, and wash again, until the last stain is gone, and not a trace of my defilement is left. *Wash me thoroughly from mine iniquity.* The one sin against Bathsheba served to show the psalmist the whole mountain of his iniquity, of which that foul deed was but

---
9. willingly desires

one falling stone. He desires to be rid of the whole mass of his filthiness, which though once so little observed, had then become a hideous and haunting terror to his mind.

And cleanse me from my sin. "Rid me of my sin by some means, by any means, by every means, only do purify me completely, and leave no guilt upon my soul." It is not the punishment he cries out against, but the sin. David is sick of sin as sin; his loudest outcries are against the evil of his transgression, and not against the painful consequences of it. When we deal seriously with our sin, God will deal gently with us. When we hate what the Lord hates, He will soon make an end of it, to our joy and peace.

Psalm 51:3 *For I acknowledge my transgressions: and my sin is ever before me.*

EXPOSITION: Verse 3. *For I acknowledge my transgressions.* Here he sees the plurality and immense number of his sins, and makes open declaration of them. My pleading guilty has barred me from any appeal against the sentence of justice: O Lord, I must cast myself on your mercy, refuse me not, I pray you. You have made me willing to confess. O follow up this work of grace with a full and free remission!

And my sin is ever before me. My sin as a whole is never out of my mind; it continually oppresses my spirit. I lay it before you because it is ever before me: Lord, put it away both from you and me. To an awakened conscience, pain on account of sin is not transient and occasional, but intense and permanent, and this is no sign of divine wrath, but rather a sure preface of abounding favor.

Psalm 51:4 *Against thee, thee only, have I sinned, and done this evil in thy sight: that thou mightest be justified when thou speakest, and be clear when thou judgest.*

EXPOSITION: Verse 4. *Against thee, thee only, have I sinned.* All his wrong doing centered, culminated, and came to a climax at the foot of the divine throne. To injure our fellow men is sin, mainly because in so doing we violate the law of God. The penitent's heart was so filled with a sense of the wrong done to the Lord himself that all other confession was swallowed up in a brokenhearted acknowledgment of offence against Him. *And done this evil in thy sight.* David felt that his sin was committed in all its filthiness while Jehovah himself looked on. None but a child of God cares for the eye of God, but where there is grace in the soul it reflects a fearful guilt upon every evil act, when we remember that the God whom we offend was present when the trespass was committed.

That thou mightest be justified when thou speakest, and be clear when thou judgest. He could not present any argument against divine justice, if it proceeded at once to condemn him and punish him for his crime. His own confession, and the judge's own witness of the whole transaction, places the transgression beyond all question or debate; the iniquity was indisputably committed, and was unquestionably a foul wrong, and therefore the course of justice was clear and beyond all controversy.

Psalm 51:5 *Behold, I was shapen in iniquity; and in sin did my mother conceive me.*

EXPOSITION: Verse 5. *Behold, I was shapen in iniquity.* He is thunderstruck at the discovery of his inbred sin, and proceeds to set it forth. It is as if he said, not only have I sinned this once, but I am in my very nature a sinner. The fountain of my life is polluted as well as its streams. My birth tendencies are out of the square of equity; I naturally lean to forbidden things. Mine is a constitutional disease, rendering my very person obnoxious to your wrath.

And in sin did my mother conceive me. He goes back to the earliest moment of his being, not to traduce[10] his mother, but to acknowledge the deep tap roots of his sin. It is a wicked wresting of Scripture to deny that original sin and natural depravity are here taught. Surely men who cavil[11] at this doctrine have the need to be taught of the Holy Spirit what the first principles of the faith are. David's mother was the Lord's handmaid, he was born in chaste wedlock, of a good father, and he was himself, "the man after God's own heart;" and yet his nature was as fallen as that of any other son of Adam, and there only needed the occasion for the manifesting of that sad fact. In our shaping we were put out of shape, and when we were conceived our nature conceived sin.

> **Psalm 51:6** *Behold, thou desirest truth in the inward parts: and in the hidden part thou shalt make me to know wisdom.*

EXPOSITION: **Verse 6.** *Behold, t* God desires not merely outward virtue, but inward purity, and the penitent's sense of sin is greatly deepened as with astonishment he discovers this truth, and how far he is from satisfying the divine demand. Reality, sincerity, true holiness, heart fidelity, these are the demands of God. He cares not for the pretence of purity; He looks to the mind, heart, and soul. The Holy

---
10. malign or speak unfavorably about
11. object to

One of Israel has always estimated men by their inner nature, and not by their outward professions; to Him the inward is as visible as the outward, and He rightly judges that the essential character of an action lies in the motive of him who works it.

And in the hidden parts thou shalt make me to know wisdom. The love of the heart, the mystery of its fall, and the way of its purification—this hidden wisdom we must all attain; and it is a great blessing to be able to believe that the Lord will "make us to know it." No one can teach our innermost nature but the Lord, but He can instruct us to profit. The Holy Spirit can write the law on our heart, and that is the sum of practical wisdom. He can put the fear of the Lord within, and that is the beginning of wisdom. He can reveal Christ in us, and He is essential wisdom. Such poor, foolish, disarranged souls as ours shall yet be ordered aright and truth and wisdom shall reign within us.

Psalm 51:7 *Purge me with hyssop, and I shall be clean: wash me, and I shall be whiter than snow.*

EXPOSITION: **Verse 7.** *Purge me with hyssop.* Sprinkle the atoning blood upon me with the appointed means. Give me the reality which legal ceremonies symbolize. Nothing but blood can take away my blood stains, nothing but the strongest purification can avail to cleanse me. Let the sin offering purge my sin. Let Him who was appointed to atone, execute His sacred office on me; for none can need it more than me.

The passage may be read as the voice of faith as well as a prayer, and so it runs—"Thou wilt purge me with hyssop, *and I shall be clean.*" Foul as I am, there is such power in the divine propitiation that my sin shall vanish quite away and I shall again be admitted into the assembly of your people

Psalm 51

and allowed to share in the privileges of the true Israel; while in your sight also, through Jesus my Lord, I shall be accepted. *Wash me.* Let it not merely be in type that I am clean, but by a real spiritual purification, which shall remove the pollution of my nature. Let the sanctifying as well as the pardoning process be perfected in me. Save me from the evils which my sin has created and nourished in me.

And I shall be whiter than snow. None but you can whiten me, but you can in grace outdo nature itself in its purest state and you can give me an enduring purity. Though snow is white below as well as on the outer surface, you can work the like inward purity in me, and make me so clean that only a hyperbole[12] can set forth my immaculate condition. Lord, do this; my faith believes you will, and my faith well knows you can.

Scarcely does Holy Scripture contain a verse more full of faith than this. Considering the nature of the sin and the deep sense the psalmist had of it, it is a glorious faith to be able to see in the blood all-sufficient merit entirely to purge it away. Considering also the deep natural inbred corruption which David saw and experienced within, it is a miracle of faith that he could rejoice in the hope of perfect purity in his inward parts. Yet, let it be added, the faith is no more than the word warrants, than the blood of atonement encourages, and than the promise of God deserves. O that some reader may take heart, even now while smarting under sin, to do the Lord the honor to rely thus confidently on the finished sacrifice of Calvary and the infinite mercy there revealed.

Psalm 51:8 *Make me to hear joy and gladness; that the bones which thou hast broken may rejoice.*

---

12. exaggerated figure of speech

EXPOSITION: Verse 8. *Make me to hear joy and gladness.* He prays about his sorrow late in the psalm; he began at once with his sin; he asks to hear pardon, and then to hear joy. He seeks comfort at the right time and from the right source. His ear has become heavy with sinning, and so he prays, "Make me to hear." No voice could revive his dead joys but that which quickens the dead. Pardon from God would give him double joy—"joy and gladness." No stinted bliss awaits the forgiven one; he shall not only have a double blooming joy, but he shall hear it; it shall sing with exultation. God's voice speaking peace is the sweetest music an ear can hear.

That the bones which thou hast broken may rejoice. He was like a poor wretch whose bones are crushed, and he groaned under no mere flesh wounds; his firmest and yet most tender powers were "broken in pieces all asunder;" his manhood had become a dislocated, mangled, quivering sensibility. Yet, if He who crushed would cure, every wound would become a new mouth for song; every bone quivering before with agony would become equally sensible of intense delight. The figure is bold, and so is the supplicant. He is requesting a great thing; preposterous prayer anywhere but at the throne of God! Preposterous there most of all but for the Cross where Jehovah Jesus bore our sins in His own body on the tree. A penitent need not ask to be a hired servant, or settle down in despairing content with perpetual mourning. He may ask for gladness and he shall have it; for if when prodigals return the father is glad, and the neighbors and friends rejoice and are merry with music and dancing.

Psalm 51:9 *Hide thy face from my sins, and blot out all mine iniquities.*

PSALM 51

EXPOSITION: **Verse 9.** *Hide thy face from my sins.* Do not look at them Lord, refuse to behold them, lest if you consider them, and your anger burn, and I die.

Blot out all mine iniquities. Souls in agony have no space to find variety of language: pain has to content itself with monotones. David's face was ashamed with looking on his sin, and no diverting thoughts could remove it from his memory; but he prays the Lord to do with his sin what he himself cannot. If God does not hide His face from our sin, He must hide it forever from us; and if He blots it not out, He must blot our names out of His book of life.

Psalm 51:10 *Create in me a clean heart, O God; and renew a right spirit within me.*

EXPOSITION: **Verse 10.** *Create in me, O God.* I, in my outward fabric, still exist; but I am empty, a desert, void. Come, then, and let your power be seen in a new creation within my old fallen self. You made a man in the world at first; Lord, make a new man in me! *A clean heart.* In the seventh verse he asked to be clean; now he seeks a heart suitable to that cleanliness; but he does not say, "Make my old heart clean;" he is too experienced in the hopelessness of the old nature. He wants the old man buried as a dead thing, and a new creation brought in to fill its place. None but God can create either a new heart or a new Earth.

Salvation is a marvelous display of supreme power at work in us and is wholly of Omnipotence. The affections must be rectified first, or all our nature will go amiss. The heart is the rudder of the soul, and until the Lord takes it in hand we steer in a false and foul way. O Lord, you once made me, be pleased to make me new, and in my most secret parts renew me.

And renew a right spirit within me. It was there once,

Lord, put it there again. The law on my heart has become like an inscription hard to read: write it anew, gracious Maker. Remove the evil as I have entreated you; but, O replace it with good. The two sentences make a complete prayer. Create what is not there at all; renew that which is there, but in a sadly feeble state.

Psalm 51:11 *Cast me not away from thy presence; and take not thy holy spirit from me.*

EXPOSITION: Verse 11. *Cast me not away from thy presence.* Throw me not away as worthless; permit me to sit among those who share your love, though I only am allowed to keep the door. I deserve to be forever denied admission to your courts; but, O good Lord, permit me still the privilege which is dear as life itself to me.

And take not thy Holy Spirit from me. Withdraw not His comforts, counsels, assistances, quickening, or else I am indeed as a dead man. Your Spirit is my wisdom, leave me not to my folly; He is my strength, O desert me not to my own weakness. Drive me not away from you, neither go away from me. Keep up the union between us, which is my only hope of salvation. It will be a great wonder if so pure a spirit deigns[13] to stay in so base a heart as mine; but then, Lord, all your works are a wonder, therefore do this, for your mercy's sake, I earnestly entreat with you.

Psalm 51:12 *Restore unto me the joy of thy salvation; and uphold me with thy free spirit.*

EXPOSITION: Verse 12. *Restore unto me the joy of thy salvation.* Salvation he had known, and had known it as the Lord's own; he had also felt the joy which arises from being

---
13. condescends

saved in the Lord, and therefore he longed for its restoration. None but God can give back this joy; He can do it; we may ask it; He will do it for His own glory and our benefit. This joy comes not first, but follows pardon and purity: in such order it is safe, in any other it is vain presumption.

And uphold me with thy free Spirit. Conscious of weakness, mindful of having so lately fallen, he seeks to be kept on his feet by power superior to his own. That royal Spirit, whose holiness is true dignity, is able to make us walk as kings and priests, in all the uprightness of holiness; and He will do so if we ask. Such influences will not enslave but emancipate us; for holiness is liberty, and the Holy Spirit is a free Spirit. In the roughest and most treacherous ways we are safe with such a Keeper for in the best paths we stumble if left to ourselves. The praying for joy and upholding go well together; it is all over with joy if the foot is not kept; and, on the other hand, joy is a very upholding thing, and greatly aids holiness; meanwhile, the free, noble, royal Spirit is giver of both.

Psalm 51:13 *Then will I teach transgressors thy ways; and sinners shall be converted unto thee.*

EXPOSITION: Verse 13. *Then will I teach transgressors thy ways.* It was his fixed resolve to be a teacher of others; and assuredly none instruct others as well as those who have been experimentally taught of God themselves. The pardoned sinner's matter will be good, for he has been taught in the school of experience, and his manner will be telling, for he will speak sympathetically as one who has felt what he declares. The audience the psalmist would choose is memorable—he would instruct transgressors like himself; others might despise them, but, "a fellow feeling makes us wondrous kind."[14]

---

14. quote from Alexander Pope, English poet and critic (1688–

If unworthy to edify saints, he would creep in along with the sinners, and humbly tell them of divine love. The mercy of God to one is an illustration of His usual procedure, so that our own case helps us to understand His "ways," or His general modes of action. Perhaps, too, David under that term refers to the preceptive part of the Word of God, which after having been broken and suffering thereby, he felt that he could vindicate and urge upon the reverence of other offenders.

And sinners shall be converted unto thee. You will bless my pathetic testimony to the recovery of many who, like me, have turned aside unto crooked ways. Doubtless this psalm and the whole story of David have produced for many ages the most salutary results in the conversion of transgressors, and so evil has been overruled for good.

Psalm 51:14 *Deliver me from bloodguiltiness, O God, thou God of my salvation: and my tongue shall sing aloud of thy righteousness.*

EXPOSITION: **Verse 14.** *Deliver me from bloodguiltiness.* He had been the means of the death of Uriah, the Hittite, a faithful and attached follower, and he now confesses that fact. Besides, his sin of adultery was a capital offence, and he puts himself down as one worthy to die the death. Honest penitents do not fetch a compass and confess their sins in an elegant periphrasis,[15] but they come to the point, and make a clean breast of it all. What other course is rational in dealing with the Omniscient? *O God, thou God of my salvation.* It had been, O God, up until now, but here he cries, thou God of my salvation. Faith grows

---

1744)

15. an indirect way of expressing something; in today's vernacular, "beating around the bush"

by the exercise of prayer. He confesses sin more plainly in this verse than before, and yet he deals with God more confidently: growing upward and downward at the same time are perfectly consistent. None but the King can remit the death penalty, it is therefore a joy to faith that God is King, and that He is the author and finisher of our salvation. *And my tongue shall sing aloud of thy righteousness.* One would rather have expected him to say, I will sing of your mercy; but David can see the divine way of justification that righteousness of God that Paul afterwards spoke of by which the ungodly are justified. After all, it is the righteousness of divine mercy which is its greatest wonder. Note how David would preach in the last verse, and now here he would sing. We can never do too much for the Lord to whom we owe more than all. If we could be preacher, precentor,[16] doorkeeper, pew opener, foot washer, and all in one, all would still be too little to show forth all our gratitude. We shall not sing our own praises if we are saved, but our theme will be the Lord our righteousness, in whose merits we stand righteously accepted.

Psalm 51:15 *O Lord, open thou my lips; and my mouth shall shew forth thy praise.*

EXPOSITION: Verse 15. *O Lord, open thou my lips.* How marvelously the Lord can open our lips, and what divine things can we poor simpletons pour forth under His inspiration! This prayer of a penitent is a golden petition for a preacher, Lord; I offer it for myself and my brethren. But it also stands in good stead anyone whose shame for sin makes him stammer in his prayers, and when it is fully answered, the tongue of the dumb begins to sing.

---

16. musical director

And my mouth shall shew forth thy praise. If God opens the mouth He is sure to have the fruit of it. According to the porter at the gate the foulest villainies troop out of a man's lips when vanity, anger, falsehood or lust unbar the door. But if the Holy Spirit opens the wicket gate, then grace, mercy, peace, and all the graces come forth.

Psalm 51:16 *For thou desirest not sacrifice; else would I give it: thou delightest not in burnt offering.*

EXPOSITION: Verse 16. *For thou desirest not sacrifice.* This was the subject of the last psalm. The psalmist was so illuminated as to see far beyond the symbolic ritual; his eye of faith gazed with delight upon the actual atonement. *Else I would give it.* Indeed, anything which the Lord prescribed he would cheerfully have rendered. We are ready to give up all we have if we may but be cleared of our sins; and when sin is pardoned our joyful gratitude is prepared for any sacrifice.

Thou delightest not in burnt offering. He knew that no form of burnt sacrifice was a satisfactory propitiation. His deep soul need made him look from the type to the antitype, from the external rite to the inward grace.

Psalm 51:17 *The sacrifices of God are a broken spirit: a broken and a contrite heart, O God, thou wilt not despise.*

EXPOSITION: Verse 17. *The sacrifices of God are a broken spirit.* All sacrifices are presented to you in one, by the man whose broken heart presents the Savior's merit to you. When the heart mourns for sin, you are better pleased than when the bullock bleeds beneath the axe. "A broken heart" is an expression implying deep sorrow, embittering the very life; it carries in it the idea of all but killing anguish in that region which is so vital as to be the very source of life. So excellent is a spirit humbled and mourning for sin, that it is not only a sacrifice, but it has a plurality of excellences, and is preeminently God's sacrifices.

A broken and a contrite heart, O God, thou wilt not despise. A heart crushed is a fragrant heart. Men despise those who are contemptible in their own eyes, but the Lord sees not as man sees. He despises what men esteem, and values that which they despise. Never yet has God spurned a lowly, weeping penitent, and never will He while God is love, and while Jesus is called the Man who receiveth sinners. A contrite heard He seeks for even one is better to Him than all the varied offerings of the old Jewish sanctuary.

Psalm 51:18 *Do good in thy good pleasure unto Zion: build thou the walls of Jerusalem.*

EXPOSITION: Verse 18. *Do good in thy good pleasure unto Zion.* Zion was David's favorite spot, whereon he had hoped to erect a temple. The ruling passion for the temple was strong in him for he felt he had hindered the project of honoring the Lord there as he desired. But he prayed and asked God to let the place of His ark be glorious, and to establish His worship and His worshiping people.

Build thou the walls of Jerusalem. This had been one of David's schemes, to wall in the holy city, and he desired to see it completed; but we believe he had a more spiritual meaning, and prayed for the prosperity of the Lord's cause and people. He had done mischief by his sin, and had, as it were, pulled down her walls; he, therefore, implores the Lord to undo the evil, and establish His Church. God can make His cause to prosper, and in answer to prayer He will do so. Without Him doing the building we labor in vain;

therefore we are more instant and constant in prayer. [See Psalm 127:1.] There is surely no grace in us if we do not feel for the Church of God, and take a lasting interest in its welfare.

Psalm 51:19 *Then shalt thou be pleased with the sacrifices of righteousness, with burnt offering and whole burnt offering: then shall they offer bullocks upon thine altar.*

EXPOSITION: Verse 19. *Then shalt thou be pleased with the sacrifices of righteousness.* In those days of joyful prosperity your saints shall present in great abundance the richest and holiest thank offerings to you, and you shall be pleased to accept them. A saved soul expects to see its prayers answered in a revived Church, and then is assured that God will be greatly glorified. *With burnt offering and whole burnt offering: then shall they offer bullocks upon thine altar.* Though we bring no more sacrifices for sin, yet as priests unto God our solemn praises and votive[17] gifts are thank offerings acceptable to God by Jesus Christ. We bring not the Lord our least things—our doves and pigeons; but we present Him with our best possessions—our bullocks. We are glad that in this present time we are able to fulfill in person the declaration of this verse: we also, forecasting the future, wait for days of the divine presence, when the Church of God, with unspeakable joy, shall offer gifts upon the altar of God, which will far eclipse anything seen in these less enthusiastic days. Hasten it, O Lord.

---

17. dedicated gifts

Psalm 52

Psalm 52:1–Psalm 52:9

Psalm 52:1 *Why boastest thou thyself in mischief, O mighty man? the goodness of God endureth continually.*

EXPOSITION: Verse 1. *Why boasteth thou thyself in mischief, O mighty man?* Doeg[18] had no reason for boasting in having procured the slaughter of a band of defenseless priests. He ought to have been ashamed of his cowardice. He had no right for exultation! Honorable titles are but irony where the wearer is mean and cruel. If David alluded to Saul, he meant by these words pityingly to say, "How can one by nature fitted for nobler deeds, descend to so low a level as to find a theme for boasting in a slaughter so heartless and mischievous?"

The goodness of God endureth continually. A beautiful contrast. The tyrant's fury cannot dry up the perennial stream of divine mercy, for though priests are slain, their Master lives. If Doeg triumphs for awhile, the Lord will outlive him, and right the wrongs which he has done. This ought to modify the proud exultations of the wicked, for while the Lord lives, iniquity has little cause to exalt itself.

Psalm 52:2 *The tongue deviseth mischiefs; like a sharp razor, working deceitfully.*

EXPOSITION: Verse 2. *Thy tongue deviseth mischiefs.*

---

18. an Edomite and chief herdsman for King Saul

You speak with an ulterior design.[19] The information given was for Saul's assistance apparently, but in very deed in his heart the Edomite hated the priests of the God of Jacob. It is a mark of deep depravity, when the evil spoken is craftily intended to promote a yet greater evil.

Like a sharp razor, working deceitfully. David is saying here that the false tongue as being effectual for mischief is like a razor which, unawares to the person operated on, is making him bald. Or he may mean that as with a razor a man's throat may be cut very speedily, under the pretence of shaving him. Whetted by malice, and guided by craft, Doeg destroyed the band of priests with cruel and accursed thoroughness.

Psalm 52:3 *Thou lovest evil more than good; and lying rather than to speak righteousness. Selah.*

EXPOSITION: Verse 3. *Thou lovest evil more than good.* He loved not good at all. If both had been equally profitable and pleasant, he would have preferred evil.

And lying rather than to speak righteousness. He was more at home at lying than at truth. He spoke not the truth except by accident, but he delighted heartily in falsehood. *Selah.* Let us pause and look at the proud blustering liar. Doeg is gone, but other dogs bark at the Lord's people. Saul's cattle master is buried, but the devil still has his drovers, who fain[20] would hurry the saints like sheep to the slaughter.

Psalm 52:4 *Thou lovest all devouring words, O thou deceitful tongue.*

EXPOSITION: Verse 4. *Thou lovest.* The tongue has a taste for evil language. *All devouring words.* There are

---
19. motive
20. desire to

words that, like boa constrictors, swallow men whole, or like lions, rend men to pieces; evil minds are fond of these words. Their oratory is evermore furious and bloody. That which will most readily provoke the lowest passions they are sure to employ, and they think such pandering to the madness of the wicked to be eloquence of a high order.

O thou deceitful tongue. Men can manage to say a great many furious things under the pretext of justice. They claim they are jealous for right, but the truth is they are determined to put down truth and holiness, and craftily go about it under this transparent pretence.

Psalm 52:5 *God shall likewise destroy thee for ever, he shall take thee away, and pluck thee out of thy dwelling place, and root thee out of the land of the living. Selah.*

EXPOSITION: Verse 5. *God shall likewise destroy thee for ever.* The desire of the persecutor is to destroy the Church, and therefore God shall destroy him, pull down his house, pluck up his roots, and make an end of him. *He shall take thee away.* God shall extinguish his coal and sweep him away like the ashes of the hearth. He who quenches the truth, God shall quench.

And pluck thee out of his dwelling place, like a captive dragged from his home. Abimelech and his brother priests were cut off from their abode, and so should those be who compassed and contrived their murder.

And root thee out of the land of the living. The persecutor shall be eradicated, pulled up by the root, cut up root and branch. He sought the death of others and death shall fall upon him he shall be banished to that land where the wicked cease from troubling. Those who will not "let live" have no right to "live." God will turn the tables on malicious men, and mete to them a portion with their own measure.

Selah. Pause again, and behold the divine justice proving itself more than a match for human sin.

Psalm 52:6 *The righteous also shall see, and fear, and shall laugh at him*

EXPOSITION: Verse 6. *The righteous*—the object of the tyrant's hatred—shall outlive his enmity, and *also shall see,* before his own face, the end of the ungodly oppressor. God permits Mordecai to see Haman hanging on the gallows. David had brought to him the tokens of Saul's death on Gilboa. *And fear.* Holy awe shall sober the mind of the good man; he shall reverently adore the God of providence.

And shall laugh at him with solemn contempt. Schemes so far reaching all baffled, plans so deep, all thwarted. Mephistopheles outwitted the old serpent taken in his own subtlety. This is a good theme for that deep-seated laughter which is more akin to solemnity than merriment.

Psalm 52:7 *Lo, this is the man that made not God his strength; but trusted in the abundance of his riches, and strengthened himself in his wickedness.*

EXPOSITION: Verse 7. *Lo.* Look here, and read the epitaph of a mighty man, who lorded it proudly during his little hour, and set his heel upon the necks of the Lord's chosen.

This is the man that made not God his strength. Behold the man! The great vainglorious man. He found a fortress, but not in God; he gloried in his might, but not in the Almighty. Behold his ruin, and be instructed.

But trusted in the abundance of his riches, and strengthened himself in his wickedness. The substance he had gathered, and the mischief he wrought, was his boast and glory. Wealth and wickedness are dreadful companions; when combined they make a monster. When the devil is master of money bags, he is a devil indeed. Beelzebub and Mammon together heat the furnace seven times hotter for the child of God, but in the end that brings their own destruction. Wherever we see a man great in sin and substance, we shall do well to anticipate his end, and view this verse as the divine in memoriam.

Psalm 52:8 *But I am like a green olive tree in the house of God: I trust in the mercy of God for ever and ever.*

EXPOSITION: Verse 8. But I, hunted and persecuted though I am, *am like a green olive tree*. I am not plucked up or destroyed, but am like a flourishing olive, which draws oil out of the rock, and amid the drought still lives and grows. *In the house of God*. He was one of the divine family, and could not be expelled from it; his place was near his God, and there was he safe and happy, despite all the machinations of his foes. He was bearing fruit, and would continue to do so when all his proud enemies were withered like branches cut from the tree.

I trust in the mercy of God for ever and ever. Eternal mercy is my present confidence. David knew God's mercy to be eternal and perpetual, and in that he trusted. What a rock to build on! What a fortress to fly to!

Psalm 52:9 *I will praise thee for ever, because thou hast done it: and I will wait on thy name; for it is good before thy saints.*

EXPOSITION: Verse 9. *I will praise thee for ever.* Like your mercy shall my thankfulness be. While others boast in their riches I will boast in my God; and when their glorying is silenced forever in the tomb, my song shall continue to proclaim the lovingkindness of Jehovah. *Because thou hast done it.* God has vindicated the righteous, and punished the wicked. God's memorable acts of providence, to saints and sinners, deserve, and must have our gratitude. David views his prayer as already answered, the promise of God as already fulfilled, and therefore at once lifts up sacred praise.

And I will wait on thy name. God shall still be the psalmist's hope; he will not look elsewhere in the future. He, whose name has been so gloriously made known in truth and righteousness, is justly chosen as our expectation for years to come.

For it is good before thy saints. Before or among the saints David intended to wait, feeling it to be good both for him and them to look to the Lord alone, and wait for the manifestation of His character in due season. Our strength is to sit still. Let the mighty ones boast, we will wait on the Lord; and if their haste brings them present honor, our patience will have its turn by and by, and bring us the honor that excels.

Psalm 53
Psalm 53:1–Psalm 53:6

Psalm 53:1 *The fool hath said in his heart, There is no God. Corrupt are they, and have done abominable iniquity: there is none that doeth good.*

EXPOSITION: Verse 1. *The fool hath said in his heart, There is no God.* This he does because he is a fool. Being a fool he speaks according to his nature; being a great fool he meddles with a great subject, and comes to a wild conclusion. The atheist is, morally and mentally a fool. A fool in the heart, head, morals and in philosophy. With the denial of God as a starting point, we may well conclude that the fool's progress is a rapid, riotous, raving, and ruinous one. He who begins at impiety is ready for anything.

No God, being interpreted, means no law, no order, no restraint to lust, and no limit to passion. Who but a fool would be of this mind? What a Bedlam, or rather what an Aceldama[21] would the world become if such lawless principles came to be universal! He who heartily entertains an irreligious spirit, and follows it out to its legitimate issues is a son of Belial, dangerous to the commonwealth, irrational, and despicable. Every natural man is, more or less a denier of God. Practical atheism is the religion of the race.

Corrupt are they. It is idle talk to compliment them as sincere doubters, and amiable thinkers—they are putrid. There is too much dainty dealing nowadays with atheism; it is not a harmless error, it is an offensive, putrid sin, and righteous

---
21. Potter's Field, Field of Blood

men should look upon it in that light. All men being more or less atheistic in spirit are also in that degree corrupt; their heart is foul, their moral nature is decayed.

And have done abominable iniquity. Bad principles soon lead to bad lives. One does not find virtue promoted by the example of Voltaire[22] and Tom Paine.[23] Those who talk so abominably as to deny their Maker will act abominably when it serves their turn. It is the abounding denial and forgetfulness of God among men which is the source of the unrighteousness and crime that we see around us. If all men are not outwardly vicious it is because of the power of other and better principles, but left to itself the "No God" spirit so universal in mankind would produce nothing but the most loathsome actions.

There is none that doeth good. The one typical fool is reproduced in the whole race; without a single exception men have forgotten the right way. This accusation twice made in the psalm, and repeated a third time by the inspired Apostle Paul, is an indictment most solemn and sweeping, but He who makes it cannot err, He knows what is in man; neither will He lay more to man's charge than He can prove.

Psalm 53:2 *God looked down from heaven upon the children of men, to see if there were any that did understand, that did seek God.*

EXPOSITION: Verse 2. *God looked down from heaven upon the children of men.* He did so in ages past, and He has continued His steadfast gaze from His all surveying observatory *to see if there were any that did understand, that did seek God.* Had there been one understanding man, one true lover of his God, the divine eye would have discovered

---
22. eighteenth-century French Enlightenment philosopher
23. philosopher and political activist in Revolutionary America

him. Those pure heathens and admirable savages that men talk so much of, do not appear to have been visible to the eye of Omniscience, the fact being that they live nowhere but in the realm of fiction. The Lord did not look for great grace, but only for sincerity and right desire, but these He found not. He saw all nations, all men, all hearts, and the motives of all hearts, but He saw neither a clear head nor a clean heart among them all. Where God's eyes see no favorable sign we may rest assured there is none.

> **Psalm 53:3** *Every one of them is gone back: they are altogether become filthy; there is none that doeth good, no, not one.*

EXPOSITION: Verse 3. *Every one of them is gone back.* The whole mass of manhood, all of it, is gone back. In the fourteenth psalm it was said to turn aside, but here it is described as running in a diametrically opposite direction. The life of unregenerate manhood is in direct defiance of the law of God, not merely apart from it but opposed to it.

They are altogether become filthy. The whole lump is soured with an evil leaven, fouled with an all pervading pollution, made rank with general putrefaction. Thus, in God's sight, our atheistic nature is not the pardoned thing that we think it to be. Errors as to God are not the mild diseases which some account them, they are abominable evils. Fair is the world to blind eyes, but to the all-seeing Jehovah it is otherwise.

There is none that doeth good, no, not one. How could there be when the whole mass was leavened with so evil a leaven? This puts an end to the fictions of the innocent savage, the lone patriarch, "the Indian whose untutored mind," etc. Pope's verse evaporates in smoke:

Father of all, in every age;
In every clime adored,
By saint, by savage, or by sage,
Jehovah, Jove, or Lord.[24]

The fallen race of man, left to its own energy, has not produced a single lover of God or doer of holiness, nor will it ever do so. Grace must interpose, or not one specimen of humanity will be found to follow after the good and true. This is God's verdict after looking down upon the race. Who shall dispute it?

Psalm 53:4 *Have the workers of iniquity no knowledge? who eat up my people as they eat bread: they have not called upon God.*

EXPOSITION: Verse 4. *Have the workers of iniquity no knowledge?* They have no wisdom, certainly, but even so common a thing as knowledge might have restrained them. Can they not see that there is a God? That sin is an evil thing? That persecution recoils upon a man's own head? Are they such utter fools as not to know that they are their own enemies, and are ruining themselves?

Who eat up my people as they eat bread. Do they not see that such food will be hard to digest, and will bring on them a horrible vomit when God deals with them in justice? Can they imagine that the Lord will allow them to devour His people with impunity? They must be insane indeed.

They have not called upon God. They carry on their cruel enterprises against the saints, and use every means but that which is essential to success in every case, namely, the invocation of God. In this respect persecutors are rather more consistent than Pharisees who devoured widow's houses, and

---

24. Alexander Pope, British poet (1688–1744)

prayed too. The natural man, like Ishmael, loves not and is jealous of the spiritual seed, and desires to destroy it because it is beloved of God; yet the natural man does not seek after the same favor from God. The carnal mind envies those who obtain mercy, and yet it will not seek mercy itself. It plays the dog in the manger. Sinners will out of a malicious jealousy devour those who pray, but yet they will not pray themselves.

> **Psalm 53:5** *There were they in great fear, where no fear was: for God hath scattered the bones of him that encampeth against thee: thou hast put them to shame, because God hath despised them.*

EXPOSITION: **Verse 5.** *There were they in great fear, where no fear was.* David sees the end of the ungodly, and the ultimate triumph of the spiritual seed. The rebellious march in fury against the gracious, but suddenly they are seized with a causeless panic. Without cause the wicked are alarmed. He who denies God is at bottom a coward, and in his infidelity he is like the boy in the churchyard who "whistles to keep his courage up."

For God hath scattered the bones of him that encampeth against thee. Mighty were the hosts which besieged Zion, but they were defeated, and their unburied carcasses proved the prowess of the God whose being they dared to deny.

Thou hast put them to shame, because God hath despised them. God's people may well look with derision upon their enemies since they are the objects of divine contempt.

> **Psalm 53:6** *Oh that the salvation of Israel were come out of Zion! When God bringeth back the captivity of his people, Jacob shall rejoice, and Israel shall be glad.*

EXPOSITION: Verse 6. *Oh that the salvation of Israel were come out of Zion!* I pray to God the final battle were well over. When will the Lord avenge His own elect? When will the long oppression of the saints come to its close and glory crown their heads? The word salvation is in the plural, to show its greatness.

When God bringeth back the captivity of his people, Jacob shall rejoice, and Israel shall be glad. Inasmuch as the yoke has been heavy, and the bondage cruel, the liberty will be happy and the triumph joyous. The Second Advent and the restoration of Israel are our hope and expectation. We have attempted to throw into rhyme the last two verses of this psalm:

> The foes of Zion quake for fright.
> Where no fear was they quail;
> For well they know that sword of might
> Which cuts through coats of mail.

> The Lord of old defiled their shields,
> And all their spears he scorned;
> Their bones lay scattered over the fields,
> Unburied and unmourned.

> Let Zion's foes be filled with shame;
> Her sons are blessed of God;
> Though scoffers now despise their name,
> The Lord shall break the rod.

> Oh! would our God to Zion turn,
> God with salvation clad;
> Then Judah's harps should music learn,
> And Israel be glad.

Psalm 54
Psalm 54:1–Psalm 54:7

Psalm 54:1 *Save me, O God, by thy name, and judge me by thy strength.*

EXPOSITION: Verse 1. *Save me, O God.* You are my Savior; all around me are my foes and their eager helpers. Every land rejects me and denies me rest. But you, O God, will give me refuge, and deliver me from all my enemies.

By thy name, by your great and glorious nature. Let every one of the perfections which are blended in your divine name work for me. Is not your honor pledged for my defense?

And judge me by thy strength. Render justice to me, for none else will or can. We dare not appeal to God in a bad cause, but when we know that we can fearlessly carry our cause before His justice we may well commit it to His power.

Psalm 54:2 *Hear my prayer, O God; give ear to the words of my mouth.*

EXPOSITION: Verse 2. *Hear my prayer, O God.* This has ever been the defense of saints. As long as God has an open ear we cannot be shut up in trouble. All other weapons may be useless, but all prayer is evermore available. *Give ear to the words of my mouth.* Vocal prayer helps the supplicant, and we keep our minds more fully awake when we can use our tongues as well as our hearts. It is all one whether we babble nonsense or plead arguments if our God grant us not a hearing. When His case had become dangerous, David could not afford to pray out of mere custom, he must succeed in his pleadings, or become the prey of his adversary.

Psalm 54:3 *For strangers are risen up against me, and oppressors seek after my soul: they have not set God before them. Selah.*

EXPOSITION: Verse 3. *For strangers are risen up against me.* Those who had no cause for ill will had gone against him, for they were strangers to him. They were aliens to his God also, and should these be allowed to worry and destroy him? A child may well complain to his father when strangers come in to molest him.

And oppressors seek after my soul. Saul, led the way, and others followed seeking David's soul, his blood, his life, his very existence. They were cruel and intense in their malice, they would utterly crush the good man; no half measure would content them.

They have not set God before them. Had they regarded God they would not have betrayed the innocent to be hunted down like a poor harmless stag. David felt that atheism lay at the bottom of the enmity which pursued him. Good men are hated for God's sake, and this is a good plea for them to urge in prayer.

Selah. He is out of breath with indignation. A sense of wrong bids him suspend the music awhile. It may also be observed, that more pauses would, as a rule, improve our devotions: we are usually too much in a hurry: a little more holy meditation would make our words more suitable and our emotions more fervent.

Psalm 54:4 *Behold, God is mine helper: the Lord is with them that uphold my soul.*

EXPOSITION: **Verse 4.** *Behold, God is mine helper:* David looks over the heads of his defenders and sees one whose aid is better than all the help of men; he is overwhelmed with joy at recognizing his divine champion, and cries, *Behold.* And is this not a theme for pious exultation in all time, that the great God protects us, His own people: no matter the number or violence of our foes when He uplifts the shield of His omnipotence to guard us, and the sword of His power to aid us? Little do we care for the defiance of the foe while we have the defense of God.

The Lord is with them that uphold my soul. The reigning Lord, the great Adonai, is in the camp of my defenders. Here was a greater champion than any of the "three mighties,"[25] or than all the valiant men who chose David for their captain. The psalmist was very confident, he felt so thoroughly that his heart was on the Lord's side that he was sure God was on his side. He asked in the first verse for deliverance, and here he returns thanks for upholding: while we are seeking one mercy which we have not, we must not be unmindful of another which we have. It is a great mercy to have some friends left us, but a greater mercy still to see the Lord among them, for like so many numbers of friends they stand for nothing until the Lord sets himself as a great unit in the front of them.

Psalm 54:5 *He shall reward evil unto mine enemies: cut them off in thy truth.*

EXPOSITION: **Verse 5.** *He shall reward evil unto mine enemies.* It cannot be that malice should go unavenged. It would be cruelty to the good to be lenient to their persecutors.

---

25. Jashobeam, Chief of the Captains, a Hachmonte. Eleazar, the son of Dodo, an Alohite. Abishai, brother of Joab, Chief of the three

It is appointed, and so it must ever be, that those who shoot upward the arrows of malice shall find them fall upon themselves. *Cut them off in thy truth.* This is spoken as an Amen to the just sentence of the just Judge not in ferocious revenge. It is not a private desire, but the solemn utterance of a military man, a grossly injured man, a public leader destined to be a monarch, and a man well trained in the school of Moses, whose Law ordains "eye for eye, and tooth for tooth" [see Leviticus 24:20].

Psalm 54:6 *I will freely sacrifice unto thee: I will praise thy name, O LORD; for it is good.*

EXPOSITION: Verse 6. *I will freely sacrifice unto thee:* So certain is he of deliverance that he offers a vow by anticipation. The more we receive, the more we ought to render. The spontaneity of our gifts is a great element in their acceptance; the Lord loveth a cheerful giver. [See 2 Corinthians 9:7.]

I will praise thy name, O Lord. The name which he invoked in prayer [See Psalm 54:1], he will now magnify in praise. Note how roundly he brings it out: *O Jehovah.*

This is ever the grand name of the revealed God of Israel, a name which awakens the most sublime sentiments, and so nourishes the most acceptable praise. None can praise the Lord as well as those who have tried and proved the preciousness of His name in seasons of adversity. The psalmist adds, *for it is good,* and surely we may read this with a double nominative, God's name is good, and so is His praise. It is of great use to our souls to be much in praise; we are never so holy or as happy David's enemies are described in Psalm 54:3 as not setting God before them, as for David, he resolves to have the Lord in perpetual remembrance in his sacrifices and praises.

Psalm 54:7 *For he hath delivered me out of all trouble: and mine eye hath seen his desire upon mine enemies.*

EXPOSITION: Verse 7. *For he hath delivered me out of all trouble.* David lived a life of dangers and hairbreadth escapes, yet he was always safe. In the retrospect of his very many deliverances he feels that he must praise God, and looking upon the mercy which he sought as though it were already received, he sang this song over it—

> And a new song is in my mouth,
> To long loved music set,
> Glory to thee for all the grace
> I have not tasted yet.[26]

Our covenant God is pledged to bring us out of our troubles, therefore let us uplift the note of triumph unto Jehovah, the faithful preserver of them that put their trust in Him. Thus far have we proved His promise good; He changes not, and therefore in all the unknown future He will be equally our guardian and defense, "showing himself strong in the behalf of them whose heart is perfect toward him."

And mine eye hath seen his desire upon mine enemies. He desired this as a matter of justice, and not of personal anger. His righteous soul exulted because he knew that unprovoked and gratuitous malice would meet with a righteous punishment. If we could keep out of our hearts all personal enmity as fully as the psalmist did in this psalm, we might yet equally feel with him a sacred acquiescence and delight in that divine justice which will save the righteous and overthrow the malicious. In closing, let us trust that if we find we are friendless, we to, shall find ourselves before long singing the same joyous hymn of praise.

---

26. Hymn: "God is the Strength of My Heart and My Portion Forever," by Anita L. Waring

PSALM 55

PSALM 55:1–PSALM 55:23

Psalm 55:1 *Give ear to my prayer, O God; and hide not thyself from my supplication.*

EXPOSITION: Verse 1. *Give ear to my prayer, O God.* The fact is so commonly before us, otherwise we would be surprised to observe how universally and constantly the saints resort to prayer in seasons of distress. From the Great Elder Brother down to the very least of the divine family, all of them delight in prayer. They run as naturally to the mercy seat in time of trouble, but note well that it is never the bare act of prayer that satisfies the godly, they crave an audience with Heaven, and an answer from the throne and nothing less will content them.

Hide not thyself from my supplication. When a man saw his neighbor in distress, and deliberately passed him by, he was said to hide himself from him; and the psalmist begs that the Lord would not so treat him. In that dread hour when Jesus bore our sins upon the tree, His Father did hide himself, and this was the most dreadful part of all the Son of David's agony. Well may each of us deprecate such a calamity as God should refusing to hear our cries.

Psalm 55:2 *Attend unto me, and hear me: I mourn in my complaint, and make a noise*

EXPOSITION: Verse 2. *Attend unto me, and hear me.* He is in deep bitter earnest. If his God does not hear, he feels that all is over with him. He begs for his God to be a listener and an answerer.

I mourn in my complaint, and make a noise. He gives loose to his sorrows, permits his mind to rehearse its griefs, and to pour them out in an almost incoherent language. What a comfort that we may be thus familiar with our God! We may not complain of Him, but we may complain to Him.

When we are distracted with grief and bring our rambling thoughts and noisy wordless utterances before Him, He hears and understand us and often fulfills our desires. "Groanings that cannot be uttered," are often prayers which cannot be refused. [See Romans 8:26.] Our Lord himself used strong crying and tears, *"and was heard in that he feared"* [Hebrews 5:7].

Psalm 55:3 *Because of the voice of the enemy, because of the oppression of the wicked: for they cast iniquity upon me, and in wrath they hate me.*

EXPOSITION: **Verse 3.** *Because of the voice of the enemy.* The enemy was vocal, and found a voice where his godly victim had nothing better than a "noise." Slander is seldom short of expression, it prates and prattles evermore. Neither David, nor our Lord, nor any of the saints were allowed to escape the attacks of venomous tongues that caused acute anguish.

Because of the oppression of the wicked: the unjust press and oppress the righteous; like an intolerable burden they crushed them down, and brought to their knees before the Lord. He that is born after the flesh will persecute him that is born after the Spirit. The great seed of the woman suffered from a bruised heel. *For they cast iniquity upon me,* they throw the black dust of their lying and verbal abuse of their slander over me. They endeavor to trip me, and if I do not fall they lie and say I do.

And in wrath they hate me. With a hearty ill will they detested the holy man and this was no small animosity, but a moral bitter anger that reigned in their bosoms. Note how applicable this is to our Lord.

Psalm 55:4 *My heart is sore pained within me: and the terrors of death are fallen upon me.*

EXPOSITION: Verse 4. *My heart is sore pained within me.* His spirit writhed in agony and was mentally in as much pain as a woman in travail physically. His inmost soul was touched; and a wounded spirit who can bear? If this were written when David was attacked by his own favorite son, and ignominiously driven from his capital, he had reason enough for using these expressions.

And the terrors of death are fallen upon me. Mortal fears seized him, he felt like he was surrounded with the glooms of the shadow of death, upon whom the eternal night suddenly descends. Within and without he was afflicted, and his chief terror seemed to come from above, for he uses the expression, "Fallen upon me." He gave himself up for lost feeling he was as good as dead. The inmost center of his nature was moved with dismay. Think of our Lord in the Garden of Gethsemane with His soul *"exceeding sorrowful, even unto death"* [Matthew 26:38] and you have a parallel to the griefs of the psalmist. Perchance, dear reader, if you have not trodden this gloomy way, you will soon; then be sure to see the footprints of your Lord in this miry part of the road.

Psalm 55:5 *Fearfulness and trembling are come upon me, and horror hath overwhelmed me.*

EXPOSITION: **Verse 5.** *Fearfulness and trembling are come upon me.* Like housebreakers these robbers were entering his soul. Like one who feels a fainting fit coming over him, David was falling into a state of terror. His fear was so great that he trembled. He did not know what would happen next, or how soon the worst should come. The sly, mysterious whisperings of slander often cause a noble mind more fear than open antagonism; we can be brave against an open foe, but cowardly, plotting conspiracies bewilder and distract us.

And horror hath overwhelmed me. He was as one enveloped in a darkness that might be felt. As Jonah went down into the sea, so did David appear to go down into deeps of horror. He was unmanned, confounded, brought into a hideous state of suspense and mortal apprehension.

Psalm 55:6 *And I said, Oh that I had wings like a dove! for then would I fly away, and be at rest.*

EXPOSITION: **Verse 6.** *And I said, Oh that I had wings like a dove! for then would I fly away, and be at rest.* If he could not resist as an eagle, he would escape as a dove. Swiftly, and unobserved, on strong, untiring pinions he would fly away from the abodes of slander and wickedness. His love of peace made him sigh for an escape from the scene of strife.

> O for a lodge in some vast wilderness,[27]
> Some boundless contiguity of shade,
> Where rumour of oppression and deceit
> Might never reach me more.

---

27. from "Slavery," poem by William Cowper

We are all too apt to utter this vain desire, for no wings of doves or eagles could bear us away from the sorrows of a trembling heart. Moreover, it is cowardly to shun the battle which God would have us fight. It is better to face danger, for our back has no armor. We need a swifter conveyance than doves' pinions to outfly slander. He who does not fly but commends his case to God may find rest. Even the dove of old found no rest until she returned to her ark, and we amid all our sorrow may find rest in Jesus. We need not depart; all will be well if we trust in Him.

Psalm 55:7 *Lo, then would I wander far off, and remain in the wilderness. Selah.*

EXPOSITION: Verse 7. *Lo, then would I wander far off.* Yet when David was far off, he longed to be near Jerusalem; thus, in our ill estate we often think the past is better than the present. We shall be called to fly far away soon enough, and maybe we shall not be ready to go; we need not indulge vain notions of premature escape from Earth.

And remain in the wilderness. He found it not such a dear abode when there, yet resolves now to make it his permanent abode. Had he been condemned to receive his wish he would before long have felt like Selkirk, in the poet's verse—

> O solitude, where are the charms
> That sages have found in thy face?
> Better dwell in the midst of alarms
> Than reign in this horrible place.[28]

Free from all idle wishes, our Lord found much strength in solitude, loved the mountain's brow at midnight, and the quiet shade of the olives of Gethsemane. Yet it is natural,

---
28. Verse one of the poem, "The Solitude of Alexander Selkirk," by William Cowper

when all men do us wrong, to wish to separate ourselves from their society. However, nature must yield to grace, and we must endure the contradiction of sinners against us and not be weary and faint in our minds.

Selah. When we are going too fast, and giving way too freely to regrets, it is good to cry, "Halt," and pause awhile, until more sober thoughts return.

Psalm 55:8 *I would hasten my escape from the windy storm and tempest.*

EXPOSITION: Verse 8. *I would hasten my escape.* David declares that he would not waste a moment, or stay to bid adieu to his friends for fear he would be too late, and because he could bear no longer the clamor of his foes.

From the windy storm and tempest. A storm was brewing, and, like a dove, he would outfly it and reach a calmer region. Swifter than the storm cloud would he fly, to avoid the deluge of rain, and the flash of the lightning. Alas! poor soul, you have no such wings, and you must tarry here and feel the tempest; but be of good cheer, you shall stretch your wings before long for a bolder flight, Heaven shall receive you, and there your sorrows shall have a finale of blessedness among the birds of paradise.

Psalm 55:9 *Destroy, O Lord, and divide their tongues: for I have seen violence and strife in the city.*

EXPOSITION: Verse 9. *Destroy, O Lord.* Let them be devoured by the sword, since they have unsheathed it against me. How could we expect the exiled monarch to offer any other prayer than this against the rebellious bands of Absalom and the crafty devices of Ahithophel?

Divide their tongues. Make another Babel in their debates

and councils of war. Set them at cross-purposes. Divide the pack that the hunted one may escape. The divisions of error are the hope of truth.

For I have seen violence and strife in the city. The rabble and their leaders were plotting and planning, raging and contending against their king: anarchy had fermented among them, and David hoped that now it might come to pass that the very lawlessness which had exiled him would create weakness among his foes. They who are strong through violence will soon find that their strength is their death. Absalom and Ahithophel may raise the mob, but they cannot rule it, nor settle their own policy as to remain firm friends. The prayer of David was heard, the rebels were soon divided in their councils; Ahithophel went his way to be hanged with a rope, and Absalom to be hanged without one.

Psalm 55:10 *Day and night they go about it upon the walls thereof: mischief also and sorrow are in the midst of it.*

EXPOSITION: Verse 10. *Day and night they go about it upon the walls thereof.* The holy city had become a den of wickedness; conspirators met in the dark, and talked even in broad daylight. Meanwhile the country was being roused to revolt, traitors outside the city threatened to surround the city, and act in concert with the rebels within. No doubt there was a smothered fire of insurrection that Absalom kindled and fanned. David perceived it before he left Jerusalem; and when he left the city it broke out into an open flame.

Mischief also and sorrow are in the midst of it. Now an unhappy capital thus beset by foes, left by her monarch, and filled with all those elements of turbulence that breed evil and trouble. Unhappy king to be compelled to see the mischief which he could not avert laying waste the city he loved so well. There was another King whose many tears watered the rebellious city, and who said, "*O Jerusalem, Jerusalem,... how often would I have gathered thy children together, even as a hen gathereth her chickens under her wings, and ye would not!*" [Matthew 23:37].

Psalm 55:11 *Wickedness is in the midst thereof: deceit and guile depart not from her streets.*

EXPOSITION: **Verse 11.** *Wickedness is in the midst thereof.* The very heart of the city was base. In her places of authority crime went hand in hand with calamity. All the wilder and more wicked elements were uppermost; the canaille[29] were commanders; the scum floated uppermost; justice was at a discount; the people were utterly demoralized; prosperity and order had vanished.

Deceit and guile depart not from her streets. In all the places of concourse crafty tongues were busy persuading the people with cozening[30] phrases. Crafty demagogues led the people by the nose. The forum was the fortress of fraud; the congress was the convention of cunning. Alas, poor Jerusalem, to be the victim of sin and shame! Virtue reviled and vice regnant![31] Her solemn assemblies broken up, her priests fled, her king banished, and troops of reckless villains parading her streets, sunning themselves on her walls, and vomiting their blasphemies in her sacred shrines. Here was cause enough for the sorrow that so plaintively utters itself in these verses.

---

29. rabble
30. deceiving
31. reigning

> **Psalm 55:12** *For it was not an enemy that reproached me; then I could have borne it: neither was it he that hated me that did magnify himself against me; then I would have hid myself from him*

EXPOSITION: Verse 12. *For it was not an enemy that reproached me; then I could have borne it.* It was not an open foe, but a pretended friend; he went over to the other camp and tried to prove the reality of his treachery by calumniating his old friend. None are such real enemies as false friends. Reproaches from those who have been intimate with us, and trusted by us, cut us to the quick; and they are usually so well acquainted with our peculiar weaknesses that they know how to touch us where we are most sensitive. The slanders of an avowed antagonist are seldom as mean and dastardly as those of a traitor, and the absence of the elements of ingratitude and treachery renders them less hard to bear. We can bear from Shimei[32] what we cannot endure from Ahithophel.[33]

Neither was it he that hated me that did magnify himself against me; then I would have hid myself from him. We can find a hiding place from open foes, but who can escape from treachery? If our enemies proudly boast over us we nerve our souls for resistance, but when those who pretended to love us leer at us with contempt, where shall we go? Our blessed Lord had to endure at its worst the deceit and faithlessness of a favored disciple; let us not marvel when we are called to tread the road which is marked by His pierced feet.

---

32. Shimei was of Saul's family. He hated David because he had succeeded Saul as king.
33. a counselor to King David who later sided with Absalom against David

Psalm 55:13 *But it was thou, a man mine equal, my guide, and mine acquaintance.*

EXPOSITION: Verse 13. *But it was thou.* He sees him. He singles him out, he points his finger at him, and he challenges him to his face. But you. *Et tu, Brute.* And you, Ahithophel, are you here? Judas, do you betray the Son of Man?

A man mine equal. Treated by me as one of my own rank, never looked upon as an inferior, but as a trusted friend. *My guide,* a counselor so sage that I trusted your advice and found it prudent to do so. *And mine acquaintance,* with whom I was on most intimate terms, who knew me even as I knew him by mutual disclosures of heart. It was fiendish treason for such a one to prove falsehearted. There was no excuse for such villainy. Judas stood very much in this relation to our Lord; he was treated as an equal, trusted as treasurer, and in that capacity often consulted with. He knew the place where the Master went to spend His solitude; in fact, he knew all the Master's movements, and yet he betrayed Him to His remorseless adversaries. How justly might the Lord have pointed at him and said, "But thou..."; but His gentle spirit warned the son of perdition in the mildest manner, and had not Iscariot been tenfold a child of hell he would have relinquished his detestable purpose.

Psalm 55:14 *We took sweet counsel together, and walked unto the house of God in company.*

EXPOSITION: Verse 14. *We took sweet counsel together.* The traitor had been treated lovingly, and trusted much. Solace, mutual and cheering, had grown out of their intimate communing. There were secrets between them of no common kind. Soul had been in converse with soul, at least on David's part. However feigned might have been the affection of the treacherous one, the betrayed friend had not dealt with him coldly, or guarded his utterance before him. Shame on the wretch who could belie such fellowship, and betray such confidence! *And walked unto the house of God in company.* Religion had rendered their conversation sacred; they had mingled their worship, and communed on heavenly themes. If ever any bonds ought to be held inviolable, religious connections should be. There is a measure of impiety, of a detestable sort, in the deceit which debases the union of men who make profession of godliness. Shall the very altar of God be defiled with hypocrisy? Shall the gatherings of the temple be polluted by the presence of treachery? All this was true of Ahithophel, and in a measure of Judas. His union with the Lord was on the score of faith, they were joined in the holiest of enterprises, he had been sent on the most gracious of errands.

His cooperation with Jesus to serve his own abominable ends stamped him as the firstborn of hell. It would have been better for him if he had not been born. Let all deceitful professors be warned by his doom, for like Ahithophel he went to his own place by his own hand, and retains a horrible preeminence in the calendar of notorious crime. Here was one source of heartbreak for the Redeemer, and it is shared in by His followers. Some vipers still remain of the serpent's brood and they will sting the hands that cherish them and sell them for silver.

Psalm 55:15 *Let death seize upon them, and let them go down quick into hell: for wickedness is in their dwellings, and among them.*

EXPOSITION: Verse 15. Not thus would Jesus pray,

but the rough soldier David so poured out the anguish of his spirit, under treachery and malice seldom equaled and altogether unprovoked. David was right in his wish; he was waging a just, defensive war against men utterly regardless of truth and justice. Read the words as a warrior's imprecation.

Let death seize upon them. Traitors such as these deserve to die, there is no living with them, and Earth is polluted by their tread; if spies are shot, much more these sneaking villains.

Let them go down quick into hell. While in the vigor of life in Sheol let them sink, let them suddenly exchange the enjoyment of the quick or living for the sepulcher of the dead. There is, however, no need to read this verse as an imprecation; it is rather a confident expectation or prophecy for David was sure that God would desolate them, and cast them out of the land of the living into the regions of the dead.

For wickedness is in their dwellings, and among them. They are too bad to be spared, for their houses are dens of infamy, and their hearts fountains of mischief. They are a pest to the commonwealth, a moral plague, a spiritual pestilence, to be stamped out by the laws of men and the providence of God. Both Ahithophel and Judas soon ended their own lives; Absalom was hanged in the oak, and the rebels perished in the wood in great numbers. There is justice in the universe, love itself demands it; pity to rebels against God, as such, is no virtue—we pray for them as creatures, we abhor them as enemies of God. We need in these days far more to guard against the disguised iniquity which sympathizes with evil, and counts punishment to be cruelty, than against the harshness of a former age. We have steered so far from Scylla[34] that Charybdis[35] is absorbing us.

---

34. mythical Greek sea monster said to live on one side of the Strait of Messina between Sicily and the Italian mainland
35. mythical Greek sea monster said to live on the opposite side of Scylla on the Strait of Messina

Psalm 55:16 *As for me, I will call upon God; and the* LORD *shall save me.*

EXPOSITION: Verse 16. *As for me, I will call upon God.* The psalmist would not endeavor to meet the plots of his adversaries by counterplots, or imitate their incessant violence, but in direct opposition to their godless behavior would continually resort to his God. Thus Jesus did, and it has been the wisdom of all believers to do the same. As this exemplifies the contrast of their character, so it will foretell the contrast of their end—the righteous shall ascend to their God, the wicked shall sink to ruin.

And the Lord shall save me. Jehovah will fulfill my desire, and glorify himself in my deliverance. The psalmist is quite sure. He knows that he will pray, and is equally clear that he will be heard. The covenant name is the pledge of the covenant promise.

Psalm 55:17 *Evening, and morning, and at noon, will I pray, and cry aloud: and he shall hear my voice.*

Exposition: **Verse 17.** *Evening and morning, and at noon, will I pray.* Seasons of great need call for frequent seasons of devotion. The three periods chosen are most fitting; to begin, continue, and end the day with God is supreme wisdom. Where time has naturally set up a boundary, there let us set up an altar stone. The psalmist will run a line of prayer right along the day, and track the sun with his petitions. Day and night he saw his enemies busy [see Psalm 55:10], and therefore he would match their activity by continuous prayer.

And cry aloud. He would give voice to his complaint in earnest pleas with Heaven. Some cry aloud who never say a word. It is the bell of the heart that rings loudest in Heaven.

Blessed be God, moaning is translatable in Heaven. A father's heart reads a child's heart.

And he shall hear my voice. He is confident that he will prevail; he makes no question that he would be heard, he speaks as if he were already answered. When our window is opened towards Heaven, the windows of Heaven are open to us. Have but a pleading heart and God will have a plenteous hand.

Psalm 55:18 *He hath delivered my soul in peace from the battle that was against me: for there were many with me.*

EXPOSITION: Verse 18. *He hath delivered my soul in peace from the battle that was against me.* The deliverance has come. Joab[36] has routed the rebels. The Lord has justified the cause of His anointed. Faith sees as well as foresees; to her foresight is sight.

For there were many with me; he thankfully acknowledges that the Lord raised him up unexpected allies, fetched him assistance when he most needed it, and made the friendless monarch once more the head of a great army. The crisis of life is usually the secret place of wrestling. Jabbok[37] makes Jacob a prevailing prince. He who strips us of all friends to make us see ourselves in their absence, can give them back again in greater numbers that we may see Him more joyfully in the fact of their presence.

Psalm 55:19 *God shall hear, and afflict them, even he that abideth of old. Selah. Because they have no changes, therefore they fear not God.*

---

36. son of Zeruiah, David's sister, commander of David's army
37. the ford of Jabbok, at which Jacob wrestled with the Lord

PSALM 55

EXPOSITION: Verse 19. *God shall hear, and afflict them.* The voice of slander, malice, and pride, is not heard alone by those whom it grieves, it reaches to Heaven, it penetrates the divine ear, it demands vengeance, and shall have it. God hears and delivers His people; He hears and destroys the wicked. Their cruel jests, their base falsehoods, their cowardly insults, their daring blasphemies are heard, and shall be repaid to them by the eternal judge.

Even he that abideth of old. He sits in eternity, enthroned judge forevermore; all the prayers of saints and profanities of sinners are before His judgment seat, and He will see that justice is done.

Selah. The singer pauses, overwhelmed with awe in the presence of the everlasting God.

Because they have no changes, therefore they fear not God. His own reverential feeling causes him to remember the daring godlessness of the wicked; he feels that his trials have driven him to his God, and he declares that their uninterrupted prosperity was the cause of their living in such neglect of the Most High. It is a very manifest fact that long continued ease and pleasure are sure to produce the worst influences upon graceless men: though troubles do not convert them, yet the absence of them makes their corrupt nature more readily develop itself. He who is without trouble is often without God. It is a forcible proof of human depravity that man turns the mercy of God into nutriment for sin: the Lord save us from this.

Psalm 55:20 *He hath put forth his hands against such as be at peace with him: he hath broken his covenant.*

EXPOSITION: Verse 20. *He hath put forth his hands against such as be at peace with him.* He smites those to whom he had given the hand of friendship, he breaks the bonds of alliance, and he is perfidious to those who dwell at ease because of his friendly profession.

He hath broken his covenant. The most solemn league he has profaned, he is regardless of oaths and promises.

Psalm 55:21 *The words of his mouth were smoother than butter, but war was in his heart: his words were softer than oil, yet were they drawn swords.*

EXPOSITION: Verse 21. *The words of his mouth were smoother than butter.* He lauded the man he hoped to devour, buttered him with flattery and then battered him with malice. Beware of a man who has too much honey on his tongue; soft, smooth, oily words are most plentiful where truth and sincerity are most scarce.

But war was in his heart. But he had a tent pin ready for the temples of his guest. When heart and lip so widely differ, the man is a monster, and those whom he assails are afflicted indeed.

His words were softer than oil. Nothing could be more unctuous and fluent, his words were as yielding as the best juice of the olive; *yet were they drawn swords*, rapiers unsheathed, weapons brandished for the fray.

Psalm 55:22 *Cast thy burden upon the* LORD, *and he shall sustain thee: he shall never suffer the righteous to be moved.*

EXPOSITION: Verse 22. *Cast thy burden,* or what the God lays upon you, lay thou it *upon the Lord.* His wisdom casts it on you; it is your wisdom to cast it on Him. He cast your lot for you; cast your lot on Him. He gives you your portion of suffering, accept it with cheerful resignation, and then take it back to Him by your assured confidence.

He shall sustain thee. Your bread and water shall be given you. Abundant nourishment shall help you to bear all your labors and trials. *"As thy days, so shall thy strength be"* [Deuteronomy 33:25].
He shall never suffer the righteous to be moved. He may move like the boughs of a tree in the tempest, but He shall never be moved like a tree torn up by the roots. He stands firm who stands in God. Many desire to destroy the saints, but God has not allowed it, and never will. Like pillars, the godly stand immoveable, to the glory of the Great Architect.

Psalm 55:23 *But thou, O God, shalt bring them down into the pit of destruction: bloody and deceitful men shall not live out half their days; but I will trust in thee.*

EXPOSITION: Verse 23. *Bloody and deceitful men,* with double iniquity of cruelty and craft upon them, *shall not live out half their days;* they shall be cut off in their quarrels, and vexation shall end them. They were in heart murderers of others, and they became in reality self-murderers. Virtue lengthens life, and vice tends to shorten it.
But I will trust in thee. A very wise, practical conclusion. We can have no better ground of confidence. The Lord is all, and more than all that faith can need as the foundation of peaceful dependence. Lord, increase our faith evermore.

Psalm 56
Psalm 56:1–Psalm 56:13

Psalm 56:1 *Be merciful unto me, O God: for man would swallow me up; he fighting daily oppresseth me.*

EXPOSITION: Verse 1. *Be merciful unto me, O God.* My soul turns to you in my deep distress, my God. Man has no mercy on me; therefore double your mercy to me. If your justice has let loose my enemies, let your mercy shorten their chain. It is sweet to see how the tender dove-like spirit of the psalmist flies to the tenderest attribute for help in the hour of peril.

For man would swallow me up. He is but your creature, a mere man, yet like a monster he is eager for blood, he pants, gapes at me, and desires to swallow me altogether, and so make an end of me. The open mouths of sinners when they rage against us should open our mouths in prayer. We may plead the cruelty of men as a reason for the divine interposition—a father is soon aroused when his children are shamefully entreated.

He fighting daily oppresseth me. He gives me no rest—he fights daily and oppresses me and wants to crush me and press me sorely. David has his eye on the leader of his foes, and lays his complaint against him in the right place. If we may thus plead against man, and much more against that great enemy of souls, the devil. We ask the Lord to forgive us our trespasses, and then we say, "Lead us not into temptation, but deliver us from the evil one." [See Matthew 6:13.]

Psalm 56:2 *Mine enemies would daily swallow me up: for they be many that fight against me, O thou most High.*

EXPOSITION: **Verse 2.** *Mine enemies would daily swallow me up.* Their appetite for blood never fails them. Unless they can quite devour me they will never be content. The ogres of nursery tales exist in reality in the enemies of the Church, who would crush the bones of the godly, and make a mouthful of them if they could.

For they be many that fight against me. Sinners are gregarious creatures. Persecutors hunt in packs. These wolves of the Church seldom come down upon us singly. The number of our foes is a powerful plea for the interposition of the one Defender of the faithful, who is mightier than all their bands. These foes of the gracious are also keen eyed, and ever on the watch, hence the margin calls them "observers."

O thou most High. Thus he invokes against the lofty ones of the Earth the aid of one who is higher than the highest. Saul, his great foe, attacked him from his throne with all the force which his high position placed at his disposal: our comfort in such a case is near to hand, for God will help us from a higher place than our proudest foes can occupy. The greatness of God as the Most High is a fertile source of consolation to weak saints oppressed by mighty enemies.

Psalm 56:3 *What time I am afraid, I will trust in thee.*

EXPOSITION: **Verse 3.** *What time I am afraid.* David's intelligence deprived him of the stupid heedlessness of ignorance, he saw the imminence of his peril, and was afraid. We are men, and therefore liable to overthrow; we are feeble, and therefore unable to prevent it; we are sinful men, and therefore deserving it, and for all these reasons we are afraid. But the condition of the psalmist's mind was complex—he feared, but that fear did not fill the whole area of his mind, for he adds, *I will trust in thee.* It is possible, then, for fear and faith to occupy the mind at the same moment. We are strange beings, and our experience in the divine life is stranger still. We are often in twilight, where light and darkness are both present, and it is hard to tell which predominates. It is a blessed fear which drives us to trust. Unregenerate fear drives from God, gracious fear drives to Him. If I fear man I have only to trust God, and I have the best antidote. To trust when there is no cause for fear, is but the name of faith, but to be reliant upon God when occasions for alarm are abundant and pressing, is the conquering faith of God's elect. Though the verse is in the form of a resolve, it became a fact in David's life, let us make it so in ours. Whether the fear arise from without or within, from past, present, or future, from temporal, or spiritual, from men or devils, let us maintain faith, and we shall soon recover courage.

Psalm 56:4 *In God I will praise his word, in God I have put my trust; I will not fear what flesh can do unto me.*

EXPOSITION: Verse 4. *In God I will praise his word.* Faith brings forth praise. God's promise, when fulfilled, is a noble subject for praise, and even before fulfillment it should be the theme of song. It is in or through God that we are able to praise. We praise as well as pray in the Spirit. In extolling the Lord one of the main points for thanksgiving is His revealed will in the Scriptures, and the fidelity with which He keeps His word of promise.

In God I have put my trust. Altogether and alone we should stay ourselves on God. What was a gracious resolve in the former verse is here asserted as already done.

I will not fear what flesh can do unto me. Faith exercised, fear is banished, and holy triumph ensues, so that the soul asks, "What can flesh do unto me?" What indeed? He can do me no real injury; all his malice shall be overruled for my good. Man is flesh, flesh is grass—Lord, in your name I defy its utmost wrath. There were two verses of complaint, and here is two of confidence; it is good to weigh out a sufficient quantity of the sweet to counteract the sour.

Psalm 56:5 *Every day they wrest my words: all their thoughts are against me for evil.*

EXPOSITION: **Verse 5.** *Every day they wrest my words.* This is a common mode of warfare among the ungodly. They extort meanings from the word which it cannot be made to contain. Thus our Savior's prophecy concerning the temple of His body, and countless accusations against His servants, were founded on willful perversions. They who do this every day become very adept in the art. A wolf can always find in a lamb's discourse a reason for eating him. Prayers are blasphemies if you choose to read them the wrong way upwards.

All their thoughts are against me for evil. No mixture of good will tone down their malice. Whether they viewed him as a king, a psalmist, a man, a father, a warrior, a sufferer, it was all the same, they saw through colored glass, and could not think a good thought towards him. Even those actions of his which were an undoubted blessing to the commonwealth, they endeavored to undervalue.

Psalm 56:6 *They gather themselves together, they hide themselves, they mark my steps, when they wait for my soul.*

EXPOSITION: **Verse 6.** *They gather themselves together.* Firebrands burn fiercer when pushed together. They are afraid to meet the good man until their numbers place terrible odds against him. Come out, you cowards, man to man, and fight the old hero! No, you wait until you are assembled like thieves in bands, and even then you waylay the man. There is nothing brave about you.

They hide themselves. In ambush they wait their opportunity. Men of malice are men of cowardice. He who dares not meet his man on the king's highway is a villain. Reputations of good men are constantly assailed with deep laid schemes, and diabolical plots, in which the anonymous enemies stab in the dark.

They mark my steps, as hunters mark the trail of their game, and so track them. Malicious men are frequently very sharp-sighted to detect the supposed failings of the righteous. Spies and mouchards[38] are not all in the pay of earthly governments, some of them will have wages to take in red hot coin from one who himself is more subtle than all the beasts of the field.

When they wait for my soul. Only his present and eternal ruin could altogether satisfy them. The good man is no fool, he sees that he has many crafty enemies; he sees also his own danger, and shows his wisdom by spreading the whole case before the Lord, thereby putting himself under divine protection.

---

38. undercover investigators

Psalm 56:7 *Shall they escape by iniquity? in thine anger cast down the people, O God.*

EXPOSITION: **Verse 7.** *Shall they escape by iniquity?* They slander the good man to screen themselves—will this avail them? They have cunningly managed so far, but will there not be an end to their games?

In thine anger cast down the people, O God. Trip them up in their tricks. Hurl them from the Tarpeian[39] rock. A persecuted man finds a friend even in an angry God, how much more in the God of love! When men seek to cast us down, it is natural and not unlawful to pray that they may be disabled from the accomplishment of their infamous designs. What God often does we may safely ask Him to do.

Psalm 56:8 *Thou tellest my wanderings: put thou my tears into thy bottle: are they not in thy book?*

EXPOSITION: **Verse 8.** *Thou tellest my wanderings.* Every step the fugitive had taken when pursued by his enemies, was not only observed but thought worthy of counting and recording. We perhaps are confused after a long course of trouble, but the omniscient and considerate Father of our spirits remembers all in detail; for He has counted them over as men count their gold, even the trial of our faith is precious in His sight.

Put thou my tears into thy bottle. His sorrows were so many that there would be need of a great wineskin to hold them all. There is no allusion to the little complimentary lachrymators[40] for fashionable and fanciful Romans. It is a more robust metaphor by far; such floods of tears had

---

39. a steep cliff of the southern summit of the Capitoline Hill overlooking the ancient Roman forum
40. a substance that causes tears to flow from the eyes

David wept that a leathern bottle would scarce hold them. He trusts that the Lord will be so considerate of his tears as to store them up as men do the juice of the vine, and he hopes that the place of storage will be a special one—*thy bottle*, not *a bottle*.

Are they not in thy book? Yes, they are recorded there, but let not only the record but the grief itself be present to you. Look on my griefs as real things, for they move the heart more than a mere account, however exact. How condescending is the Lord! How exact His knowledge of us! How generous His estimation! How tender His regard!

Psalm 56:9 *When I cry unto thee, then shall mine enemies turn back: this I know; for God is for me.*

EXPOSITION: **Verse 9.** *When I cry unto thee, then shall mine enemies turn back.* As soon as I pray they shall fly. As surely as I cry they shall be routed.

So swift is prayer to reach the sky,[41]
So kind is God to me.

The machinery of prayer is not always visible, but it is most efficient. God inclines us to pray, we cry in anguish of heart, He hears, He acts, and the enemy is turned back. What irresistible artillery this is to protect His children, for in a moment He delivers them from the mightiest adversaries!

This I know. This is one of the believer's certainties, his axioms, and his infallible, indisputable verities.

For God is for me. This, we know, and we know, therefore, that none can be against us who are worth a moment's fear. "If God be for us, who can be against us?" [Romans 8:31]. Who will not pray when it is so potent? Who will seek any other ally than God, who is instantly present as soon as

---

41. verse two of the hymn "Psalm LXXVI," by Isaac Watts

we give the ordained signal, by which we testify both our need and our confidence?

Psalm 56:10 *In God will I praise his word: in the* LORD *will I praise his word.*

EXPOSITION: **Verse 10.** *In God will I praise his word.* Now comes the thanksgiving. He is a wretch who, having obtained help, forgets to return a grateful acknowledgment. The least we can do is to praise Him from whom we receive such distinguished favors. The object of David's praise is His word, and the faithfulness with which He keeps it. If so, we see how attached our hearts should be to the sure word of promise, and especially to Him who is the Word incarnate. The Lord is to be praised under every aspect, and in all His attributes and acts, but certain mercies peculiarly draw out our admiration towards special portions of the great whole. That praise which is never special in its direction cannot be very thoughtful, and it is to be feared cannot be very acceptable.

In the Lord will I praise his word. He delights to dwell on His praise, he therefore repeats His song. The change by which he brings in the glorious name of Jehovah is doubtless meant to indicate that under every aspect he delights in His God and in His word.

Psalm 56:11 *In God have I put my trust: I will not be afraid what man can do unto me.*

EXPOSITION: **Verse 11.** *In God have I put my trust.* This and the former verse are evidently the chorus of the psalm. We cannot be too careful of our faith, or see too sedulously[42] that it is grounded on the Lord alone.

I will not be afraid what man can do unto me. Faith

---
42. diligently

has banished fear. He views his foes in their most forcible character, calling them not flesh, but indicating them as man, yet he dreads them not; even if the whole race were his enemies he would not be afraid now that his trust is stayed on God. He is not afraid of what they threaten to do, for much of that they cannot do; and even what is in their power do, he defies with holy daring. He speaks for the future, "I will not," for he is sure that the security of the present will suffice for days to come.

> **Psalm 56:12** *Thy vows are upon me, O God: I will render praises unto thee.*

EXPOSITION: **Verse 12.** *Thy vows are upon me, O God.* Vows made in his trouble he does not lightly forget, nor should we. We voluntarily made them, let us cheerfully keep them. All professed Christians are men under vows, but especially those who in hours of dire distress have rededicated themselves unto the Lord.

I will render praises unto thee. With heart, voice, and gift, we should cheerfully extol the God of our salvation. The practice of making solemn vows in times of trouble is to be commended, when it is followed by the far less common custom of fulfilling them when the trouble is over.

> **Psalm 56:13** *For thou hast delivered my soul from death: wilt not thou deliver my feet from falling, that I may walk before God in the light of the living?*

EXPOSITION: **Verse 13.** *For thou hast delivered my soul from death.* His enemies were defeated in their attempts upon his life, and therefore he vowed to devote his life to God.

Wilt not thou deliver my feet from falling? One mercy is a plea for another, for indeed it may happen that the second is the necessary complement of the first. It matters little that we live, if we are made to fall in character by the thrusts of our enemies. A life cannot be, as life bereft of honor, and fallen prostrate before my enemies.

That I may walk before God in the light of the living, enjoying the favor and presence of God, and finding the joy and brightness of life therein. Walking at liberty, in holy service, in sacred communion, in constant progress in holiness, enjoying the smile of Heaven—this I seek after. Here is the loftiest reach of a good man's ambition, to dwell with God, to walk in righteousness before Him, to rejoice in His presence, and in the light and glory which it yields. Thus in this short psalm, we have climbed from the ravenous jaws of the enemy into the light of Jehovah's presence, a path which only faith can tread.

Psalm 57
Psalm 57:1–Psalm 57:11

> **Psalm 57:1** *Be merciful unto me, O God, be merciful unto me: for my soul trusteth in thee: yea, in the shadow of thy wings will I make my refuge, until these calamities be overpast.*

EXPOSITION: Verse 1. *Be merciful unto me, O God, be merciful unto me.* Urgent need suggests the repetition of the cry, for thus intense urgency of desire is expressed. "If he gives twice who gives quickly, so he who would receive quickly must ask twice."[43] For mercy the psalmist pleads at first, and he feels he cannot improve upon his plea, and therefore returns to it. God is the God of mercy, and the Father of mercies, it is most fit therefore that in distress he should seek mercy from Him in whom it dwells.

For my soul trusteth in thee. Faith urges her suit right well. How can the Lord be unmerciful to a trustful soul? Our faith does not deserve mercy, but it always wins it from the sovereign grace of God when it is sincere, as in this case where the soul of the man believed. *"With the heart man believeth unto righteousness"* [Romans 10:10].

Yea, in the shadow of thy wings will I make my refuge. Not in the cave alone would he hide, but in the cleft of the Rock of Ages. As the little birds find ample shelter beneath the parental wing, even so would the fugitive place himself beneath the secure protection of the divine power. When we

---
43. *The Facts on File Dictionary of Proverbs* By Martin H. Manser Page 117.

cannot see the sunshine of God's face, it is blessed to cower down beneath the shadow of His wings.

Until these calamities be overpast. Evil will pass away, and the eternal wings will abide over us until then. Blessed be God, our calamities are matters of time, but our safety is a matter of eternity. When we are under the divine shadow, the passing over of trouble cannot harm us; the hawk flies across the sky, but this is no evil to the chicks when they are safely nestling beneath the hen.

Psalm 57:2 *I will cry unto God most high; unto God that performeth all things for me.*

EXPOSITION: Verse 2. *I will cry.* He is quite safe, but yet he prays, for faith is never silent. We pray because we believe. We exercise by faith the spirit of adoption whereby we cry. He says I will cry, and indeed, this resolution may stand with all of us until we pass through the gates of pearl; for while we are here below we shall still have need to cry.

Unto God most high—Prayers are for God only; the greatness and sublimity of His person and character suggest and encourage prayer; however high our enemies, our heavenly Friend is higher, for He is Most high, and He can readily send from the height of His power the help we need.

Unto God that performeth all things for me. The believer waits and God works, He will go through with His covenant engagements. Our translators have very properly inserted the words, "all things," for there is a blank in the Hebrew, as if it were a carte blanche,[44] and we should write those words there. Whatsoever the Lord takes in hand He will accomplish; hence past mercies are guarantees for the future, and admirable reasons for continuing to cry unto Him.

---

44. freedom to act or say what one wishes with no fear of reprisal

Psalm 57:3 *He shall send from heaven, and save me from the reproach of him that would swallow me up. Selah. God shall send forth his mercy and his truth.*

EXPOSITION: Verse 3. *He shall send from heaven.* If there are no fit instruments on Earth, Heaven shall yield up its legions of angels for the help of the saints. We may in times of great straits expect mercies of a remarkable kind; like the Israelites in the wilderness, we shall have our bread hot from Heaven, new every morning; and for the overthrow of our enemies God shall open His celestial batteries, and put them to utter confusion. *And save me from the reproach of him that would swallow me up.* He will be in time, not only to rescue His servants from being swallowed up, but even from being reproached. Not only shall they escape the flames, but not even the smell of fire shall pass upon them. Selah. Such mercy may well make us pause to meditate and give thanks. Rest, singer, for God has given you rest!

God shall send forth his mercy and his truth. He asked for mercy, and truth came with it. Thus evermore does God give us more than we ask or think. His attributes, like angels on the wing, are ever ready to come to the rescue of His chosen.

Psalm 57:4 *My soul is among lions: and I lie even among them that are set on fire, even the sons of men, whose teeth are spears and arrows, and their tongue a sharp sword.*

EXPOSITION: Verse 4. *My soul is among lions.* He was like Daniel. Howled at, hunted, wounded, but not slain. His place was in extreme peril, yet faith made him feel secure enough to lie down. The cave may have reminded him of a lion's den, and Saul and his shouting followers were the lions; yet beneath the divine shelter he finds himself safe.

And I lie even among them that are set on fire. Perhaps Saul and his band kindled a fire in the cavern while they halted in it, and David was thus reminded of the fiercer fire of their hate which burned within their hearts. Like the bush in Horeb, the believer is often in the midst of flames, but never consumed. It is a mighty triumph of faith when we can lie down even among firebrands and find rest, because God is our defense.

Even the sons of men, whose teeth are spears and arrows, and their tongue a sharp sword. Malicious men carry a whole armory in their mouths; they have harmful mouths, whose teeth grind their own food as in a mill, but their jaws are as are canines, and their nature is canine, leonine, wolfish, and devilish. The tongue, which is compared to a sword, has the adjective sharp added to it. No weapon is so terrible as a tongue sharpened on the devil's grindstone; yet even this we need not fear, for *"No weapon that is formed against thee shall prosper; and every tongue that shall rise against thee in judgment thou shalt condemn"* [Isaiah 54:17].

Psalm 57:5 *Be thou exalted, O God, above the heavens; let thy glory be above all the earth.*

EXPOSITION: Verse 5. *Be thou exalted, O God, above the heavens.* This is the chorus of the psalm. Higher than the heavens is the Most High, and so high ought our praises to rise. Above even the power of cherubim and seraphim to express it, the glory of God is revealed and is to be acknowledged by us.

Let thy glory be above all the earth. As above, so below, let your praises, O great Jehovah, be universally proclaimed. As the air surrounds all nature, so let your praises gird the Earth with a zone of song.

Psalm 57:6 *They have prepared a net for my steps; my soul is bowed down: they have digged a pit before me, into the midst whereof they are fallen themselves. Selah.*

EXPOSITION: Verse 6. *They have prepared a net for my steps.* As for each sort of fish, or bird, or beast, a fitting net is needed, so do the ungodly suit their net to their victim's circumstances and character with a careful craftiness of malice. Whatever David might do, and whichever way he might turn, his enemies were ready to entrap him in some way or other.

My soul is bowed down. He was held down like a bird in a trap; his enemies took care to leave him no chance of comfort.

They have digged a pit before me, into the midst whereof they are fallen themselves. He likens the design of his persecutors to pits, which were commonly dug by hunters to entrap their prey; these were made in the usual path of the victim, and in this case David says, before me, i.e., in my ordinary way. He rejoices because these devices had recoiled upon themselves. Saul hunted David, but David caught him more than once and might have slain him on the spot. Evil is a stream which one day flows back to its source.

Selah. We may sit down at the pit's mouth and view with wonder the just retaliations of providence.

Psalm 57:7 *My heart is fixed, O God, my heart is fixed: I will sing and give praise.*

EXPOSITION: Verse 7. *My heart is fixed.* One would have thought he would have said, "My heart is fluttered;" but no, he is calm, firm, happy, resolute, and established. When the central axle is secure, the whole wheel is right. *O God, my heart is fixed.* I am resolved to trust you, to serve you, and to praise you. Twice he declares this to the glory of God who thus comforts the souls of His servants. Reader, it is surely well with you, if your once roving heart is now firmly fixed upon God *and the proclamation of His glory.*

I will sing and give praise. Vocally and instrumentally I will celebrate your worship. With lips and with heart will I ascribe honor to you. I will make Adullam ring with music, and all the caverns thereof echo with joyous song. Believer, make a firm decree that in all seasons your soul will magnify the Lord.

> Sing, though sense and carnal reason[45]
> Fain would stop the joyful song:
> Sing, and count it highest treason
> For a saint to hold his tongue.

Psalm 57:8 *Awake up, my glory; awake, psaltery and harp: I myself will awake early.*

EXPOSITION: Verse 8. *Awake up, my glory.* Let the noblest powers of my nature stir themselves: the intellect which conceives thought, the tongue which expresses it, and the inspired imagination which beautifies it—let all be on the alert now that the hour for praise has come.

Awake, psaltery and harp. Let all the music with which I am familiar be well attuned for the hallowed service of praise.

I myself will awake early. I will awake the dawn with my joyous notes. No sleepy verses and weary notes shall be heard from me; I will thoroughly arouse myself for this high employ. When we are at our best we fall short of the Lord's deserts, let us, therefore, make sure that what we bring Him is our best, and, if marred with infirmity, at least let it not be deteriorated by indolence. Three times the psalmist calls

---

45. from hymn by Isaac Watts titled "Sing Ye Saints," as found in *Our Own Hymn-Book.*

upon himself to awake. Do we need so much arousing, and for such work? Then let us not spare it, for the engagement is too honorable, too needful to be left undone or ill done for want of arousing ourselves.

> **Psalm 57:9** *I will praise thee, O Lord, among the people: I will sing unto thee among the nations.*

EXPOSITION: Verse 9. *I will praise thee, O Lord, among the people.* Gentiles shall hear my praise. The ordinary Jew would never wish the Gentile dogs to hear Jehovah's name, except to tremble at it; but this grace-taught psalmist has a missionary spirit, and would spread the praise and fame of his God.

I will sing unto thee among the nations. However far off they may be, I would make them hear of you through my glad psalmody.

> **Psalm 57:10** *For thy mercy is great unto the heavens, and thy truth unto the clouds.*

EXPOSITION: Verse 10. *For thy mercy is great unto the heavens.* Mercy reaches right up from man's lowliness to heaven's loftiness. The riches of mercy exceed our highest thoughts. As he sits at the cave's mouth, the psalmist looks up to the firmament, rejoices that God's goodness is vaster and more sublime than even the vaulted skies.

And thy truth unto the clouds. Upon the cloud He sets the seal of His truth, the rainbow, which ratifies His covenant; in the cloud He hides His rain and snow, which prove His truth by bringing to us seedtime and harvest, cold and heat. Creation is great, but the Creator is far greater. Heaven cannot contain Him; and His goodness far exceeds above clouds and stars.

Psalm 57:11 *Be thou exalted, O God, above the heavens: let thy glory be above all the earth.*

EXPOSITION: Verse 11. *Be thou exalted, O God, above the heavens.* A grand chorus. Take it up, you angels and you spirits made perfect, and join in it, you sons of men below, as you say,

Let thy glory be above all the earth. The prophet in the previous verse spoke of mercy "unto the heavens," but here his song flies "above the heavens;" praise rises higher, and knows no bound.

Psalm 58

Psalm 58:1–Psalm 58:11

Psalm 58:1 *Do ye indeed speak righteousness, O congregation? do ye judge uprightly, O ye sons of men?*

EXPOSITION: Verse 1. *Do ye indeed speak righteousness, O congregation?* The enemies of David were a numerous and united band, and because they so unanimously condemned the persecuted one, they were apt to take it for granted that their verdict was a right one. "What everybody says must be true," is a lying proverb based upon the presumption that comes of large combinations. Yet the persecuted one lays the axe at the root by requiring his judges to answer the question whether or not they were acting according to justice. It would be good if men would sometimes pause, and candidly consider this. Some of those who surrounded Saul were rather passive than active persecutors. They held their tongues when the object of royal hate was slandered; in the original, this first sentence appears to be addressed to them, and they are asked to justify their silence. Silence gives consent. He who refrains from defending the right is himself an accomplice in the wrong.

Do ye judge uprightly, O ye sons of men? You too are only men though dressed in a little brief authority. Your office for men and your relation to men both bind you to rectitude; but have you remembered this? Have you not put aside all truth when you have condemned the godly, and united in seeking the overthrow of the innocent? Yet in doing this be not too sure of success, or you are only the "sons of men," and there is a God who can and will reverse your verdicts.

Psalm 58:2 *Yea, in heart ye work wickedness; ye weigh the violence of your hands in the earth.*

EXPOSITION: Verse 2. *Yea, in heart ye work wickedness.* Down deep in your very souls you hold a rehearsal of the injustice you intend to practice, for those very men who sat as judges, and pretended to so much indignation at the faults imputed to their victim, were in their hearts perpetrating all manner of evil. *Ye weigh the violence of your hands in the earth.* As righteous judges ponder the law, balance the evidence, and weigh the case, so the malicious dispense injustice with malice aforethought in cold blood. Note in this verse that the men described sinned with heart and hand; privately in their heart, publicly in the Earth; they worked and they weighed—they were active, and yet deliberate. See what a generation saints have to deal with! Such were the foes of our Lord, a generation of vipers, an evil and adulterous generation; they sought to kill Him because He was righteousness itself, yet they masked their hatred to His goodness by charging Him with sin.

Psalm 58:3 *The wicked are estranged from the womb: they go astray as soon as they be born, speaking lies.*

EXPOSITION: Verse 3. *The wicked are estranged from the womb.* It is small wonder that some men persecute the righteous seed of the woman, since all of them are of the serpent's brood, and enmity is set between them. No sooner born than alienated from God—what a condition to be found in! *They go astray as soon as they be born, speaking lies.* Every observer may see how very soon infants act lies.

Before they can speak they practice little deceptive arts. This is especially the case in those who grow up to be adept in slander, they begin their evil trade early, and there is no marvel that they become adept in it. He who starts early in the morning will go far before night. To be untruthful is one of the surest proofs of a fallen state, and since falsehood is universal, so also is human depravity.

> **Psalm 58:4** *Their poison is like the poison of a serpent: they are like the deaf adder that stoppeth her ear*

EXPOSITION: **Verse 4.** *Their poison is like the poison of a serpent.* Is man also a poisonous reptile? Yes, and his venom is even as that of a serpent. The viper has but death for the body in his fangs; but unregenerate man carries poison under his tongue, destructive to the nobler nature.

They are like the deaf adder that stoppeth her ear. While speaking of serpents the psalmist remembers that many of them have been conquered by the charmer's art, but men such as he had to deal with no art could tame or restrain. Therefore, he likens them to a serpent less susceptible than others to the charmer's music, and says that they refused to hear reason, even as the adder shuts her ear to those incantations that fascinate other reptiles.

> **Psalm 58:5** *Which will not hearken to the voice of charmers, charming never so wisely.*

EXPOSITION: **Verse 5.** *Which will not hearken to the voice of charmers, charming never so wisely.* Try all your arts, you preachers of the word! Lay yourselves out to meet the prejudices and tastes of sinners, and you shall yet have to cry, *"Who hath believed our report?"* [John 12:38]. It is not in your music, but in the sinner's ear that the cause of failure lies, and it is only the power of God that can remove it.

> You can call spirits from the vast deep,[46]
> But will they come when you do call for them?

No, we call and call, and call in vain, until the arm of the Lord is revealed. This is at once the sinner's guilt and danger. He ought to hear but will not, and because he will not hear, he cannot escape the damnation of hell.

Psalm 58: *Break their teeth, O God, in their mouth: break out the great teeth of the young lions, O LORD.*

EXPOSITION: Verse 6. *Break their teeth, O God, in their mouth.* If they have no capacity for good, at least deprive them of their ability for evil. Treat them as the snake charmers do their serpents, extract their fangs, and break their teeth. The Lord can do this, and He will.

Break out the great teeth of the young lions, O Lord. As if one brute creature had not enough of evil in it to complete the emblem of ungodly nature, another specimen of *ferae naturae*[47] is fetched in. For fierce cruelty the wicked are likened to young lions, monsters in the prime of their vigor, and the fury of their lustiness; and it is asked that their teeth be dashed out, rendering them harmless. One can well understand how the banished son of Jesse, while poisoned by the venomous slander of his foes, and worried by their cruel power, would appeal to Heaven for a speedy and complete riddance from his enemies.

---

46. quote from Shakespeare's play, *King Richard II.*
47. wild by nature and not usually tamed

Psalm 58:7 *Let them melt away as waters which run continually: when he bendeth his bow to shoot his arrows, let them be as cut in pieces.*

EXPOSITION: Verse 7. *Let them melt away as waters which run continually.* Like mountain torrents dried up by the summer heats let them disappear.

When he bendeth his bow to shoot his arrows, let them be as cut in pieces. When the Lord goes forth to war, let His judgments so tell upon these persecutors that they may be utterly cut in pieces as a mark shattered by many shafts. The prayer of the psalm has often become fact, and will be again fulfilled as often as need arises.

Psalm 58:8 *As a snail which melteth, let every one of them pass away: like the untimely birth of a woman, that they may not see the sun.*

EXPOSITION: Verse 8. *As a snail which melteth, let every one of them pass away.* As the snail makes its own way by its slime, and so dissolves as it goes, so shall the malicious eat out their own strength and disappear.

Like the untimely birth of a woman, that they may not see the sun. Solemn is this curse, but how surely does it fall on many graceless wretches! They are as if they had never been. Their character is shapeless, hideous, revolting. Their life never reaches ripeness, their aims are abortive, their only achievement is to have brought misery to others, and horror to themselves. Such men as Herod, Judas, Alva, Bonner, had it not been better for them if they had never been born? Better for the lands they cursed? Every unregenerate man is an abortion. He misses the true form of God-made manhood; corrupts in the darkness of sin; and he never shall see the light of God in purity, in Heaven.

Psalm 58:9 *Before your pots can feel the thorns, he shall take them away as with a whirlwind, both living, and in his wrath.*

EXPOSITION: Verse 9. *Before your pots can feel the thorns.* So sudden is the overthrow of the wicked, before any heat can be brought to bear upon the pot, yea, even as soon as the fuel has touched the cooking vessel, a storm comes and sweeps all away; the pot is overturned, the fuel is scattered far and wide.

He shall take them away as with a whirlwind. Cook, fire, pot, meat and all, disappear at once, whirled away to destruction.

Both living, and in his wrath. In the very midst of the man's life, the persecutor is overwhelmed with a tornado, his designs are baffled, and himself destroyed. The unexpected tempest removes all trace of him, his fire, and his feast, in just a moment.

Psalm 58:10 *The righteous shall rejoice when he seeth the vengeance: he shall wash his feet in the blood of the wicked.*

EXPOSITION: Verse 10. *The righteous shall rejoice when he seeth the vengeance.* He will have no hand in meting out, neither will he rejoice in the spirit of revenge, but his righteous soul shall acquiesce in the judgments of God, and he shall rejoice to see justice triumphant. There is nothing in Scripture of that sympathy with God's enemies that modern traitors are so fond of parading as the finest species of benevolence. We shall at the last say, "Amen," to the condemnation of the wicked, and feel no disposition to question the ways of God with the impenitent. Remember how John, the loving disciple, puts it in Revelation 19:1–3.

PSALM 58

And after these things I heard a great voice of much people in heaven, saying, Alleluia; Salvation and glory, and honour, and power, unto the Lord our God: for true and righteous are his judgments: for he hath judged the great whore, which did corrupt the earth with her fornication, and hath avenged the blood of his servants at her hand. And again they said, Alleluia. And her smoke rose up for ever and ever.

He shall wash his feet in the blood of the wicked. He shall triumph over them, they shall be so utterly vanquished that their overthrow shall be final and fatal, and his deliverance complete and crowning. The damnation of sinners shall not mar the happiness of saints.

Psalm 58:11 *So that a man shall say, Verily there is a reward for the righteous: verily he is a God that judgeth in the earth.*

EXPOSITION: **Verse 11.** *So that a man shall say.* Every man however ignorant shall be compelled to say, *Verily, in very deed, assuredly, there is a reward for the righteous.* If nothing else is true this is. The godly are not forsaken and given over to their enemies; the wicked are not to have the best of it, truth and goodness are recompensed in the long run.

Verily he is a God that judgeth in the earth. All men shall be forced by the sight of the final judgment to see that there is a God, and that He is the righteous ruler of the universe. Two things will come out clearly after all—there is a God and there is a reward for the righteous. Time will remove doubts, solve difficulties, and reveal secrets; meanwhile faith's foreseeing eye discerns the truth even now, and is glad.

Psalm 59

Psalm 59:1–Psalm 59:17

Psalm 59:1 *Deliver me from mine enemies, O my God: defend me from them that rise up against me.*

EXPOSITION: Verse 1. *Deliver me from mine enemies, O my God.* He was to be taken dead or alive, well or ill, and carried to the slaughter. Unbelief would have suggested that prayer was a waste of breath, but not so thought the good man, for he makes it his sole resort. He cries for deliverance and leaves ways and means with his God.

Defend me from them that rise up against me. David asks to be lifted up, as into a lofty tower, beyond the reach of his adversary. God is our God, and therefore deliverance and defense are ours.

Psalm 59:2 *Deliver me from the workers of iniquity, and save me from bloody men.*

EXPOSITION: Verse 2. *Deliver me from the workers of iniquity* When a habitation is beset by thieves, the good man of the house rings the alarm bell; and in these verses we may hear it ring out loudly, "deliver me," "defend me," "deliver me," "save me." Saul had more cause to fear than David had, for the invincible weapon of prayer was being used against him, and Heaven was being aroused to give him battle.

And save me from bloody men. As David remembers how often Saul had sought to assassinate him, he knows what he has to expect from that quarter and from the king's creatures and minions who were watching for him. David represents his enemy in his true colors before God; the bloodthirstiness of the foe is a fit reason for the interposition of the righteous God, for the Lord abhors all those who delight in blood.

Psalm 59:3 *For, lo, they lie in wait for my soul: the mighty are gathered against me; not for my transgression, nor for my sin, O LORD.*

EXPOSITION: Verse 3. *For, lo, they lie in wait for my soul.* They were in ambush for the good man's life. He knew their design and cried to God to be rescued from them. Their victim used effectual means to baffle them, for he laid the matter before the Lord. While the enemy lies waiting in the posture of a beast, we wait before God in the posture of prayer, for God waits to be gracious to us and terrible towards our foes.

The mighty are gathered against me. None of them were absent from the muster when a saint was to be murdered. They were too fond of such sport to be away. Saul, the gigantic monarch is spending all his strength to slay a faithful follower.

Not for my transgression, not for my sin, O Lord. David appeals to Jehovah that he had done no ill. His only fault was that he was too valiant and too gracious, and was, besides, the chosen of the Lord. We shall always find it to be a great thing to be innocent; if it does not carry our cause before an earthly tribunal, it will ever prove the best of arguments in the court of conscience, and a standing consolation when we are under persecution.

> **Psalm 59:4** *They run and prepare themselves without my fault: awake to help me, and behold.*

EXPOSITION: Verse 4. *They run and prepare themselves without my fault.* So quick are they to obey their cruel master that they never stay to consider whether their errand is a good one or not; they run at once, and buckle on their harness as they run. To be thus gratuitously attacked is a great grief. To a brave man the danger causes little distress of mind compared with the injustice to which he is subjected. It was a cruel and crying shame that such a hero as David should be hounded down as if he were a monster, and beset in his house like a wild beast in its den.

Awake to help me, and behold. When others go to sleep, keep watch, O God. Only look at your servant's sad condition and your hand will be sure to deliver me. We see how thorough the psalmist's faith was in the mercy of his Lord, for he is satisfied that if the Lord does but look on his case it will move his active compassion.

> **Psalm 59:5** *Thou therefore, O LORD God of hosts, the God of Israel, awake to visit all the heathen: be not merciful to any wicked transgressors. Selah.*

EXPOSITION: Verse 5. *Thou,* thyself, work for me personally, for the case needs thine interposition. *Therefore,* because I am unjustly assailed, and cannot help myself. O Lord, ever living, *God of Hosts,* able to rescue me; the God of Israel, pledged by covenant to redeem your oppressed servant; *awake to visit all the heathen,* arouse your holy mind, bestow your sacred energies, punish the heathen among your Israel, the falsehearted who say they are Jews and are not, but do lie. It is the mark of a thoughtful prayer that the titles which are in it applied to God are appropriate, and are, as it were, congruous to the matter, and fitted to add force to the argument. The name of God is, even in a literal sense, a fortress and high tower for all His people. What a forceful petition is contained in the words, *"awake to visit"!* Actively punish, in wisdom judge, chastise with force.

Be not merciful to any wicked transgressors. Be merciful to them as men, but not as transgressors; if they continue hardened in their sin, do not wink at their oppression. The psalmist feels that the overthrow of oppression which was so needful for himself must be equally desirable for multitudes of the godly placed in like positions, and therefore he prays for the whole company of the faithful, and against the entire confraternity[48] of traitors.

Selah. With such a subject before us we may well pause.

Psalm 59:6 *They return at evening: they make a noise like a dog, and go round about the city.*

EXPOSITION: Verse 6. *They return at evening.* Like wild beasts that roam at night, they come forth to do mischief. If foiled in the light, they seek the more congenial darkness in which to accomplish their designs. They mean to break into the house in the dead of night.

They make a noise like a dog, and go round about the

---

48. a brotherhood of men united for some purpose

city. David compares his foes to Eastern dogs, not owned, loathsome, degraded, lean, and hungry, and he represents them as howling with disappointment, because they cannot find the food they seek. Saul's watchmen and the cruel king himself must have raved and raged fiercely when they found the image and the pillow of goat's hair in the bed instead of David. Their surveillance time was in vain, the victim had been delivered by the daughter of the man who desired his blood.

Psalm 59:7 *Behold, they belch out with their mouth: swords are in their lips: for who, say they, doth hear?*

EXPOSITION: Verse 7. *Behold they belch out with their mouth.* The noisy creatures are so remarkable in their way, that attention is called to them with a "behold." *Ecce homines,*[49] might we not say, *Ecce canes!* [50] Their malicious speech gushes from them as from a bubbling fountain. The wicked are voluble in slander; their vocabulary of abuse is copious, and as detestable as it is abundant. *Swords are in their lips.* They speak daggers. Their words pierce like rapiers, and cleave like cutlasses. As the cushion of a lions' paw conceals his claw, so their soft ruby lips contain bloody words.

For who, say they, doth hear? They are free from all restraint, they fear no God in Heaven, and the government on Earth is with them. He who neither fears God nor regards man sets out on errands of oppression with gusto, and uses language of the most atrociously cruel sort. David must have been in a singular plight when he could hear the foul talk and hideous bragging of Saul's black guards around the house. After the style in which a Cavalier would have cursed

---

49. behold the man
50. behold the dog

a Puritan, or Claverhouse[51] a Covenanter,[52] the Saulites swore at the upstarts whom the king's majesty had sent them to arrest. David called them dogs, and no doubt a pretty pack they were, a cursed cursing company of curs. When they said, "Who doth hear?" God was listening, and this David knew, and therefore took courage.

Psalm 59:8 *But thou, O LORD, shalt laugh at them; thou shalt have all the heathen in derision.*

EXPOSITION: Verse 8. *But thou, O Lord, shalt laugh at them.* They are laughing at me, and longing for my destruction, but you are laughing at them for you have determined to send them away without their victim, and made fools of by Michal. *Thou shalt have all the heathen in derision.* If not only these but all the heathen nations were besetting the house, yet Jehovah would readily enough disappoint them and deliver them. In the end of all things it will be seen how utterly contemptible and despicable are all the enemies of the cause and Kingdom of God.

Psalm 59:9 *Because of his strength will I wait upon thee: for God is my defence.*

EXPOSITION: Verse 9. *Because of his strength will I wait upon thee.* Is my persecutor strong? Then, my God, for this very reason I will turn myself to you, and leave my matters in your hand. It is a wise thing to find in the greatness of our difficulties a reason for casting ourselves on the Lord.

---

51. a Jacobite hero and enemy of Scottish Presbyterians in the 17th century
52. Christians in Scotland who opposed the interference of the Stuart kings in the affairs of the Scottish Presbyterian Church

And when it seems no chance nor change[53]
From grief can set me free,
Hope finds its strength in helplessness,
And, patient, waits on thee.

For God is my defence, my high place, my fortress, the place of my resort in the time of my danger.

Psalm 59:10 *The God of my mercy shall prevent me: God shall let me see my desire upon mine enemies.*

EXPOSITION: Verse 10. *The God of my mercy shall prevent me.* God, who is the giver and fountain of all the undeserved goodness I have received, will go before me and lead my way as I march onward. He will meet me in my time of need. How frequently have we met with preventing mercy—the supply prepared before the need occurred, the refuge built before the danger arose. Far ahead into the future the foreseeing grace of Heaven has projected itself, and forestalled every difficulty.

God shall let me see my desire upon mine enemies. From the Hebrew we are taught that David expected to see his enemies without fear. God will enable His servant to gaze steadily upon the foe without trepidation; he shall be calm, and self-possessed in the hour of peril; and before long he shall look down on the same foes discomfited, overthrown, and destroyed. When Jehovah leads the way victory follows at his heels. See God, and you need not fear to see your enemies.

Psalm 59:11 *Slay them not, lest my people forget: scatter them by thy power; and bring them down, O Lord our shield.*

---
53. Hymn 662 in the *Service of Song for Baptist Churches*, by F.W. Faber

EXPOSITION: Verse 11. *Slay them not, lest my people forget.* It argues great faith on David's part, that even while his house was surrounded by his enemies he is yet so fully sure of their overthrow, and so completely realizes it in his own mind, that he puts in a detailed petition that they may not be too soon or too fully exterminated. No, let the righteous be buffeted a little longer, and let the boasting oppressor puff and brag through his little hour, it will help to keep Israel in mind of the Lord's justice, and make the brave party who side with God's champion accustomed to divine interpositions. Enemies help to keep the Lord's servants awake.

Scatter them by thy power. Let the enemy live as a vagabond race. Make Cains of them. Let them be living monuments of divine power, advertisements of Heaven's truth. To the fullest extent let divine justice be illustrated in them.

And bring them down. From the seats of power which they disgrace, and the positions of influence which they pollute, let them be hurled into humiliation. This was a righteous wish, and if it is untempered by the gentleness of Jesus, we must remember that it is a soldier's prayer, and the wish of one who was smarting under injustice and malice of no ordinary kind.

O Lord, our shield. David felt himself to be the representative of the religious party in Israel, and therefore he says, our shield, speaking in the name of all those who make Jehovah their defense. We are in good company when we hide beneath the buckler of the Eternal; meanwhile He who is the shield of His people is the scatterer of their enemies.

Psalm 59:12 *For the sin of their mouth and the words of their lips let them even be taken in their pride: and for cursing and lying which they speak.*

EXPOSITION: Verse 12. *For the sin of their mouth and*

the words of their lips let them even be taken in their pride. Such dreadful language of atheism and insolence deserves a fit return. Sins of the lips are real sins, and punishable sins. Men must not think because their hatred gets no further than railing and blasphemy that therefore they shall be excused. He, who takes the will for the deed, will take the word for the deed and deal with men accordingly. Pride though it does not show itself in clothes, but only in speech, is a sin; and persecuting pride, though it piles no faggots at Smithfield, but only revile with its lips, shall have to answer for it among the unholy crew of inquisitors.

And for cursing and lying which they speak. Sins, like hounds, often hunt in couples. He, who is not ashamed to curse before God, will be sure to lie unto men. Every swearer is a liar. Persecution leads on to perjury. They lie and swear to it. This shall not go unnoticed of the Lord, but shall bring down its recompense.

Psalm 59:13 *Consume them in wrath, consume them, that they may not be: and let them know that God ruleth in Jacob unto the ends of the earth. Selah.*

EXPOSITION: **Verse 13.** *Consume them in wrath.* Revilers of God whose mouths pour forth such filth as David was on this occasion obliged to hear, are not to be tolerated by a holy soul; indignation must flame forth, and cry to God against them. *Consume them, that they may not be.* When men curse the age and the place in which they live, common humanity leads the righteous to desire that they may be removed. *And let them know;* i.e., let all the nations know, *that God ruleth in Jacob unto the ends of the earth.* He whose government is universal fixes His headquarters among His chosen people, and there in special He punishes sin. So David would have all men see. Let even the most remote nations know that the great moral Governor has power to destroy ungodliness, and does not wink at iniquity in any, at any time, or in any place. *Selah.*

Psalm 59:14 *And at evening let them return; and let them make a noise like a dog, and go round about the city.*

EXPOSITION: Verse 14. *And at evening let them return; and let them make a noise like a dog, and go round about the city.* He laughs to think that all the city would know how they were deceived, and all Israel would ring with the story of the image and the goats' hair in the bed. Nothing was more a subject of Oriental merriment than a case in which the crafty are deceived, and nothing more makes a man the object of derision than to be outwitted by a woman, as in this instance Saul and his base minions were by Michal.

Psalm 59:15 *Let them wander up and down for meat, and grudge if they be not satisfied.*

EXPOSITION: Verse 16. *Let them wander up and down for meat.* Like dogs that have missed the expected carcass, let them go up and down dissatisfied, snapping at one another, and too disappointed to be quiet and take the matter easily.

And grudge if they be not satisfied. Let them act like those who cannot believe that they have lost their prey: like a herd of Oriental dogs, no homes, and no kennels, let them prowl about seeking a prey which they shall never find. Thus the menial followers of Saul paraded the city in vain hope of satisfying their malice and their master. "Surely," say they, "we shall have him yet. We cannot endure to miss him. We grudge him his life. See the restlessness of wicked men; this will increase as their enmity to God increases, and in hell it will be their infinite torment. What is the state of the lost, but the condition of an ambitious camp of rebels, who have espoused a hopeless cause, and will not give it up, but are impelled by their raging passions to rave on against the cause of God, of truth, and of His people.

> **Psalm 59:16** *But I will sing of thy power; yea, I will sing aloud of thy mercy in the morning: for thou hast been my defence and refuge in the day of my trouble.*

EXPOSITION: **Verse 16.** *But I will sing of thy power.* The wicked howl, but I sing and will sing. Their power is weakness, but yours is omnipotence; I see them vanquished and your power victorious, and forever and ever will I sing of you.

Yea, I will sing aloud of thy mercy in the morning. What a blessed morning will soon break for the righteous, and what a song will be theirs! Sons of the morning, you may sigh tonight, but joy will come on the wings of the rising sun. Tune your harps even now, for the signal to commence the eternal music will soon be given; the morning comes and your sun shall go no more down for ever.

For thou hast been my defence. The song is for God alone, and it is one which none can sing but those who have experienced the lovingkindness of their God. Looking back upon a past all full of mercy, the saints will bless the Lord with their whole hearts, and triumph in Him as the high place of their security.

And refuge in the day of my trouble. The greater our present trials the louder will our future songs be, and the more intense our joyful gratitude. David's besetment by Saul's bloodhounds creates an opportunity for divine interposition and so for triumphant praise.

Psalm 59:17 *Unto thee, O my strength, will I sing: for God is my defence, and the God of my mercy.*

EXPOSITION: Verse 17. *Unto thee, O my strength, will I sing.* What transport is here! What a monopolizing of all his emotions for the one object of praising God! Strength has been overcome by strength; not by the hero's own prowess, but by the might of God alone. See how the singer girds himself with the almightiness of God, and calls it all his own by faith. Sweet is the music of experience, but it is all for God; there is not even a stray note for man, for self, or for human helpers.

For God is my defence, and the God of my mercy. With full assurance he claims possession of the Infinite as his protection and security. He sees God in all, and all his own. Mercy rises before him, undisturbed and manifold, for he feels he is undeserving, and security is with him, undisturbed and impregnable, for he knows that he is safe in divine keeping. Oh, choice song! My soul would sing it now in defiance of all the dogs of hell. Away, away, ye adversaries of my soul, the God of my mercy will keep you all at bay—"Nor shall the infernal lion rend whom he designs to keep."

Psalm 60

Psalm 60:1–Psalm 60:12

Psalm 60:1 *O God, thou hast cast us off, thou hast scattered us, thou hast been displeased; O turn thyself to us again.*

EXPOSITION: Verse 1. David found himself the possessor of a tottering throne, troubled with the double evil of factions at home, and invasion from abroad. He traced at once the evil to its true source, and began at the fountainhead. His were the politics of piety, which after all are the wisest and most profound. He knew that the displeasure of the Lord had brought calamity upon the nation, and to the removal of that displeasure he set himself by earnest prayer.

O God, thou hast cast us off. God has treated us as foul and offensive things, to be put away; as mean and beggarly persons, to be shunned with contempt; as useless dead boughs, to be torn away from the tree, which they disfigure. When the divine desertion causes mourning and repentance, it will be but partial and temporary. Whoever might be the secondary agent of these disasters; he beholds the Lord's hand as the prime moving cause, and pleads with the Lord concerning the matter. Israel was like a city with a breach made in its wall, because her God was wroth with her.

Thou hast been displeased. This is the secret of our miseries. Had we pleased Him, He would have pleased us; but as we have walked contrary to Him, He has walked contrary to us.

O turn thyself to us again. Forgive the sin and smile

once more. Turn us to you, and turn you to us. At one time your face was towards your people, be pleased to look on us again with your favor and grace. A truehearted prayer brings a blessing so soon that it is no presumption to consider it already obtained. There was more need for God to turn to His people than for Judah's troops to be brave, or Joab and the commanders wise. God with us is better than strong battalions; God displeased is more terrible than all the Edomites[54] that ever marched into the Valley of Salt, or all the devils that ever opposed the Church. If the Lord turns to us, what care we for Aramnaharaim[55] or Aramzobah,[56] or death, or hell? But if He withdraws His presence we tremble at the fall of a leaf.

Psalm 60:2 *Thou hast made the earth to tremble; thou hast broken it: heal the breaches thereof; for it shaketh.*

EXPOSITION: Verse 2. *Thou hast made the earth to tremble.* Things were as unsettled as though the solid ground had been made to quake; nothing was stable; the priests had been murdered by Saul, the worst men had been put in office, the military power had been broken by the Philistines, and the civil authority had grown despicable through insurrections and rebellious contests.

Thou hast broken it. As the ground cracks, and opens itself in rifts during violent earthquakes, so was the kingdom rent with strife and calamity.

Heal the breaches thereof. As a house in time of earthquake is shaken, and the walls begin to crack, and gape with

---
54. a nation of people descended from Esau
55. located in Old Testament times in Mesopotamia
56. Aram-Zobah was the capital of an early Aramean state in southern Syria, at one time of considerable importance.

threatening fissures, so was it with the kingdom.

For it shaketh. It tottered to a fall; if not soon propped up and repaired it would come down in complete ruin. So far gone was Israel, that only God's interposition could preserve it from utter destruction. How often have we seen churches in this condition, and how suitable is the prayer before us, in which the extremity of the need is used as an argument for help. The same may be said of our personal religion, it is sometimes so tried, that like a house shaken by earthquake it is ready to come down with a crash, and none but the Lord himself can repair its breaches, and save us from utter destruction.

Psalm 60:3 *Thou hast shewed thy people hard things: thou hast made us to drink the wine of astonishment.*

EXPOSITION: Verse 3. *Thou hast showed thy people hard things.* Hardships had been heaped upon them, and the psalmist traces these rigorous providences to their fountainhead. Nothing had happened by chance, but all had come by divine design and with a purpose, yet for all that things had gone hard with Israel. The psalmist claims that they were still the Lord's own people, though in the first verse he had said, "thou hast cast us off." The language of complaint is usually confused, and faith in time of trouble before long contradicts the desponding statements of the flesh.

Thou hast made us to drink the wine of astonishment. Our afflictions have made us like men drunken with some potent and bitter wine; we are in amazement, confusion, delirium; our steps reel, and we stagger as those about to fall. The Great Physician gives His patients potent potions to purge out their abounding and deep seated diseases. Astonishing evils bring with them astonishing results. The grapes of the vineyard of sin produce a wine which fills the most hardened with anguish when justice compels them to quaff[57] the cup. There is a fire water of anguish of soul which even to the righteous makes a cup of trembling, which causes them to be exceeding sorrowful almost unto death.

Psalm 60:4 *Thou hast given a banner to them that fear thee, that it may be displayed because of the truth. Selah.*

EXPOSITION: Verse 4. *Thou hast given a banner to them that fear thee.* Their afflictions had led them to exhibit holy fear, and then being fitted for the Lord's favor, He gave them an ensign, which would be both a rallying point for their hosts, a proof that He had sent them to fight, and a guarantee of victory. The Lord has given us the standard of the gospel, let us live to uphold it, and if needful die to defend it. Our right to contend for God, and our reason for expecting success, are found in the fact that the faith has been once committed to the saints, and that by the Lord himself.

That it may be displayed because of the truth. Israel might well come forth boldly, for a sacred standard was borne aloft before them. To publish the gospel is a sacred duty, to be ashamed of it a deadly sin. The truth of God was involved in the triumph of David's armies, he had promised them victory; and so in the proclamation of the gospel we need feel no hesitancy, for as surely as God is true He will give success to His own word. For the truth's sake, and because the true God is on our side, let us in these modern days of warfare emulate the warriors of Israel, and unfurl our banners to the breeze with confident joy. Dark signs of present or coming ill must not dishearten us; if the Lord had meant to destroy us He would not have given us the gospel; the very

---

57. gulp down in large swallows

fact that He has revealed himself in Christ Jesus involves the certainty of victory. *Magna est veritas et praevalebit.*[58]

> Hard things thou hast upon us laid,
> And made us drink most bitter wine;
> But still thy banner we have displayed,
> And borne aloft thy truth divine.
>
> Our courage fails not, though the night
> No earthly lamp avails to break,
> For thou wilt soon arise in might,
> And of our captors captives make.

Psalm 60:5 *That thy beloved may be delivered; save with thy right hand, and hear me.*

EXPOSITION: Verse 5. *That thy beloved may be delivered.* David was the Lord's beloved, his name signifies "dear, or beloved," and there was in Israel a remnant according to the election of grace, who were the beloved of the Lord; for their sakes the Lord wrought great marvels, and He had an eye to them in all His mighty acts. God's beloved are the inner seed, for whose sake He preserves the entire nation, which acts as a husk to the vital part. This is the main design of providence, *"That your beloved may be delivered."* If it were not for their sakes He would neither give a banner nor send victory to it.

Save with thy right hand, and hear me. Tarry not, O Lord, until I am done pleading: save first and hear afterwards. The salvation must be a right royal and eminent one, such as only the omnipotent hand of God linked with His dexterous wisdom can achieve. Urgent distress puts men upon pressing and bold petitions such as this. He, the Lord's David, pleads

---

58. Truth is mighty and will prevail.

for the rest of the beloved, beloved and accepted in Him the Chief Beloved; He seeks salvation as though it were for himself, but His eye is ever upon all those who are one with Him in the Father's love. When divine interposition is necessary for the rescue of the elect it must occur, for the first and greatest necessity of providence is the honor of God, and the salvation of His chosen. This is fixed fate, the center of the immutable decree, the inmost thought of the unchangeable Jehovah.

> **Psalm 60:6** *God hath spoken in his holiness; I will rejoice, I will divide Shechem, and mete out the valley of Succoth.*

EXPOSITION: Verse 6. *God hath spoken in his holiness.* Faith is never happier than when it can fall back upon the promise of God. God had promised Israel victory, and David the kingdom; the holiness of God secured the fulfillment of His own covenant, and therefore the king spoke confidently. The goodly land had been secured to the tribes by the promise made to Abraham, and that divine grant was an abundantly sufficient warrant for the belief that Israel's arms would be successful in battle.

I will rejoice, or "I will triumph." Faith regards the promise not as fiction but fact, and therefore drinks in joy from it, and grasps victory by it. "*God hath spoken; I will rejoice*" here is a fit motto for every soldier of the Cross.

I will divide Shechem. As a victor David would allot the conquered territory to those to whom God had given it by lot. Shechem was an important portion of the country, which as yet had not yielded to his government; but he saw that by Jehovah's help it would be, and indeed was all his own. Faith divides the spoil, she is sure of what God has promised, and enters at once into possession.

And mete out the valley of Succoth. As the east so the west of Jordan should be allotted to the proper persons. Enemies should be expelled, and the landmarks of peaceful ownership set up. Where Jacob had pitched his tent, there his rightful heirs should till the soil. When God has spoken, His divine "shall," our "I will," becomes no idle boast, but the fit echo of the Lord's decree. Believer, rise up and take possession of covenant mercies. Divide Shechem, and mete out the valley of Succoth. Let not Canaanitish doubts and legalisms keep you out of the inheritance of grace. Live up to your privileges; take the good which God provides you.

Psalm 60:7 *Gilead is mine, and Manasseh is mine; Ephraim also is the strength of mine head; Judah is my lawgiver*

EXPOSITION: Verse 7. *Gilead is mine, and Manasseh is mine.* Two other great divisions of the country he mentions, evidently delighting to survey the goodly land which the Lord had given him. All things are ours, whether things present or things to come; no small portion belongs to the believer, and let him not think little of it. No enemy shall withhold from true faith what God has given her, for grace makes her mighty to wrest it from the foe. Life is mine, death is mine, for Christ is mine.

Ephraim also is the strength of mine head. All the military power of the valiant tribe was at the command of David, and he praises God for it. God will bow to the accomplishment of His purposes all the valor of men; the Church may cry, "the prowess of armies is mine," but God will overrule all their achievements for the progress of His cause.

Judah is my lawgiver. There the civil power was concentrated: the king being of that tribe sent forth his laws out of her midst. We know no lawgiver, but the King who came out of Judah. To all the claims of Rome, or Oxford, or the councils of men, we pay no attention; we are free from all other ecclesiastical rule, but that of Christ: but we yield joyful obedience to Him: *Judah is my lawgiver.* Amid distractions it is a great thing to have good and sound legislation, it was a balm for Israel's wounds, and it is our joy in the Church of Christ.

Psalm 60:8 *Moab is my washpot; over Edom will I cast out my shoe: Philistia, triumph thou because of me.*

EXPOSITION: Verse 8. *Moab,* so injurious to me in former years, *is my washpot.* The basin into which the water falls when it is poured from an ewer[59] upon my feet. Once she defiled Israel, according to the counsel of Balaam, the son of Beor; but she shall no longer be able to perpetrate such baseness; she shall be a washpot for those whom she sought to pollute. David treats his foes as but insignificant and inconsiderable; a whole nation he counts but as a footbath for his kingdom.

Over Edom will I cast out my shoe. As a man when bathing throws his shoes on one side, so would he obtain his dominion over haughty Esau's descendants as easily as a man casts a shoe. Easily are we victors when Omnipotence leads the way. The day shall come when the Church shall with equal ease subdue China and Ethiopia to the scepter of the Son of David. Every believer also may by faith triumph over all difficulties, and reign with Him who has made us kings and priests. *"They overcame through the blood of the Lamb,"* shall yet be said of all who rest in the power of Jesus. [See Revelation 12:11.]

---

59. pitcher

Philistia, triumph thou because of me. Be so subdued as to rejoice in my victories over my other foes. O proud Philistia, where are your vaunts? Where now your haughty looks, and promised conquests? Therefore do we dare defy the last enemy, *"O death, where is thy sting? O grave, where is thy victory?"* [1 Corinthians 15:55]. When the Lord speaks the promise, we will not be slow to rejoice and glory in it.

Psalm 60:9 *Who will bring me into the strong city? who will lead me into Edom?*

EXPOSITION: Verse 9. *Who will bring me into the strong city?* It was all but inaccessible, and hence the question of David. When we have achieved great success it must be a stimulus to greater efforts, but it must not become a reason for self-confidence.

Who will lead me into Edom? No heights of grace are too elevated for us, the Lord being our leader, but we must beware of high things attempted in self-reliance. *Excelsior*[60] is well enough as a cry, but we must look to the Highest of All for guidance. Joab could not bring David into Edom. The city of the seven hills must yet hear the gospel. Who will give the Church the power to accomplish this? The answer is not far to seek.

Psalm 60:10 *Wilt not thou, O God, which hadst cast us off? and thou, O God, which didst not go out with our armies?*

EXPOSITION: Verse 10. *Wilt not thou, O God, which hadst cast us off?* Yes, the chastising God is our only hope. He loves us still. For a small moment he does forsake us,

---

60. higher, always upward (Latin)

but with great mercy He gathers His people. Strong to smite, He is also strong to save. He who proved to us our need of Him by showing us what poor creatures we are without Him, will now reveal the glory of His help by conducting great enterprises to a noble issue.

And thou, O God, which didst not go out with our armies? The selfsame God you are, and to you faith cleaves. Though you slay us, we will trust in you, and look for your merciful help.

Psalm 60:11 *Give us help from trouble: for vain is the help of man.*

EXPOSITION: Verse 11. *Give us help from trouble.* Help us to overcome the disasters of civil strife and foreign invasion; save us from further incursions from without and division within. Do work this deliverance, O Lord, *for vain is the help of man.* How sweetly will this verse suit the tried people of God as a frequent emphatic exclamation. We know how true it is.

Psalm 60:12 *Through God we shall do valiantly: for he it is that shall tread down our enemies.*

EXPOSITION: Verse 12. *Through God we shall do valiantly.* From God all power proceeds, and all we do well is done by divine operation; but still we, as soldiers of the great king, are to fight, and to fight valiantly too. Divine working is not an argument for human inaction, but rather is it the best excitement for courageous effort.

For he it is that shall tread down our enemies. From Him shall the might proceed; to Him shall the honor be given. Like straw on the threshing floor beneath the feet of the oxen shall we tread upon our abject foes, but it shall rather be His foot which presses them down than ours; His hand shall go out against them so as to put them down and keep them in subjection

We shall do valiantly; we will not be ashamed of our colors, afraid of our foes, or fearful of our cause. The Lord is with us, omnipotence sustains us, and we will not hesitate, we dare not be cowards. O that our King, the true David, were come to claim the Earth, for the kingdom is the Lord's, and He is the governor among the nations.

PSALM 61
PSALM 61:1–PSALM 61:8

Psalm 61:1 *Hear my cry, O God; attend unto my prayer.*

EXPOSITION: Verse 1. *Hear my cry, O God.* He was in terrible earnest; he shouted, he lifted up his voice on high. He is not, however, content with the expression of his need: to give his sorrows vent is not enough for him, he wants an actual audience from Heaven, and manifold help as the result. Pharisees may rest in their prayers; true believers are eager for an answer to them: Ritualists may be satisfied when they have, "said or sung" their litanies and short prayers, but living children of God will never rest until their supplications have entered the ears of the Lord God of Sabaoth.

Attend unto my prayer. Give it your consideration and such an answer as your wisdom sees fit. Our heavenly Father is not hardened against the cries of His own children. What a consoling thought it is that the Lord at all times hears His people's cries, and is never forgetful of their prayers; whatever else fails to move Him, praying breath is never spent in vain!

Psalm 61:2 *From the end of the earth will I cry unto thee, when my heart is overwhelmed: lead me to the rock that is higher than I.*

EXPOSITION: Verse 2. *From the end of the earth will I cry unto thee.* He was banished from the spot which was the center of his delight, and at the same time his mind was in a depressed and melancholy condition; both actually and figuratively he was an outcast, yet he does not therefore restrain prayer, but rather finds therein a reason for the louder and more importunate cries. There may be an end of the Earth, but there must not be an end to devotion. On creation's verge we may call upon God, for even there He is within call. No spot is too dreary; no condition too deplorable; whether it be the world's end or life's end, prayer is equally available. To pray in some circumstances needs resolve, and the psalmist here expresses it.

I will cry. It was a wise resolution, for had he ceased to pray he would have become the victim of despair; there is an end to a man when he makes an end to prayer. Observe that David never dreamed of seeking any other God: he was at the end of the Promised Land, but he knew himself to be still in the territory of the Great King; to Him only does he address his petitions.

When my heart is overwhelmed—when the huge waves of trouble wash over me, and I am completely submerged, not only as to my head, but also my heart. It is hard to pray when the very heart is drowning, yet gracious men plead best at such times. Tribulation brings us to God, and brings God to us. Mark how our psalmist tells the Lord, as if he knew He were hearing him, that he intended to call upon Him: our prayer by reason of our distress may be like to a call upon a far-off friend, but our inmost faith has its quiet heart whispers to the Lord as to one who is assuredly our very present help.

Lead me to the rock that is higher than I. I see you to be my refuge, sure and strong; but alas! I am confused, and cannot find you; I am weak, and cannot climb to you. You are so steadfast, guide me; you are so high, uplift me. There is a mint of meaning in this brief prayer. A clergyman of one of the coast villages has, with immense labor, cut steps up from the beach to a large chamber, which he has excavated in the chalk cliffs; here many mariners have been saved; they have climbed the rock, which had been too high for them, and they have escaped. We have heard of late, however, that the steps have been worn away by the storms, and that poor sailors have perished miserably within sight of the refuge which they could not reach, for it was too high for them, Therefore, it is proposed to drive in iron stanchions, and to hang up chain ladders so that shipwrecked mariners may reach the chambers in the rock. The illustration is self-interpreting. Our experience leads us to understand this verse right well, for the time was with us when we were in such amazement of soul by reason of sin, and though we knew the Lord Jesus to be a sure salvation for sinners, yet we could not come at Him because of our many doubts and forebodings. A Savior would have been of no use to us if the Holy Spirit had not gently led us to Him, and enabled us to rest upon Him.

A seeking soul should at once believe in Jesus, but it is legitimate for a man to ask to be led to Jesus. The Holy Spirit is able to effect such a leading, and He can do it even though the heart is on the borders of despair. Hence we are led to cry for grace upon grace, and to see how dependent we are for everything, not only for the Savior, but for the power to believe on Him.

Psalm 61:3 *For thou hast been a shelter for me, and a strong tower from the enemy.*

EXPOSITION: **Verse 3.** *For thou hast been a shelter for me.* Observe how the psalmist rings the changes on: *Thou hast,* and *I will. And a strong tower from the enemy.* As in an impregnable fort, David had dwelt because he was surrounded by omnipotence. It is sweet beyond expression to remember the lovingkindnesses of the Lord in our former days, for He is unchangeable, and therefore will continue to guard us from all evil.

Psalm 61:4 *I will abide in thy tabernacle for ever: I will trust in the covert of thy wings. Selah.*

EXPOSITION: Verse 4. *I will abide in thy tabernacle for ever.* Let me once get back to your courts, and nothing shall again expel me from them: even now in my banishment my heart is there; and ever will I continue to worship you in spirit wherever my lot may be cast.

> There would I find a settled rest,
> While others go and come;
> No more a stranger or a guest,
> But like a child at home.[61]

He who communes with God is always at home. The divine omnipresence surrounds such a one consciously; his faith sees all around him the palace of the King, in which he walks with exulting security and overflowing delight. The best of all is that our residence with God is not for a limited period of time, but for ages; yes, for ages of ages, for time and for eternity: this is our highest and most heavenly privilege; I will abide in your tabernacle forever.

I will trust in the covert of thy wings. Often does our sweet singer use this figure; and far better is it to repeat one apt and instructive image, than for the sake of novelty to ransack creation for poor, strained metaphors. O for more trust; it cannot be too implicit: such a covert invites us to the most unbroken repose.

Selah. Rest we well may when we reach this point. Even the harp may be eloquently silent when deep, profound calm

---

61. from the hymn, "My Shepherd Will Supply My Need," by Isaac Watts

completely fills the bosom, and sorrow has sobbed itself into a peaceful slumber.

> **Psalm 61:5** *For thou, O God, hast heard my vows: thou hast given me the heritage of those that fear thy name.*

EXPOSITION: Verse 5. *For thou, O God, hast heard my vows.* Proofs of divine faithfulness are to be had in remembrance, and to be mentioned to the Lord's honor. The prayer of Psalm 61:1 is certain of an answer because of the experience of Psalm 61:5, since we deal with an immutable God.

Vows may rightly be joined with prayers when they are lawful, well considered, and truly for God's glory. It is great mercy on God's part to take any notice of the vows and promises of such faithless and deceitful creatures as we are.

Thou hast given me the heritage of those that fear thy name. We are made heirs, joint heirs with all the saints, partakers of the same portion. With this we ought to be delighted. If we suffer, it is the heritage of the saints; if we are persecuted, in poverty, or in temptation, all this is contained in the title deeds of the heritage of the chosen. Those we are to sup with we may well be content to dine with. We have the same inheritance as the Firstborn himself; what better is conceivable? Saints are described as fearing the name of God; they are reverent worshippers; they stand in awe of the Lord's authority; they are afraid of offending Him, they feel their own nothingness in the sight of the Infinite One. To share with such men, to be treated by God with the same favor as He metes out to them, is matter for endless thanksgiving. All the privileges of all the saints are also the privileges of each one.

Psalm 61:6 *Thou wilt prolong the king's life: and his years as many generations.*

EXPOSITION: **Verse 6.** *Thou wilt prolong the king's life;* death threatened, but God preserved His beloved. David, considering his many perils, enjoyed a long and prosperous reign.

And his years as many generations. He lived to see generation after generation personally; in his descendants he lived as king through a very long period; his dynasty continued for many generations; and in Christ Jesus, his seed and son, spiritually David reigns on evermore. Thus he who began at the foot of the rock, half drowned, and almost dead, is here led to the summit. He sings as a priest abiding in the tabernacle, a king ruling with God forever, and a prophet foretelling good things to come (Psalm 61:7). See the uplifting power of faith and prayer.

Psalm 61:7 *He shall abide before God for ever: O prepare mercy and truth, which may preserve him.*

EXPOSITION: **Verse 7.** *He shall abide before God for ever.* Though this is true of David in a modified sense, we prefer to view the Lord Jesus as here intended as the lineal descendant of David, and the representative of His royal race. Jesus is enthroned Him we are made to sit together in the heavens. *O prepare mercy and truth, which may preserve him.* As men cry, "Long live the king," so we hail with acclamation our enthroned Immanuel, and cry, "*Let mercy and truth preserve him.*" Eternal love and immutable faithfulness are the bodyguards of Jesus' throne, and they are both the providers and the preservers of all those who in Him are made kings and priests unto God.

Psalm 61:8 *So will I sing praise unto thy name for ever, that I may daily perform my vows.*

EXPOSITION: Verse 8. *So will I sing praise unto thy name for ever.* David had given vocal utterance to his prayer by a cry; he will now give expression to his praise by a song: there should be a parallel between our supplications and our thanksgivings. We ought not to leap in prayer, and limp in praise.

That I may daily perform my vows. To God who adds days to our days we will devote all our days. We vowed perpetual praise, and we desire to render it without intermission. We would worship God *de die in diem*,[62] going right on as the days roll on. God daily performs His promises; let us daily perform our vows: He keeps His covenant, let us not forget ours. Blessed be the name of the Lord from this time forth, even forevermore.

---

62. from day to day

Psalm 62
Psalm 62:1–Psalm 62:12

Psalm 62:1 *Truly my soul waiteth upon God: from him cometh my salvation.*

EXPOSITION: Verse 1. *Truly* faith alone is true which rests on God alone, that confidence which relies but partly on the Lord is vain confidence. If we Anglicized the word by our word verily, as some do, we would have here a striking reminder of our blessed Lord's frequent use of that adverb.

My soul waiteth upon God. My inmost self draws near in reverent obedience to God. To wait upon God, and for God, is the habitual position of faith; to wait on Him truly is sincerity; to wait on Him only is spiritual chastity. The original is, "only to God is my soul silence." It is an eminent work of grace to bring down the will and subdue the affections to such a degree, that the whole mind lies before the Lord like the sea beneath the wind, ready to be moved by every breath of His mouth, but free from all inward and self-caused emotion.

From him cometh my salvation. Faith can hear the footsteps of coming salvation, because she has learned to be silent. Our salvation in no measure or degree comes to us from any inferior source; let us, therefore, look alone to the true fountain, and avoid the detestable crime of ascribing to the creature what belongs alone to the Creator.

Psalm 62:2 *He only is my rock and my salvation; he is my defence; I shall not be greatly moved.*

EXPOSITION: Verse 2. *He only is my rock and my salvation.* David had often lain concealed in rocky caverns, and here he compares his God to such a secure refuge; and, indeed, declares Him to be his only real protection, all-sufficient in himself and never failing. At the same time, as if to show us that what he wrote was not mere poetic sentiment but blessed reality, the literal word salvation follows the figurative expression: that our God is our refuge is no fiction; nothing in the world is more a matter of fact.

He is my defence, Here we have another and bolder image; the tried believer not only abides in God as in a cavernous rock; but dwells in him as a warrior in some bravely defiant tower or lordly castle.

I shall not be greatly moved. His personal weakness might cause him to be somewhat moved; but his faith would come in to prevent any very great disturbance; he would not be much tossed about.

Psalm 62:3 *How long will ye imagine mischief against a man? ye shall be slain all of you: as a bowing wall shall ye be, and as a tottering fence.*

EXPOSITION: Verse 3. *How long will ye imagine mischief against a man?* It is always best to begin with God, and then we may confront our enemies. Make all sure with Heaven, and then you may grapple with Earth and hell The persistence of those who oppose the people of God are so strange that we may well expostulate with them and say, "How long will you thus display your malice?" A hint is given in the text as to the cowardliness of so many pressing upon one man; but none are less likely to act a fair and manly part than those who are opposed to God's people for righteousness' sake.

Ye shall be slain all of you. Your edged tools will cut your own fingers. Those who take the sword shall perish with the sword. [See Matthew 26:52.]
As a bowing wall shall ye be, and as a tottering fence. Boastful persecutors bulge and swell with pride, but they are only as a bulging wall ready to fall in a heap. They expect men to bow to them, and quake for fear in their presence; but men made bold by faith see nothing in them to honor, and very, very much to despise.

Psalm 62:4 *They only consult to cast him down from his excellency: they delight in lies: they bless with their mouth, but they curse inwardly. Selah.*

EXPOSITION: Verse 4. *They only consult to cast him down from his excellency.* The excellencies of the righteous are obnoxious to the wicked, and the main object of their fury. If the wicked could but ruin the work of grace in us, they would be content; for to crush our character and overturn our influence is the object of their consultation. *They delight in lies;* hence they hate the truth and the truthful, and by falsehood endeavor to cause their overthrow.

They bless with their mouth, but they curse inwardly. Flattery has ever been a favorite weapon with the enemies of good men; they can curse bitterly enough when it serves their turn; meanwhile, since it answers their purpose, they mask their wrath, and with smooth words pretend to bless those whom they would willingly tear in pieces *Selah.* Here pause, and the perfect security of such as rest themselves upon the Lord.

Psalm 62:5 *My soul, wait thou only upon God; for my expectation is from him.*

EXPOSITION: **Verse 5.** *My soul, wait thou only upon God.* When we have already practiced a virtue, it is yet needful that we commit ourselves to a continuance in it. Be still silent, O my soul! Submit yourself completely, trust immovably, and wait patiently. Let none of your enemies' imaginings, consulting, flatteries, or maledictions cause you to break the King's peace. Be like the sheep before her shearers, and like your Lord, conquer by the passive resistance of victorious patience. You can only achieve this as you are inwardly persuaded of God's presence, and as you wait solely and alone on Him.

For my expectation is from him. We expect from God because we believe in Him. Expectation is the child of prayer and faith, and is given by the Lord as an acceptable grace. We should desire nothing but what would be right for God to give, then our expectation would be all from God. Concerning truly good things we should not look to second causes, but to the Lord alone, and so again our expectation would be all from Him.

Psalm 62:6 *He only is my rock and my salvation: he is my defence; I shall not be moved.*

EXPOSITION: **Verse 6.** *He only is my rock and my salvation.* Alone, and without other help, God is the foundation and completion of my safety.

He is my defence. Not my defender only, but my actual protection. I am secure, because He is faithful.

I shall not be moved. A living faith grows; experience develops the spiritual muscles of the saint, and gives a manly force which our religious childhood has not yet reached.

Psalm 62:7 *In God is my salvation and my glory: the rock of my strength, and my refuge, is in God.*

EXPOSITION: Verse 7. *In God is my salvation and my glory.* Wherein should we glory but in Him who saves us?

The rock of my strength, and my refuge, is in God. He multiplies titles, for He would render much honor to the Lord, whom He had tried, and proved to be a faithful God under so many aspects.

Psalm 62:8 *Trust in him at all times; ye people, pour out your heart before him: God is a refuge for us. Selah.*

EXPOSITION: Verse 8. *Trust in him at all times.* Faith is an abiding duty, a perpetual privilege. We should trust when we can see, as well as when we are utterly in the dark. God at all times deserves our confidence. We at all times need to place our confidence in Him.

Ye people, pour out your heart before him. You, to whom His love is revealed, reveal yourselves to Him. His heart is set on you; lay bare your hearts to Him. Unburden your soul to the Lord; let Him be your only father confessor, for He only can absolve you when He has heard your confession. We need sympathy, and if we unload our hearts at Jesus' feet, we shall obtain a sympathy as practical as it is sincere, as consolatory as it is ennobling.

God is a refuge for us. Whatever He may be to others, for us He is undoubtedly a refuge: here then is the best of reasons for resorting to Him whenever sorrows weigh upon our bosoms. Prayer is peculiarly the duty of those to whom the Lord has specially revealed himself as their defense.

Selah. Precious pause! Timely silence!

Psalm 62:9 *Surely men of low degree are vanity, and men of high degree are a lie: to be laid in the balance, they are altogether lighter than vanity.*

EXPOSITION: Verse 9. *Surely men of low degree are vanity.* They are many and enthusiastic, but they are not to be depended on. As the first son of Adam was called Abel or vanity, so here we are taught that all the sons of Adam are Abels; it would be well if they were all the same in character as well as in name; but alas, in this respect, too many of them are Cains!

And men of high degree are a lie. How wretched is that poor man who puts his trust in princes. The more we rely upon God, the more we shall perceive the utter hollowness of every other confidence.

To be laid in the balance, they are altogether lighter than vanity. Calmly deliberate, quietly ponder, and your verdict will be that which inspiration here records. Vainer than vanity itself are all human confidences: the great and the small alike are unworthy of our trust. A feather has some weight in the scale, vanity has none, and creature confidence has less than that.

Psalm 62:10 *Trust not in oppression, and become not vain in robbery: if riches increase, set not your heart upon them.*

EXPOSITION: Verse 10. *Trust not in oppression, and become not vain in robbery.* Wealth ill-gotten is the trust only of fools, for the deadly pest lies in it; it is full of canker, it reeks with God's curse. To tread down the poor and silence their cries for justice is the delight of many a braggart bully, who in his arrogance imagines that he may defy both God and man. *If riches increase, set not your heart upon them.* If they grow in an honest, providential manner, as the result of industry or commercial success, do not make much account of the circumstance; nor be unduly elated or fix your love upon your money bags. As we must not rest in men, so neither must we repose in money. Gain and fame are only so much foam of the sea. All the wealth and honor the whole world can afford would be too slender a thread to bear up the happiness of an immortal soul.

Psalm 62:11 *God hath spoken once; twice have I heard this; that power belongeth unto God.*

EXPOSITION: Verse 11. *God hath spoken once.* So immutable is God that He need not speak twice, as though He had changed; so infallible, that one utterance suffices, for He cannot err; so omnipotent, that His solitary word achieves all His designs. We speak often and say nothing; God speaks once and utters eternal verities. All our speaking may yet end in sound; but He speaks, and it is done; He commands, and it stands fast.

Twice have I heard this. Our meditative soul should hear the echo of God's voice again and again. What He speaks once in revelation, we should be always hearing. Creation and providence are evermore echoing the voice of God; *"He that hath ears to hear, let him hear"* [Matthew 11:15]. We have two ears, so that we may hear attentively, and the spiritual have inner ears with which they hear indeed. He hears twice in the best sense who hears with his heart as well as his ears.

That power belongeth unto God. He is the source of it, and in Him it actually abides. This one voice of God we ought always to hear, so as to be preserved from putting our trust in creatures in whom there can be no power, since all power is in God. May our souls hear the thunder of Jehovah's voice as He claims all power, and henceforth may we wait only upon God!

Psalm 62:12 *Also unto thee, O Lord, belongeth mercy: for thou renderest to every man according to his work.*

EXPOSITION: Verse 12. *Also unto thee, O Lord, belongeth mercy.* God is so full of mercy that it belongs to Him, as if all the mercy in the universe came from God, and still was claimed by Him as His possession. His mercy, like His power, endures forever, and is ever present in Him, ready to be revealed,

For thou renderest to every man according to his work. This looks rather like justice than mercy; but if we understand it to mean that God graciously rewards the poor, imperfect works of His people, we see in it a clear display of mercy. He metes out to us strength equal to our day. Man neither helps us nor rewards us; God will do both. In Him power and grace eternally reside; our faith should therefore patiently hope and quietly wait, for we shall surely see the salvation of God. *Deo soli gloria.* All glory be to God only.

Psalm 63
Psalm 63:1–Psalm 63:11

Psalm 63:1 *O God, thou art my God; early will I seek thee: my soul thirsteth for thee, my flesh longeth for thee in a dry and thirsty land, where no water is;*

EXPOSITION: **Verse 1.** *O God, thou art my God.* Strong affiance bids the fugitive poet to confess his allegiance to the only living God; and firm faith enables him to claim Him as his own. How sweet is such language! Is there any other word comparable to it for delights? *Meus Deus.*[63] Can angels say more?

Early will I seek thee. Observe the eagerness implied in the time mentioned; he will not wait for noon or the cool eventide; he is up at cockcrowing to meet his God. Communion with God is so sweet that the chill of the morning is forgotten, and the luxury of the couch is despised. The morning is the time for dew and freshness, and the psalmist consecrates it to prayer and devout fellowship. The best of men have been on their knees long before the morning dawns.

My soul thirsteth for thee. Thirst is an insatiable longing after that which is one of the most essential supports of life; there is no reasoning with it, no forgetting it, no despising it, no overcoming it by stoical indifference. Thirst will be heard; the whole man must yield to its power; it is even so with that divine desire which the grace of God creates in regenerate men; only God himself can satisfy the craving of

---

63. my God

a soul really aroused by the Holy Spirit.

My flesh longeth for thee; by the two words soul and flesh, he denotes the whole of his being. The flesh, in the New Testament sense of it, never longs after the Lord, but rather it "lusts against the spirit" [see Galatians 5:17]. David only refers to that sympathy which is sometimes created in our bodily frame by vehement emotions of the soul. When the wilderness caused David weariness, discomfort, and thirst, his flesh cried out in unison with the desire of his soul.

In a dry and thirsty land, where no water is. The absence of outward comforts can be borne with serenity when we walk with God; and the most lavish multiplication of them does not avail when He withdraws. Therefore, let us pant only after God. Let all desires be gathered into one. Seeking first the kingdom of God—all else shall be added unto us. [See Matthew 6:33.]

Psalm 63:2 *To see thy power and thy glory, so as I have seen thee in the sanctuary.*

EXPOSITION: Verse 2. *To see thy power and thy glory, so as I have seen thee in the sanctuary.* He looked through the veil of ceremonies to the invisible One. Often had his heart been gladdened by communion with God in the outward ordinances, and for this great blessing he sighs again; as well he might, for it is the weightiest of all Earth's sorrows for a Christian man to lose the conscious presence of his covenant God. It is a precious thought that the divine power and glory are not confined in their manifestation to any places or localities; they are to be heard above the roaring of the sea, seen amid the glare of the tempest, felt in the forest and the prairie, and enjoyed wherever there is a heart that longs and thirsts to behold them. David did not thirst for water or any earthly thing, but only for spiritual manifestations. The sight of God was enough for him, but nothing short of that would content him. How great a friend is He, the very sight of whom is consolation. Oh, my soul, imitate the psalmist, and let all thy desires ascend towards the highest good; longing here to see God, and having no higher joy even for eternity.

Psalm 63:3 *Because thy lovingkindness is better than life, my lips shall praise thee.*

EXPOSITION: Verse 3. *Because thy lovingkindness is better than life.* Life is dear, but God's love is dearer. To dwell with God is better than life at its best; life at ease, in a palace, in health, in honor, in wealth, and in pleasure. Oh yes, a thousand lives are not equal to the eternal life that abides in Jehovah's smile. In him we truly live, and move, and have our being. [See Acts 17:28.] The withdrawal of the light of His countenance is as the shadow of death to us; hence we cannot but long after the Lord's gracious appearing.

My lips shall praise thee, I will tell of your goodness. We ought not to make our praises of God depend upon our own personal reception of benefits; this would be mere selfishness; even publicans and sinners have a good word for those whose hands are enriching them with gifts. It is the true believer only who will bless the Lord when He takes away His gifts or hides His face.

Psalm 63:4 *Thus will I bless thee while I live: I will lift up my hands in thy name.*

EXPOSITION: Verse 4. *Thus will I bless thee while I live.* As I bless you now, I will ever do so. As thou reveal your lovingkindness to me, I will in return continue to extol you. While we live we will love. If no others bless God, yet His people will; His very nature, as being the infinitely good God, is a sufficient argument for our praising Him as long as we exist.

I will lift up my hands in thy name. For worship the hands were uplifted, also in joy, in thanksgiving, in labor, and in confidence; in all these senses we would lift up our hands in Jehovah's name alone. No hands need hang down when God draws near in love. The name of Jesus has often made lame men leap as a hart,[64] and it has made sad men clap their hands for joy.

Psalm 63:5 *My soul shall be satisfied as with marrow and fatness; and my mouth shall praise thee with joyful lips:*

EXPOSITION: **Verse 5.** *My soul shall be satisfied as with marrow and fatness.* There is in the love of God richness, a sumptuousness, a fullness of soul filling joy, comparable to the richest food with which the body can be nourished. The Hebrews were fonder of fat than we are, and their highest idea of festive provision is embodied in the two words, marrow and fatness: a soul hopeful in God and full of His favor is thus represented as feeding upon the best of the best, the dainties of a royal banquet.

And my mouth shall praise thee with joyful lips. More joy, more praise. When the mouth is full of mercy, it should also be full of thanksgiving. When God gives us the marrow of His love, we must present to Him the marrow of our hearts. Vocal praise should be rendered to God as well as mental adoration; others see our mercies, let them also hear our thanks.

---

64. a male red deer

Psalm 63:6 *When I remember thee upon my bed, and meditate on thee in the night watches.*

EXPOSITION: Verse 6. *When I remember thee upon my bed.* Lying awake, the good man began to meditate, and then began to sing. His praise anticipated the place of which it is written, "There is no night there."[65] Perhaps the wilderness helped to keep him awake, and if so, all the ages are debtors to it for this delightful hymn. If day's cares tempt us to forget God, it is well that night's quiet should lead us to remember Him. We see best in the dark if it is there we see God best.

And meditate on thee in the night watches. Keeping up sacred worship in my heart as the priests and Levites celebrated it in the sanctuary. Perhaps David had formerly united with those "who by night stand in the house of the Lord,"[66] and now as he could not be with them in person, he remembers the hours as they pass, and unites with the choristers in spirit, blessing Jehovah as they did. We read of beds of ivory, but beds of piety are far better. Some revel in the night, but they are not one-tenth as happy as those who meditate on God.

Psalm 63:7 *Because thou hast been my help, therefore in the shadow of thy wings will I rejoice.*

EXPOSITION: Verse 7. *Because thou hast been my help.* Meditation had refreshed his memory and recalled to him his past deliverances. This is the grand use of memory, to furnish us with proofs of the Lord's faithfulness, and lead us onward to a growing confidence in Him.

Therefore in the shadow of thy wings will I rejoice. The

---

65. from a hymn titled "No Night There" by John Clements
66. Psalm 134:1 sung as a song of praise

very shade of God is sweet to a believer. Under the eagle wings of Jehovah we hide from all fear, and we do this naturally and at once, because we have already tried and proved both His love and His power. We are not only safe, but happy in God: we rejoice as well as repose.

Psalm 63:8 *My soul followeth hard after thee: thy right hand upholdeth me.*

EXPOSITION: Verse 8. *My soul followeth hard after thee*, we follow close at the Lord's heels, because we are one with Him. Who shall divide us from His love? If we cannot walk with Him with equal footsteps, we will at least follow after with all the strength He lends us, earnestly panting to reach Him and abide in His fellowship.

Thy right hand upholdeth me. The divine power, that has so often been dwelt upon in this and the preceding psalms, is here mentioned as the source of man's attachment to God. How strong we are when the Lord works in us by His own right hand, and how utterly helpless if He withhold His aid!

Psalm 63:9 *But those that seek my soul, to destroy it, shall go into the lower parts of the earth.*

EXPOSITION: Verse 9. *But those that seek my soul, to destroy it.* At his life they aimed, at his honor, his best welfare; and this they would not merely injure but utterly ruin. Destroyers shall be destroyed. Those who hunt souls shall themselves be the victims.

Shall go into the lower parts of the earth. Into the pits they dug for others they shall fall. The slayers shall be slain, and the grave shall cover them. The hell which they in their curse invoked for others shall shut its mouth upon them. Every blow aimed against the godly will recoil on the persecutor; he who smites a believer drives a nail in his own coffin.

> **Psalm 63:10** *They shall fall by the sword: they shall be a portion for foxes.*

EXPOSITION: Verse 10. *They shall fall by the sword.* So David's enemies did. They that take the sword shall perish with the sword.

They shall be a portion for foxes. Too mean to be fit food for the lions, the foxes shall sniff around their corpses, and the jackals shall hold carnival over their carcasses. Unburied and unhonored they shall be meat for the dogs of war. Frequently have malicious men met with a fate so dire as to be evidently the award of retributive justice.

> **Psalm 63:11** *But the king shall rejoice in God; every one that sweareth by him shall glory: but the mouth of them that speak lies shall be stopped.*

EXPOSITION: Verse 11. *But the king shall rejoice in God.* The Lord's anointed shall not fail to offer his joyful thanksgiving: his well-established throne shall own the superior lordship of the King of kings; his rejoicing shall be alone in God. When his subjects sing, *"Io triumphe,"*[67] he will bid them chant, *"Te Deum."*[68]

Every one that sweareth by him shall glory. His faithful followers shall have occasion for triumph; they shall never need to blush for the oath of their allegiance. The heathen swore by their gods, and the Israelite called Jehovah to witness to his asseveration; those, therefore, who owned the Lord as their God should have reason to glory when He proved

---
67. hail, triumphal procession
68. God, we praise You

himself the defender of the king's righteous cause, and the destroyer of traitors.

But the mouth of them that speak lies shall be stopped. For a liar is a human devil, he is the curse of men, and accursed of God, who has comprehensively said, *"all liars shall have their part in the lake which burneth with fire and brimstone"* [Revelation 21:8].

See the difference between the mouth that praises God, and the mouth that forges lies: the first shall never be stopped, but shall sing on forever; the second shall be made speechless at the bar of God. O Lord, we seek you and your truth; deliver us from all malice and slander, and reveal to us your own self, for Jesus' sake. Amen.

Psalm 64
Psalm 64:1–Psalm 64:10

Psalm 64:1 *Hear my voice, O God, in my prayer: preserve my life from fear of the enemy.*

EXPOSITION: Verse 1. *Hear my voice, O God, in my prayer.* It often helps devotion if we are able to use the voice and speak audibly; but even mental prayer has a voice with God which He will hear. We do not read that Moses had spoken with his lips at the Red Sea, and yet the Lord said to him, *"Why criest thou unto me?"* [Exodus 14:15]. Prayers which are unheard on Earth may be among the best heard in Heaven. It is our duty to note how constantly David turns to prayer; it is his battle-ax and weapon of war; he uses it under every pressure, whether of inward sin or outward wrath, foreign invasion or domestic rebellion. We shall act wisely if we make prayer to God our first and best trusted resource in every hour of need.

Preserve my life from fear of the enemy. From harm and dread of harm protect me. With all our sacrifices of prayer we should offer the salt of faith.

Psalm 64:2 *Hide me from the secret counsel of the wicked; from the insurrection of the workers of iniquity:*

EXPOSITION: Verse 2. *Hide me from the secret counsel of the wicked.* From their hidden snares hide me. Circumvent their counsel; let their secrets be met by your secret providence, their counsels of malice by your counsels of love.

From the insurrection of the workers of iniquity. When their secret counsels break forth into clamorous tumults, be still my preserver. It is a good thing to conquer malicious foes, but a better thing still to be screened from all conflict with them, by being hidden from the strife. The Lord knows how to give His people peace, and when He wills to make quiet, He is more than a match for all disturbers, and can defeat their deep laid plots and their overt hostilities.

Psalm 64:3 *Who whet their tongue like a sword, and bend their bows to shoot their arrows, even bitter words:*

EXPOSITION: **Verse 3.** *Who whet their tongue like a sword.* As warriors grind their swords, to give them an edge which will cut deep and wound desperately, so do the unscrupulous invent falsehoods which shall be calculated to inflict pain, to stab the reputation, to kill the honor of the righteous. *And bend their bows to shoot their arrows, even bitter words.* Far off they dart their calumnies, as archers shoot their poisoned arrows. They studiously and with force prepare their speech as bent bows, and then with cool, deliberate aim, they let fly the shaft which they have dipped in bitterness. To sting, to inflict anguish, to destroy, is their one design. However, in all cases, let us fly to the Lord for help. David had but the one resource of prayer against the twofold weapons of the wicked, for defense against sword or arrow he used the one defense of faith in God.

Psalm 64:4 *That they may shoot in secret at the perfect: suddenly do they shoot at him, and fear not.*

EXPOSITION: Verse 4. *That they may shoot in secret at the perfect.* Sincere and upright conduct will not secure us from the assaults of slander. The devil shot at our Lord himself, and we may rest assured he has a fiery dart in reserve for us; He was absolutely perfect, we are only so in a relative sense, hence in us there is fuel for fiery darts to kindle on.

Suddenly do they shoot at him, and fear not. To secrecy they add suddenness. They give their unsuspecting victim no chance of defending himself. Is it possible for justice to invent a punishment sufficiently severe to meet the case of the dastard[69] who defiles my good name, and remains himself in concealment?

Psalm 64:5 *They encourage themselves in an evil matter: they commune of laying snares privily; they say, Who shall see them?*

EXPOSITION: Verse 5. *They encourage themselves in an evil matter.* The children of darkness are wise in their generation and keep their spirits up, and each one has a cheering word to say to his fellow villain.

They commune of laying snares privily. Laying their heads together they count and recount their various devices, so as to come at some new and masterly device.

They say, Who shall see them? So sedulously do they mask their attacks and themselves too carefully concealed to be found out. So they think, but they forget the all-seeing eye, and the all-discovering hand, which are ever close by them. As in the Gunpowder Plot,[70] there is usually a breakdown somewhere or other; among the conspirators themselves truth

---

69. despicable coward
70. In the infamous Gunpowder Plot (November 1605), some Catholics, most famously Guy Fawkes, plotted to blow up James I, the first of the Stuart kings of England.

finds an ally, or the stones of the field cry out against them. Fear not, ye tremblers; for the Lord is at your right hand, and you shall not be hurt by the enemy.

> **Psalm 64:6** *They search out iniquities; they accomplish a diligent search: both the inward thought of every one of them, and the heart, is deep.*

EXPOSITION: Verse 6. *They search out iniquities.* Diligently they consider, invent, devise, and seek for wicked plans to wreak their malice. The Inquisition could display instruments of torture, revealing as much skill as the machinery of our modern exhibitions.

They accomplish a diligent search. Their design is perfected, consummated, and brought into working order. Hell's craft furnishes inspiration to the artistes who fashion deceit. Earth and the places under it are ransacked for the material of war, and profound skill turns all to account.

Both the inward thought of every one of them, and the heart, is deep. Wicked men frequently have the craft to hasten slowly, to please in order to ruin, to flatter that before long they may devour, and to bow the knee that they may ultimately crush beneath their foot. Alas, how dangerous is the believer's condition, and how readily may he be overcome if left to himself! This is the complaint of reason and the moan of unbelief. When faith comes in, we see that even in all this the saints are still secure, for they are all in the hands of God.

> **Psalm 64:7** *But God shall shoot at them with an arrow; suddenly shall they be wounded.*

EXPOSITION: Verse 7. *But God shall shoot at them with an arrow.* They shot, and shall be shot. A greater archer than they are shall take sure aim at their hearts. One of His arrows shall be enough, for He never misses His aim.

Suddenly shall they be wounded. They were looking to surprise the saint, but they are taken unawares themselves; they desired to inflict deadly wounds, and are smitten themselves with wounds which none can heal. *"Vengeance is mine; I will repay, saith the Lord."* [Romans 12:19]. The righteous need not learn the arts of self-defense or of attack; their avenging is in better hands than their own.

Psalm 64:8 *So they shall make their own tongue to fall upon themselves: all that see them shall flee away.*

EXPOSITION: Verse 8. *So they shall make their own tongue to fall upon themselves.* Their tongue shall cut their throats. It was both sword, and bow and arrow; it shall be turned against them, and bring home to them full punishment.

All that see them shall flee away. Afraid, both of them and their overthrow, their former friends shall give them wide space, lest they perish with them. Those who crowded around a powerful persecutor, and cringed at his feet, are among the first to desert him in the day of wrath. Woe unto you, ye liars! "Who will desire fellowship with you in your seething lake of fire?"

Psalm 64:9 *And all men shall fear, and shall declare the work of God; for they shall wisely consider of his doing.*

EXPOSITION: Verse 9. *And all men shall fear.* Those who might have been bold in sin shall be made to tremble and to stand in awe of the righteous Judge.

And shall declare the work of God. They sinned secretly, but their punishment shall be wrought before the face of the sun.

For they shall wisely consider of his doing. The judgments of God are frequently so clear and manifest that men cannot misread them, and if they have any thought at all, they must extract the true teaching from them.

Psalm 64:10 *The righteous shall be glad in the* LORD, *and shall trust in him; and all the upright in heart shall glory.*

EXPOSITION: Verse 10. *The righteous shall be glad in the Lord.* Admiring His justice and fully acquiescing in its displays, they shall also rejoice at the rescue of injured innocence yet, their joy shall not be selfish or sensual, but altogether in reference to the Lord.

And shall trust in him. Their observation of providence shall increase their faith; since He who fulfils His threatenings will not forget His promises.

And all the upright in heart shall glory. The victory of the oppressed shall be the victory of all upright men; the whole host of the elect shall rejoice in the triumph of virtue. Lord God of mercy, grant to us to be preserved from all our enemies, and saved in your Son with an everlasting salvation.

Psalm 65
Psalm 65:1–Psalm 65:13

Psalm 65:1 *Praise waiteth for thee, O God, in Sion: and unto thee shall the vow be performed.*

EXPOSITION: Verse 1. *Praise waiteth for thee, O God, in Sion.* Zion remains faithful to her King; to Him, and to Him only, she brings her perpetual oblation of worship. Those who have seen in Zion the blood of sprinkling, and know themselves to belong to the church of the firstborn, can never think of her without presenting humble praise to Zion's God; His mercies are too numerous and precious to be forgotten. We reserve our best praises until the Lord reveals himself in the assembly of His saints; and, indeed, until He shall descend from Heaven in the day of His appearing. Praise attends the Lord's pleasure, and continues to bless Him, whether He shows tokens of present favor or not; she is not soon wearied, but all through the night she sings on in sure hope that the morning comes. We shall continue to wait on, tuning our harps, amid the tears of Earth; but O what harmonies will those be which we will pour forth, when the home bringing is come, and the King shall appear in His glory. Perhaps the poet best expressed the thought of the psalmist when he said—

> A sacred reverence checks our songs,[71]
> And praise sits silent on our tongues.

---
71. from hymn #5 in the *Hymns for Divine Worship: Compiled for the Use of the Methodist New Connexion*, written by Isaac Watts.

A church, bowed in silent adoration by a profound sense of divine mercy, would certainly offer more real praise than the sweetest voices aided by pipes and strings; yet, vocal music is not to be neglected, for this sacred hymn was meant to be sung. It is would be good before singing to have the soul placed in a waiting attitude, and to be humbly conscious that our best praise is but silence compared with Jehovah's glory.

And unto thee shall the vow be performed. Perhaps a special vow made during a season of drought and political danger. Nations and churches must be honest and prompt in redeeming their promises to the Lord, who cannot be mocked with impunity. We ought to be very deliberate in promising, and very punctilious in performing. A vow not kept will burn the conscience like a hot iron. Vows of service, of donation, of praise, or whatever they may be, are no trifles; and in the day of grateful praise they should, without fail, be fulfilled to the utmost of our power.

Psalm 65:2 *O thou that hearest prayer, unto thee shall all flesh come.*

EXPOSITION: Verse 2. *O thou that hearest prayer.* This is your name, your nature, your glory. God not only has heard, but is now hearing prayer, and always must hear prayer, since He is an immutable being and never changes in His attributes. What a delightful title for the God and Father of our Lord Jesus Christ! Every right and sincere prayer is as surely heard as it is offered. Here the psalmist brings in the personal pronoun "thou," and we beg the reader to notice how often "thou," "thee," and "thy" occur in this hymn; David evidently believed in a personal God, and did not adore a mere idea or abstraction.

Unto thee shall all flesh come. This shall encourage men of all nations to seek His face. Flesh they are, and therefore weak; frail and sinful, they need to pray; and you are such a God as they need, for you are touched with compassion, and do condescend to hear the cries of poor flesh and blood. Many come to you now in humble faith, and are filled with good, but more shall be drawn to you by the attractiveness of your love, and at length the whole Earth shall bow at your feet. To come to God is the life of true religion; we come weeping in conversion, hoping in supplication, rejoicing in praise, and delighting in service.

Psalm 65:3 *Iniquities prevail against me: as for our transgressions, thou shalt purge them away.*

EXPOSITION: Verse 3. *Iniquities prevail against me.* Were it not for the remembrance of the atonement which covers every one of my iniquities. Our sins would, but for grace, prevail against us in the court of divine justice, in the court of conscience, and in the battle of life. *As for our transgressions, thou shalt purge them away.* God covers them all, for He has provided a covering propitiation, a mercy seat which wholly covers His law. What a comfort that iniquities which prevail against us, do not prevail against God. They would keep us away from God, but He sweeps them away from before himself and us; they are too strong for us, but not for our Redeemer, who is mighty, yes, and almighty to save. It is worthy of note that as the priest washed in the laver before he sacrificed, so David leads us to obtain purification from sin before we enter upon the service of song. When we have washed our robes and made them white in His blood, then shall we acceptably sing, *"Worthy is the Lamb that was slain"* [Revelation 5:12].

Psalm 65:4 *Blessed is the man whom thou choosest, and causest to approach unto thee, that he may dwell in thy courts: we shall be satisfied with the goodness of thy house, even of thy holy temple.*

EXPOSITION: **Verse 4.** *Blessed is the man whom thou choosest, and causest to approach unto thee.* After cleansing comes benediction, it comprehends both election, effectual calling, access, acceptance, and sonship. First, we are chosen of God, according to the good pleasure of His will, and this alone is blessedness. Then, since we cannot and will not come to God of ourselves, He attracts us powerfully; subdues our unwillingness, and removes our inability by the almighty workings of His transforming grace. This also is no slight blessedness.

We, by His divine drawings, are made nigh by the blood of His Son and brought close by His Spirit into intimate fellowship and we approach as chosen and accepted ones, to become dwellers in the divine household: this is heaped up blessedness, vast beyond conception. But dwelling in the house we are treated as sons, for *"the servant abideth not in the house for ever, but the son abideth ever"* [John 8:35]. Behold what manner of love and blessedness the Father has bestowed upon us that we may dwell in His house, and go no more out for ever. Happy are the men who dwell at home with God. May both writer and reader be such men.

That he may dwell in thy courts. Acceptance leads to abiding: God does not make a temporary choice, or give and take; his gifts and calling are without repentance. *We shall be satisfied with the goodness of thy house, even of thy holy temple.* He who is once admitted to God's courts shall inhabit them forever; he shall be

No more a stranger or a guest,[72]
But like a child at home.

Psalm 65:5 *By terrible things in righteousness wilt thou answer us, O God of our salvation; who art the confidence of all the ends of the earth, and of them that are afar off upon the sea*

EXPOSITION: Verse 5. *By terrible things in righteousness wilt thou answer us, O God of our salvation.* God's memorial is that He hears prayer, and His glory is that He answers it in a manner fitted to inspire awe in the hearts of His people. The saints, in the commencement of the psalm, offered praise in reverential silence; and now, in the like awestricken spirit, they receive answers to their prayers. We do not always know what we are asking for when we pray; when the answer comes, the veritable answer, it is possible that we may be terrified by it. We seek sanctification, and trial will be the reply: we ask for more faith, and more affliction is the result: we pray for the spread of the gospel, and persecution scatters us. Nevertheless, it is good to ask, for nothing which the Lord grants in His love can do us any harm. Terrible things will turn out to be blessed things after all, when they come in answer to prayer. He who is terrible is also our refuge from terror when we see Him in the Well-Beloved.

Who art the confidence of all the ends of the earth. The dwellers in the far-off isles trust in God; those most remote from Zion yet confide in the ever-living Jehovah. His arm is strong to smite, but also strong to save.

And of them that are afar off upon the sea. Both elements have their elect band of believers. If the land gave Moses

---

72. from hymn, "My Shepherd Will Supply My Need" by Isaac Watts

elders, the sea gave Jesus apostles. Noah, when all was ocean, was as calm with God as Abraham in his tent. All men are equally dependent upon God; the seafaring man is usually most conscious of this, but in reality he is not more so than the husbandman, nor the husbandman than anyone else. There is no room for self-confidence on land or sea, since God is the only true confidence of men on land or ocean.

Psalm 65:6 *Which by his strength setteth fast the mountains; being girded with power*

EXPOSITION: Verse 6. *Which by his strength setteth fast the mountains.* He fixed them in their sockets, and preserved them from falling by earthquake or storm. The firmest owe their stability to Him. Our poet sees God's hand settling Alps and Andes on their bases, and therefore he sings in His praise.

Being girded with power. The Lord is so himself, and He therefore casts a girdle of strength around the hills, and there they stand, braced, belted, and bulwarked with His might. The poetry is such as would naturally suggest itself to one familiar with mountain scenery; power everywhere meets you, sublimity, massive grandeur, and stupendous force are all around you; and God is there, the author and source of all. Without Him, the everlasting hills would crumble; how much more shall all our plans, projects, and labors come to decay. Repose, O believer, where the mountains find their bases, namely in the undiminished might of the Lord God.

Psalm 65:7 *Which stilleth the noise of the seas, the noise of their waves, and the tumult of the people.*

EXPOSITION: Verse 7. *Which stilleth the noise of the seas.* His soft breath smoothes the sea into a glass, and the mountainous waves into ripples. God does this. Let mariners magnify the God who rules the waves.

The noise of their waves. Each separate brawler amid the riot of the storm is quieted by the divine voice.

And the tumult of the people. Nations are as difficult to rule as the sea itself, they are as fitful, treacherous, restless, and furious; they will not brook the bridle nor be restrained by laws. Canute[73] had not a more perilous seat by the rising billows than many a king and emperor has had when the multitude have been set on mischief, and have grown weary of their lords. God alone is King of nations. The sea obeys Him, and the yet more tumultuous nations are kept in check by Him. Human society owes its preservation to the continued power of God. Glory be unto God who maintains the fabric of social order, and stops the wicked who would rather overthrow all things. The child of God in seasons of trouble should fly at once to Him who stills the seas: nothing is too hard for Him.

Psalm 65:8 *They also that dwell in the uttermost parts are afraid at thy tokens: thou makest the outgoings of the morning and evening to rejoice.*

EXPOSITION: Verse 8. *They also that dwell in the uttermost parts are afraid of thy tokens.* These tokens are sometimes terrible phenomena in nature—such as earthquakes, pestilence, tornado, or storm; and when these are seen, even the most barbarous people tremble before God. At other times they are dread works of providence—such as the overthrow of Sodom, and the destruction of Pharaoh. The

---

73. Canute or Cnut the Great was born circa 990, the son of King Sweyn Forkbeard of Denmark. Canute was to become the ruler of an empire which, at its height, included England, Denmark, Norway, and part of Sweden.

rumor of these judgments travels to Earth's utmost verge, and impresses all people with a fear and trembling at such a just and holy God. We bless God that we are not afraid but rejoice at His tokens; with solemn awe we are glad when we behold His mighty acts.

Thou makest the outgoings of the morning and evening to rejoice. East and west are made happy by God's favor to the dwellers therein. Our rising hours are bright with hope, and our evening moments mellow with thanksgiving. Whether the sun goes forth or comes in we bless God and rejoice in the gates of the day. When the fair morning blushes with the rosy dawn we rejoice; and when the calm evening smiles restfully we rejoice still.

Psalm 65:9 *Thou visitest the earth, and waterest it: thou greatly enrichest it with the river of God, which is full of water: thou preparest them corn, when thou hast so provided for it.*

EXPOSITION: **Verse 9.** *Thou visitest the earth, and waterest it.* God's visits leave a blessing behind. When the Lord goes on visitations of mercy, He has an abundance of necessary things for all His needy creatures. He is represented here as going around the Earth, as a gardener surveys his garden, and as giving water to every plant that requires it, and that not in small quantities, but until the earth is drenched and soaked with a rich supply of refreshment. O Lord, in this manner visit your Church, and my poor, parched, and withering piety. Make your grace overflow towards my graces; water me, for no plant of your garden needs it more.

> My stock lies dead, and no increase,[74]
> Doth my dull husbandry improve;
> O let thy graces without cease
> Drop from above.

Thou greatly enrichtest it. Millions of money could not so much enrich mankind as the showers do. The soil is made rich by the rain, and then yields its riches to man; but God is the first giver of all. How truly rich are those who are enriched with grace; this is great riches.

With the river of God, which is full of water. The brooks of Earth are soon dried up, but God's provision for the supply of rain is inexhaustible; there is no bottom or shore to His River. How true this is in the realm of grace; there the River of God is full of water, and *"of his fulness have all we received, and grace for grace"* [John 1:16]. The ancients in their fables spoke of Pactolus,[75] which flowed over sands of gold; but this river of God, which flows above and from which the rain is poured, is far more enriching; for the wealth of men lies mainly in the harvest of their fields, without which even gold would be of no value whatever.

Thou preparest them corn. Corn is specially set apart to be the food of man. In its various species it is a divine provision for the nutriment of our race, and is truly called the staff of life. As surely as the manna was prepared of God for the tribes, so certainly is corn made and sent by God for our daily use.

When thou hast so provided for it. When all is prepared to produce corn, the Lord puts on the finishing stroke, and the grain is forthcoming. Blessed be the Great Householder; He does not suffer the harvest to fail, He supplies the teeming myriads of Earth with bread enough from year to year. In

---

74. first stanza of a poem titled "Grace" by George Herbert
75. a river near the Aegean coast of Turkey

this way He grants heavenly food to His redeemed ones: *"He hath given meat unto them that fear him; he is ever mindful of his covenant"* [Psalm 111:5].

Psalm 65:10 *Thou waterest the ridges thereof abundantly: thou settlest the furrows thereof: thou makest it soft with showers: thou blessest the springing thereof.*

EXPOSITION: Verse 10. *Thou waterest the ridges thereof abundantly: thou settlest the furrows thereof.* Ridge and furrow are drenched. The ridges beaten down and settled and the furrows made to stand like gutters flooded to the full.

Thou makest it soft with showers. The drought turned the clods into iron, but the plenteous showers dissolve and loosen the soil.

Thou blessest the springing thereof. Vegetation enlivened by the moisture leaps into vigor, the seed germinates and sends forth its green shoot, and the aroma is that as of a field which the Lord has blessed. All this may be likened to the operations of the Holy Spirit in beating down high thoughts, filling our lowly desires, softening the soul, and causing every holy thing to increase and spread.

Psalm 65:11 *Thou crownest the year with thy goodness; and thy paths drop fatness.*

EXPOSITION: Verse 11. *Thou crownest the year with thy goodness.* The harvest is the plainest display of the divine bounty, and the crown of the year. The Lord himself conducts the coronation, and sets the golden garland upon the brow of the year. The providence of God in its visitations makes a complete circuit, and surrounds the year.

And thy paths drop fatness. The footsteps of God, when

He visits the land with rain, create fertility. For spiritual harvests we must look to Him, for He alone can give "times of refreshing" and feasts of Pentecost.

Psalm 65:12 *They drop upon the pastures of the wilderness: and the little hills rejoice on every side.*

EXPOSITION: Verse 12. *They drop upon the pastures of the wilderness.* Ten thousand oases smile while the Lord of mercy passes by. The birds of the air, the wild goats, and the fleet stags rejoice as they drink from the pools, new filled from Heaven. The most lonely and solitary souls God will visit in love.

And the little hills rejoice on every side. On all hands the eminences are girt with gladness. Soon they languish under the effects of drought, but after a season of rain they laugh again with verdure.

Psalm 65:13 *The pastures are clothed with flocks; the valleys also are covered over with corn; they shout for joy, they also sing.*

EXPOSITION: Verse 13. *The pastures are clothed with flocks.* The clothing of man first clothes the fields. Pastures appear to be quite covered with numerous flocks when the grass is abundant.

The valleys also are covered over with corn. The arable[76] as well as the pasture land is rendered fruitful. God's clouds, like ravens, bring us both bread and flesh. Grazing flocks and waving crops are equally the gifts of the Preserver of men, and for both praise should be rendered. Sheepshearing and harvest should both be holiness unto the Lord.

They shout for joy. The bounty of God makes the Earth

---

76. tillable

vocal with His praise, and in opened ears it lifts up a joyous shout. The cattle low out the divine praises, and the rustling ears of grain sing a soft sweet melody unto the Lord.

> Ye forests bend, ye harvests wave to him;[77]
> Breathe your still song into the reaper's heart,
> As home he goes beneath the joyous moon.
> Bleat out afresh, ye hills; ye mossy rocks
> Retain the sound; the broad responsive low
> Ye valleys raise; for the Great Shepherd reigns,
> And his unsuffering kingdom yet will come.

They also sing. The voice of nature is articulate to God; it is not only a shout, but a song. Well-ordered are the sounds of animate creation as they combine with the equally well-tuned ripple of the waters, and sighing of the wind. Nature has no discords. Her airs are melodious; her chorus is full of harmony. All, all is for the Lord; the world is a hymn to the Eternal, blessed is he who, hearing, joins in it, and makes one singer in the mighty chorus.

---

77. from "The Seasons" a poem by James Thompson (1832)

Psalm 66
Psalm 66:1–Psalm 66:20

Psalm 66:1 *Make a joyful noise unto God, all ye lands*

EXPOSITION: Verse 1. *Make a joyful noise unto God.* If praise is to be widespread, it must be vocal; exulting sounds stir the soul and cause a sacred contagion of thanksgiving. Composers of tunes for the congregation should see to it that their airs are cheerful; we need joyful noise. God is to be praised with the voice, and the heart should go there in holy exultation. All praise from all nations should be rendered unto the Lord. Happy the day when no shouts shall be presented to Juggernaut[78] or Boodh,[79] but all the Earth will adore the Creator thereof.

All ye lands. Let the whole Earth rejoice before God. The languages of the lands are many, but their praises should be one, addressed to one only God.

Psalm 66:2 *Sing forth the honour of his name: make his praise glorious.*

EXPOSITION: Verse 2. *Sing forth the honour of his name.* The honor of God should be our subject, and to honor Him our object when we sing. To give glory to God is but to restore to Him His own. It is our glory to be able to give God glory; and all our true glory should be ascribed

---
78. a Hindu god; a huge, powerful, overwhelming force
79. same as Buddha

unto God, for it is His glory. "All worship is to God only," should be the motto of all true believers. The name, nature, and person of God are worthy of the highest honor.

Make his praise glorious. Let not His praise arise with grandeur and solemnity before Him We under the dispensation of Holy Spirit are to throw so much of heart and holy reverence into all our worship that it shall be the best we can render. Heart worship and spiritual joy render praise more glorious than vestments, incense, and music could do.

Psalm 66:3 *Say unto God, How terrible art thou in thy works! through the greatness of thy power shall thine enemies submit themselves unto thee.*

EXPOSITION: Verse 3. *Say unto God.* Turn all your praises to Him. Devotion, unless it is resolutely directed to the Lord, is no better than whistling to the wind.

How terrible art thou in thy works. The mind is usually first arrested by those attributes which cause fear and trembling; and, even when the heart has come to love God, and rest in Him, there is an increase of worship when the soul is awed by an extraordinary display of the more dreadful of the divine characteristics.

Through the greatness of thy power shall thine enemies submit themselves unto thee; but, as the Hebrew clearly intimates, it will be a forced and false submission. Power brings a man to his knee, but love alone wins his heart.

Psalm 66:4 *All the earth shall worship thee, and shall sing unto thee; they shall sing to thy name. Selah.*

EXPOSITION: Verse 4. *All the earth shall worship thee, and shall sing unto thee.* All men must even now prostrate themselves before you but a time will come when they shall do this cheerfully; to the worship of fear shall be added the singing of love

They shall sing to thy name. The nature and works of God will be the theme of Earth's universal song, and He himself shall be the object of the joyful adoration of our emancipated race. Acceptable worship not only praises God as the mysterious Lord, but it is rendered fragrant by some measure of knowledge of His name or character. God would not be worshipped as an unknown God, nor have it said of His people, *"Ye worship ye know not what"* [John 4:22]. May the knowledge of the Lord soon cover the Earth, *Selah.* A little pause for holy expectation is well inserted after so great a prophecy, and the uplifting of the heart is also a seasonable direction. No meditation can be more joyous than that excited by the prospect of a world reconciled to its Creator.

Psalm 66:5 *Come and see the works of God: he is terrible in his doing toward the children of men.*

EXPOSITION: Verse 5. *Come and see the works of God.* Such glorious events, as the cleaving of the Red Sea and the overthrow of Pharaoh, are standing wonders, and throughout all time a voice sounds forth concerning them—"Come and see." Even till the close of all things, the marvelous works of God at the Red Sea will be the subject of meditation and praise; for standing on the sea of glass mingled with fire, the triumphal armies of Heaven *"sing the song of Moses, the servant of God, and the song of the Lamb"* [Revelation 15:3]. It has always been the favorite subject of the inspired bards, and their choice was most natural.

He is terrible in his doing toward the children of men. For the defense of His church and the overthrow of her foes He deals terrific blows, and strikes the mighty with fear. This same God still lives, and is to be worshipped with trembling reverence.

Psalm 66:6 *He turned the sea into dry land: they went through the flood on foot: there did we rejoice in him.*

EXPOSITION: **Verse 6.** *He turned the sea into dry land.* It was no slight miracle to divide a pathway through such a sea, and to make it fit for the traffic of a whole nation. He who did this can do anything, and must be God, the worthy object of adoration. The Christian's inference is that no obstacle in his journey heavenward need hinder him, for the sea could not hinder Israel, and even death itself shall be as life; the sea shall be dry land when God's presence is felt.

They went through the flood on foot. Through the river the tribes passed dry shod, Jordan was afraid because of them.

> What ailed thee, O thou mighty sea?[80]
> Why rolled thy waves in dread?
> What bade thy tide, O Jordan, flee
> And bare its deepest bed?
>
> O earth, before the Lord, the God
> Of Jacob, tremble still;
> Who makes the waste a watered sod,
> The flint a gushing rill.

There did we rejoice in him. We participate this day in that ancient joy. The scene is so vividly before us that it seems as if we were there personally, singing unto the Lord because He has triumphed gloriously. It is to be remarked that Israel's joy was in her God, and let ours be there. It is

---
80. from hymn, "When Forth from Egypt's Trembling Strand," by George Burgess, c. 1840

not so much what He has done, as what He is that should excite in us a sacred rejoicing. *"He is my God, and I will prepare him an habitation; my father's God, and I will exalt him"* [Exodus 15:2].

Psalm 66:7 *He ruleth by his power for ever; his eyes behold the nations: let not the rebellious exalt themselves. Selah.*

EXPOSITION: Verse 7. *He ruleth by his power for ever.* He has not deceased, nor abdicated, nor suffered defeat. The prowess displayed at the Red Sea is undiminished: the divine dominion endures throughout eternity.

His eyes behold the nations. Even as He looked out of the cloud upon the Egyptians and discomfited them, so does He spy out His enemies, and mark their conspiracies. His hand rules and His eye observes, His hand has not waxed weak, nor His eye dim. He oversees all and overlooks none.

Let not the rebellious exalt themselves. Where rebellion reaches to a great head, and hopes most confidently for success, it is a sufficient reason for abating our fears, that the Omnipotent ruler is also an Omniscient observer. O proud rebels, remember that the Lord aims His arrows at the high soaring eagles and brings them down from their nest among the stars. *"He hath put down the mighty from their seats, and exalted them of low degree"* [Luke 1:52].

Selah. Pause again, and take time to bow low before the throne of the Eternal.

Psalm 66:8 *O bless our God, ye people, and make the voice of his praise to be heard*

EXPOSITION: Verse 8. *O bless our God, ye people.*

You chosen seed, peculiarly beloved, it is yours to bless your covenant God as other nations cannot.

And make the voice of his praise to be heard. Whoever else may sing with bated breath, you be sure to give full tongue and volume to the song. Compel unwilling ears to hear the praises of your covenant God.

Psalm 66:9 *Which holdeth our soul in life, and suffereth not our feet to be moved.*

EXPOSITION: Verse 9. *Which holdeth our soul in life.* At any time the preservation of life, and especially the soul's life, is a great reason for gratitude. Blessed be God, who, having put our souls into possession of life, has been pleased to preserve that Heaven given life from the destroying power of the enemy.

And suffereth not our feet to be moved. If God has enabled us not only to keep our life, but our position, we are bound to give Him double praise. Living and standing is the saint's condition through divine grace. Immortal and immoveable are those whom God preserves.

Psalm 66:10 *For thou, O God, hast proved us: thou hast tried us, as silver is tried.*

EXPOSITION: Verse 10. *For thou, O God, hast proved us.* He proved His Israel with sore trials. David had his temptations. All the saints must go to the proving house; God had one Son without sin, but He never had a son without trial. The Lord himself proves us, who then shall raise a question as to the wisdom and the love which are displayed in the operation? The day may come when, as in this case, we shall make hymns out of our griefs, and sing all the more sweetly because our mouths have been purified with bitter draughts.

Thou hast tried us, as silver is tried. Searching and repeated, severe and thorough, has been the test; for the dross and tin have been consumed, and the pure ore has been discovered. Since trial is sanctified to so desirable an end, ought we not to submit to it with abounding resignation?

> **Psalm 66:11** *Thou broughtest us into the net; thou laidst affliction upon our loins.*

EXPOSITION: **Verse 11.** *Thou broughtest us into the net.* The people of God in the olden time were often enclosed by the power of their enemies. The only comfort was that God himself had brought them there as a punishment for their transgressions; Israel in Egypt was much like a bird in the fowler's net.

Thou laidest affliction upon our loins. Not on their backs alone was the load, but their loins were pressed and squeezed with the straits and weights of adversity. God's people and affliction are intimate companions. As in Egypt every Israelite was a burden bearer, so is every believer while he is in this foreign land. As Israel cried to God by reason of their sore bondage, so also do the saints. We too often forget that God lays our afflictions upon us; if we remembered this fact, we would more patiently submit to the pressure which now pains us. The time will come when we shall receive a far more exceeding and eternal weight of glory.

> **Psalm 66:12** *Thou hast caused men to ride over our heads; we went through fire and through water: but thou broughtest us out into a wealthy place.*

EXPOSITION: **Verse 12.** *Thou hast caused men to ride over our heads.* Riding the high horse, in their arrogance, they, who were in themselves mean men, treated the Lord's people as if they were the lowest of mankind. They even turned their captives into beasts of burden, and rode upon their heads, as some read the Hebrew. Nothing is too bad for the servants of God when they fall into the hands of proud persecutors.

We went through fire and through water. Trials many and varied were endured by Israel in Egypt, and are still the portion of the saints and even thus the Church of God has outlived, and will outlive, all the artifices and cruelties of man. Fire and water are pitiless and devouring, but a divine fiat stays their fury, and forbids these or any other agents from utterly destroying the chosen seed. Many an heir of Heaven has had a dire experience of tribulation. Yet each saint has been more than conqueror thus far, and, as it has been, so it shall be. The fire is not kindled which can burn the woman's seed, neither does the dragon know how to vomit a flood which shall suffice to drown it.

But thou broughtest us out into a wealthy place. A blessed issue to a mournful story. Canaan was indeed a broad and royal domain for the once enslaved tribes: God, who took them into Egypt, also brought them into the land which flowed with milk and honey, and Egypt was in His purposes en route to Canaan. The way to Heaven is via tribulation.

> The path of sorrow and that path alone,[81]
> Leads to the land where sorrow is unknown.

How wealthy is the place of every believer, and how doubly does he feel it to be so in contrast with his former slavery: what songs shall suffice to set forth our joy and gratitude for such a glorious deliverance and such a bountiful

---

81. excerpt from a poem by William Cowper

heritage. Glory be unto Him who saw in the apparent evil the true way to the real good. With patience we will endure the present gloom, for the morning comes. Over the hills faith sees the daybreak, in whose light we shall enter into the wealthy place.

Psalm 66:13 *I will go into thy house with burnt offerings: I will pay thee my vows*

EXPOSITION: Verse 13. *I will go into thy house with burnt offerings;* the usual sacrifices of godly men. Even the thankful heart dares not come to God without a victim of grateful praise; of this as well as of every other form of worship, we may say, *"the blood is the life thereof."* Reader, never attempt to come before God without Jesus, the divinely promised, given, and accepted burnt offering. [See Leviticus 17:11, 14.]

I will pay thee my vows. He would not appear before the Lord empty, but at the same time he would not boast of what he offered, seeing it was all due on account of former vows. After all, our largest gifts are but payments; when we have given all, we must confess, *"O Lord, of thine own have we given unto thee"* [1 Chronicles 29:14]. We should be slow in making vows, but prompt in discharging them. When we are released from trouble, and can once more go up to the house of the Lord, we should take immediate occasion to fulfill our promises. How can we hope for help another time, if we prove faithless to covenants voluntarily entered upon in hours of need?

Psalm 66:14 *Which my lips have uttered, and my mouth hath spoken, when I was in trouble.*

EXPOSITION: Verse 14. *Which my lips have uttered,*

his vows had been wrung from him; extreme distress burst open the doors of his lips, and out rushed the vow like a long pent up torrent, which had at last found a vent. What we were so eager to vow, we should be equally earnest to perform; but alas, many a vow runs so fast in words that it lames itself for deeds!

And my mouth hath spoken. He had made the promise public, and had no desire to go back; an honest man is always ready to acknowledge a debt.

When I was in trouble. Distress suggested the vow; God in answer to the vow removed the distress, and now the votary desires to make good his promise. Even great Caesar, whose look did awe the world, must have his trouble and become weak as other men; so that his enemy could say in bitterness, "when the fit was on him, I did mark how he did shake."[82] Of the strong and vigorous man the nurse could tell a tale of weakness, and his wife could say of the boaster, "I did hear him groan; his coward lips did from their color fly."[83] All men have trouble, but they act not in the same manner while under it; the profane take to swearing and the godly to praying. Both bad and good have been known to resort to vowing, but the one is a liar unto God, and the other a conscientious respecter of His Word.

Psalm 66:15 *I will offer unto thee burnt sacrifices of fatlings, with the incense of rams; I will offer bullocks with goats. Selah.*

EXPOSITION: Verse 15. *I will offer unto thee burnt sacrifices of fatlings.* The good man will give his best things to God. He will present no starveling goat upon the hills

---

82. excerpt from *Julius Caesar,* act 1, scene 2, by William Shakespeare
83. Ibid.

at the altar, but the well fed bullocks of luxuriant pastures shall ascend in smoke from the sacred fire. He who is miserly with God is a wretch indeed. Few devise liberal things, but those few find a rich reward in so doing.

With the incense of rams. The smoke of burning rams should also rise from the altar; he would offer the strength and prime of his flocks as well as his herds. Of all we have we should give the Lord His portion, and that should be the choicest we can select. It was no waste to burn the fat upon Jehovah's altar, nor to pour the precious ointment upon Jesus' head; neither are large gifts and bountiful offerings to the Church of God any diminution to a man's estate: such money is put to good interest and placed where it cannot be stolen by thieves nor corroded by rust.

I will offer bullocks with goats. A perfect sacrifice, completing the circle of offerings, should show forth the intense love of his heart. We should magnify the Lord with the great and the little.

Selah. It is most fit that we should suspend the song while the smoke of the victims ascends the heavens; let the burnt offerings stand for praises while we meditate upon the infinitely greater sacrifice of Calvary.

Psalm 66:16 *Come and hear, all ye that fear God, and I will declare what he hath done for my soul.*

EXPOSITION: Verse 16. *Come and hear.* Before, they were bidden to come and see. Hearing is faith's seeing. Mercy comes to us by way of our ear gate. *"Hear, and your soul shall live"* [Isaiah 55:3]. They saw how terrible God was, but they heard how gracious He was.

All ye that fear God. These are a fit audience when a good man is about to relate his experience; and it is well to select our hearers when inward soul matters are our theme. It is forbidden us to throw pearls before swine. [See Matthew 7:6.] We do not want to furnish wanton minds with subjects for their comedies, and therefore it is wise to speak of personal spiritual matters where they can be understood

And I will declare what he hath done for my soul. I will count and recount the mercies of God to me, to my soul, my best part, my most real self. Testimonies ought to be borne by all experienced Christians, in order that the younger and feebler sort may be encouraged by the recital to put their trust in the Lord. To declare the gracious acts of God is instructive, consoling, inspiring, and beneficial in many respects. Let each man speak for himself, for a personal witness is the surest and most forcible; second hand experience is like "cauld kale het again;"[84] it lacks the flavor of first hand interest.

Psalm 66:17 *I cried unto him with my mouth, and he was extolled with my tongue.*

EXPOSITION: Verse 17. *I cried unto him with my mouth, and he was extolled with my tongue.* It is good when prayer and praise go together. Some cry who do not sing and some sing who do not cry: both together are best. Since the Lord's answers so frequently follow close at the heels of our petitions, and even overtake them, it becomes us to let our grateful praises keep pace with our humble prayers. Observe that the psalmist did both cry and speak.

Psalm 66:18 *If I regard iniquity in my heart, the Lord will not hear me*

EXPOSITION: *If I regard iniquity in my heart.* If, having seen it to be there, I continue to gaze upon it without

---
84. cold kale (green leafy vegetable), leftover and reheated

aversion; if I cherish it, have a side glance of love toward it, excuse it, and palliate it;

the Lord will not hear me. How can He? Can I desire Him to connive at my sin, and accept me while I willfully cling to any evil way? Nothing hinders prayer like iniquity harbored in the breast; as with Cain, so with us, sin lies at the door, and blocks the passage. If you refuse to hear God's commands, He will surely refuse to hear your prayers. An imperfect petition God will hear for Christ's sake, but not one which is willfully miswritten by a traitor's hand.

Psalm 66:19 *But verily God hath heard me; he hath attended to the voice of my prayer.*

EXPOSITION: Verse 19. *But verily God hath heard me.* The answer to his prayer was a fresh assurance that his heart was sincere before the Lord. See how sure the psalmist is that he has been heard; it is with him no hope, surmise, or fancy, but he seals it with a verily. Facts are blessed things when they reveal both God's heart as loving, and our own heart as sincere.

He hath attended to the voice of my prayer. He gave His mind to consider my cries, interpreted them, accepted them, and replied to them; and therein proved His grace and also my uprightness of heart. Let the reader see to it, that his inmost soul be rid of all alliance with iniquity, all toleration of secret lust, or hidden wrong.

Psalm 66:20 *Blessed be God, which hath not turned away my prayer, nor his mercy from me.*

EXPOSITION: Verse 20. *Blessed be God.* Let His name be honored and loved.

Which has not turned away my prayer, nor His mercy

from me. He has neither withdrawn His love nor my liberty to pray. He has neither cast out my prayer nor me. His mercy and my cries still meet each other. The psalm ends on its key note. Praise all through is its spirit and design. Lord enable us to enter into it. Amen.

Psalm 67

Psalm 67:1–Psalm 67:7

Psalm 67:1 *God be merciful unto us, and bless us; and cause his face to shine upon us; Selah.*

EXPOSITION: **Verse 1.** *God be merciful unto us, and bless us; and cause his face to shine upon us.* This is a fit refrain to the benediction of the High Priest in the name of the Lord, as recorded in Numbers 6:24–25. *The Lord bless thee, and keep thee: the Lord make his face shine upon thee, and be gracious unto thee."* It begins at the beginning with a cry for mercy. Forgiveness of sin is always the first link in the chain of mercies experienced by us. Mercy is a foundation attribute in our salvation. The best saints and the worst sinners may unite in this petition. It is addressed to the God of mercy, by those who feel their need of mercy, and it implies the death of all legal hopes or claims of merit. Next, the church begs for a blessing; *bless us*—a very comprehensive and far-reaching prayer. When we bless God we do but little, for *our* blessings are but words, but when God blesses He enriches us indeed, for His blessings are gifts and deeds. But His blessing alone is not all His people crave; they desire a personal consciousness of His favor, and pray for a smile from His face. These three petitions include all that we need here or hereafter. This verse may be regarded as the prayer of Israel, and spiritually of the Christian Church. The largest charity is shown in this psalm, but it begins at home. The whole Church, each church, and each little company, may rightly pray, *bless us*. It would, however, be very wrong to let our charity end where it begins, as some do; our love must make long marches, and our prayers must have a wide sweep, we must embrace the whole world in our intercessions.

Selah. Lift up the heart, lift up the voice. A higher key, a sweeter note is called for.

Psalm 67:2 *That thy way may be known upon earth, thy saving health among all nations.*

EXPOSITION: Verse 2. *That thy way may be known upon earth.* The blessing of the Most High comes upon the world through the Church. We are blessed for the sake of others as well as ourselves. God deals in a way of mercy with His saints, and then they make that way known far and wide, and the Lord's name is made famous in the Earth. Ignorance of God is the great enemy of mankind, and the testimonies of the saints, experimental and grateful, overcome this deadly foe.

Thy saving health among all nations. One likes the old words, "saving health," yet as they are not the words of the Spirit but only of our translators, they must be given up: the word is salvation, and nothing else. This, all nations need, but many of them do not know it, desire it, or seek it; our prayer and labor should be, that the knowledge of salvation may become as universal as the light of the sun. Despite the gloomy notions of some, we cling to the belief that the kingdom of Christ will embrace the whole habitable globe, and that all flesh shall see the salvation of God: we agonize in prayer for this glorious consummation.

Psalm 67:3 *Let the people praise thee, O God; let all the people praise thee.*

EXPOSITION: Verse 3. *Let the people praise thee, O God.* Cause them to honor your goodness and thank you with all their hearts

Let all the people praise thee. May every man bring his music, all are under obligations to you, to thank you will benefit all, and praise from all will greatly glorify you; therefore, O Lord, give all men the grace to adore your grace, the goodness to see your goodness. What is here expressed as a prayer in our translation may be read as a prophecy, if we follow the original Hebrew.

Psalm 67:4 *O let the nations be glad and sing for joy: for thou shalt judge the people righteously, and govern the nations upon earth. Selah.*

EXPOSITION: Verse 4. *O let the nations be glad and sing for joy,* when men know God's way and see His salvation, it brings to their hearts much happiness. Nothing creates gladness so speedily, surely, and abidingly as the salvation of God. What a sweet word it is to sing for joy! Some sing for form, others for show, some as a duty, others as an amusement, but to sing from the heart, because overflowing joy must find a vent, this is to sing indeed. Whole nations will do this when Jesus reigns over them in the power of His grace. *For thou shalt judge the people righteously.* His laws are righteousness itself. He rights all wrongs and releases all who are oppressed. Justice on the throne is a fit cause for national exultation.

And govern the nations upon earth. He will lead them as a shepherd his flock, and through His grace they shall willingly follow, then will there be peace, plenty, and prosperity. It is a great condescension on God's part to become the Shepherd of nations, and to govern them for their good

Selah.

Strings and voices, hands and hearts,[85]
In the concert bear your parts;
All that breathe, your Lord adore,
Praise him, Praise him, evermore!

Psalm 67:5 *Let the people praise thee, O God; let all the people praise thee.*

EXPOSITION: Verse 5. Let the people praise thee, O God; let all the people praise thee. These words are no vain repetition, but are a chorus worthy to be sung again and again. The great theme of the psalm is the participation of the Gentiles in the worship of Jehovah; the psalmist is full of it, he hardly knows how to contain or express his joy.

Psalm 67:6 *Then shall the earth yield her increase; and God, even our own God, shall bless us.*

EXPOSITION: Verse 6. *Then shall the earth yield her increase.* Sin first laid a curse on the soil, and grace alone can remove it. We read that the Lord turns "a fruitful land into barrenness" [see Psalm 107:34], for the wickedness of them that dwell therein, and observation confirms the truth of the divine threatening; but even under the law it was promised, *"The Lord shall make thee plenteous in every work of thine hand, in the fruit of thy cattle, and in the fruit of thy land for good"* [Deuteronomy 28:11]. There is certainly an intimate relation between moral and physical evil, and between spiritual and physical good.

And God, even our own God, shall bless us. He will make Earth's increase to be a real blessing. Men shall see in His gifts the hand of that same God whom Israel of old adored,

---

85. from a hymn titled "Praise the Lord" by Henry Francis Lyte

and Israel, especially, shall rejoice in the blessing, and exult in her own God. We never love God rightly until we know Him to be ours, and the more we love Him the more we long to be fully assured that He is ours. What dearer name can we give to Him than "mine own God." The spouse in the song has no sweeter canticle than *"my beloved is mine, and I am his"* [Song of Solomon 2:16]. Every believing Jew must feel a holy joy at the thought that the nations shall be blessed by Abraham's God; but every Gentile believer also rejoices that the whole world shall yet worship the God and Father of our Lord and Savior Jesus Christ, who is our Father and our God.

Psalm 67:7 *God shall bless us; and all the ends of the earth shall fear him.*

EXPOSITION: Verse 7. *God shall bless us.* Truly the Lord's blessing is manifold; He blesses and blesses and blesses again. How many are His beatitudes! How choice His benedictions! They are the peculiar heritage of His chosen. He is the Savior of all men, but especially of them that believe. In this verse we find a song for all future time. God shall bless us is our assured confidence; He may smite us, or strip us, or even slay us, but He must bless us. He cannot turn away from doing good to His elect.

And all the ends of the earth shall fear him. The far off shall fear. The ends of the earth shall end their idolatry, and adore their God. All tribes, without exception, shall feel a sacred awe of the God of Israel. Ignorance shall be removed, insolence subdued, injustice banished, idolatry abhorred, and the Lord's love, light, life, and liberty, shall be over all, the Lord himself being King of kings and Lord of lords. Amen and Amen.

Psalm 68
Psalm 68:1–Psalm 68:35

Psalm 68:1 *Let God arise, let his enemies be scattered: let them also that hate him flee before him.*

EXPOSITION: Verse 1. *Let God arise.* Before we move, we should always desire to see the Lord lead the way. The words suppose the Lord to have been passive for awhile, allowing His enemies to rage, but restraining His power. Israel beseeches Him to "arise," as elsewhere to "awake," "gird on His sword," and other similar expressions. We, also, may thus importunately cry unto the Lord, that He would be pleased to make bare His arm, and plead His own cause.

Let his enemies be scattered. Our glorious Captain of the vanguard clears the way readily, however many may seek to obstruct it; He has but to arise, and they flee, He has easily overthrown His foes in days of yore, and will do so all through the ages to come. Sin, death, and hell know the terror of His arm; their ranks are broken at His approach. Our enemies are His enemies, and in this is our confidence of victory.

Let them also that hate him flee before him. Hatred of God is impotent. His proudest foes can do Him no injury. Alarmed beyond measure, they shall flee before it comes to blows. Long before the army of Israel can come into the fray; the haters of God shall flee before Him who is the champion of His chosen. He comes, He sees, He conquers. How fitting a prayer this is for the commencement of a revival! How it suggests the true mode of conducting one—the Lord leads the way, His people follow, and the enemies flee.

Psalm 68:2 *As smoke is driven away, so drive them away: as wax melteth before the fire, so let the wicked perish at the presence of God.*

EXPOSITION: Verse 2. *As smoke is driven.* The wind chases the smoke easily and completely removes it, no trace is left; so, Lord, do the same to the foes of your people. They defile wherever they prevail. Lord, let your breath, your Spirit, your Providence, make them to vanish forever from the march of your people. Philosophic skepticism is as flimsy and as foul as smoke; may the Lord deliver His Church from the reek of it.

As wax melteth before the fire, so let the wicked perish at the presence of God. Wicked men are haughty until they come into contact with the Lord, and then they faint for fear; their hearts melt like wax when they feel the power of His anger. Israel saw, in the Ark, God on the mercy seat—power in connection with propitiation—and they rejoiced in the omnipotence of such a manifestation. This is even more clearly the confidence of the New Testament Church, for we see Jesus, the appointed atonement, clothed with glory and majesty, and before His advance all opposition melts like snow in the sun; the pleasure of the Lord shall prosper in his hands. When He comes by His Holy Spirit, conquest is the result; but when He arises in person, His foes shall utterly perish.

Psalm 68:3 *But let the righteous be glad; let them rejoice before God: yea, let them exceedingly rejoice.*

EXPOSITION: Verse 3. *But let the righteous be glad.* The presence of God on the throne of grace is an overflowing source of delight to the godly; and let them not fail to drink of the streams which are meant to make them glad.

Let them rejoice before God, for in His presence is fullness of joy. That presence, which is the dread and death of the wicked, is the desire and delight of the saints.

Yea, let them exceedingly rejoice. "Again, I say, rejoice," says the apostle, as if he would have us add joy to joy without measure or pause. When God is seen to shine propitiously from above the mercy seat in the person of our Immanuel, our hearts must leap within us with exultation, if we are indeed among those made righteous in His righteousness, and sanctified by His Spirit. Move on, O army of the living God, with shouts of abounding triumph, for Jesus leads the vanguard.

Psalm 68:4 *Sing unto God, sing praises to his name: extol him that rideth upon the heavens by his name JAH, and rejoice before him.*

EXPOSITION: Verse 4. *Sing unto God, sing praises to his name.* To time and tune, with order and care, celebrate the character and deeds of God, the God of His people. Sing not to the congregation, but "unto God."

Extol him that rideth upon the heavens by his name JAH. Remember His most great, incomprehensible, and awful name; reflect upon His self-existence and absolute dominion, rise to the highest pitch of joyful reverence in adoring Him. Heaven beholds Him riding on the clouds in the storm, and Earth has seen Him marching over its plains with majesty. The name JAH is an abbreviation of the name Jehovah; it is not a diminution of that name, but an intensified word, containing in it the essence of the longer, august title. It only occurs here in our version of Scripture, except in connection with other words such as Hallelujah.

And rejoice before him. In the presence of Him who

marched so gloriously at the head of the elect nation, it is most fitting that all His people should display a holy delight. It should be our wish and prayer, that in this wilderness world, a highway may be prepared for the God of grace. "Prepare ye the way of the Lord, make straight in the desert a highway for our God," is the cry of gospel heralds, and we must all zealously aim at obedience thereto; for where the God of the mercy seat comes, blessings innumerable are given to the sons of men. [See Isaiah 40:3.]

Psalm 68:5 *A father of the fatherless, and a judge of the widows, is God in his holy habitation.*

EXPOSITION: Verse 5. *A father of the fatherless, and a judge of the widows, is God in his holy habitation.* As the generation which came out of Egypt gradually died away, there were many widows and fatherless ones in the camp, but they suffered no want or wrong, for the righteous laws and the just administrators whom God had appointed, looked well to the interests of the needy. The Tabernacle was the Palace of Justice; the ark was the seat of the great King. This was a great cause for joy to Israel, that they were ruled by the One who would not suffer the poor and needy to be oppressed. To this day and forever, God is, and will be, the peculiar guardian of the defenseless. How zealously ought His Church to cherish those who are here marked out as Jehovah's especial charge. Does He not here in effect say, *"Feed my lambs"*? [John 21:15]. Blessed duty, it shall be our privilege to make this one of our life's dearest objects. The reader is warned against misquoting this verse; it is generally altered into "the husband of the widow," but Scripture had better be left as God gave it.

Psalm 68:6 *God setteth the solitary in families: he bringeth out those which are bound with chains: but the rebellious dwell in a dry land.*

EXPOSITION: **Verse 6.** *God setteth the solitary in families.* The people had been sundered and scattered over Egypt; family ties had been disregarded, and affections crushed; but when the people escaped from Pharaoh they came together again and all the fond associations of household life were restored. This was a great joy.

He bringeth out those which are bound with chains. The most oppressed in Egypt were chained and imprisoned, but the divine Emancipator brought them all forth into perfect liberty. He who did this of old continues His gracious work. The solitary heart, convinced of sin and made to pine alone, is admitted into the family of the Firstborn. The fettered spirit is set free, and its prison broken down when sin is forgiven. God is to be greatly extolled, for He has done it, and magnified the glory of His grace.

But the rebellious dwell in a dry land. Israel did not find the desert dry, for the smitten rock gave forth its streams; but even in Canaan itself men were consumed with famine, because they cast off their allegiance to their covenant God. Even where God is revealed on the mercy seat, some men persist in rebellion, and such need not wonder if they find no peace, no comfort, no joy, even where all these abound. Justice is the rule of the Lord's Kingdom, and hence there is no provision for the unjust to indulge their evil lusting: a perfect Earth, and even Heaven itself, would be a dry land to those who can only drink of the waters of sin. When a man has a rebellious heart, he must of necessity find all around him a dry land.

Psalm 68:7 *O God, when thou wentest forth before thy people, when thou didst march through the wilderness*

EXPOSITION: **Verse 7.** *O God, when thou wentest forth before thy people.* What a sweetly suitable association, "thou" and "thy people"—God before, and His people following! The Lord went before, and, therefore, whether the Red Sea or burning sand lay in the way, it mattered not; the pillar of cloud and fire always led them by a right way.

When thou didst march through the wilderness. He was the Commander-in-Chief of Israel, from whom they received all orders, and the march was therefore His march. We may speak, if we will, of the "wanderings of the children of Israel," but we must not think them purposeless straying, they were in reality a well-arranged and well-considered march.

Psalm 68:8 *The earth shook, the heavens also dropped at the presence of God: even Sinai itself was moved at the presence of God, the God of Israel.*

EXPOSITION: **Verse 8.** *The earth shook.* The solid ground trembled beneath the sublime.

The heavens also dropped at the presence of God, as if they bowed before their God, the clouds descended, and a few dark shower drops stole abroad.

Even Sinai itself was moved at the presence of God. Moses tell us, in Exodus 19, that "the whole mountain quaked greatly." That hill, so lone and high, bowed before the manifested God.

The God of Israel. The one only living and true God, whom Israel worshipped, and who had chosen that nation to be His own above all the nations of the Earth. The passage is so sublime that it would be difficult to find its equal. May the reader's heart adore the God before whom the unconscious Earth and sky act as if they recognized their Maker and were moved with a tremor of reverence.

> **Psalm 68:9** *Thou, O God, didst send a plentiful rain, whereby thou didst confirm thine inheritance, when it was weary.*

EXPOSITION: Verse 9. *Thou, O God, didst send a plentiful rain.* Such rain as never fell before dropped on the desert sand, bread from Heaven and winged fowl fell all around the host; good gifts were poured upon them, rivers leaped forth from rocks.

Whereby thou didst confirm thine inheritance, when it was weary. As at the end of each stage, when they halted, weary with the march, they found such showers of good things awaiting them that they were speedily refreshed. In like manner, to this day, the elect of God in this wilderness state are apt to become tired and faint, but their ever loving Jehovah comes in with timely help, cheers the faint, strengthens the weak, and refreshes the hungry; so that once again, when the silver trumpets sound, the Church militant advances with bold and firm step towards "the rest which remaineth." [See Hebrews 4:9.]

> **Psalm 68:10** *Thy congregation hath dwelt therein: thou, O God, hast prepared of thy goodness for the poor.*

EXPOSITION: Verse 10. *Thy congregation hath dwelt therein.* The congregation of the faithful find the Lord to be their *"dwelling place in all generations"* [Psalm 90:1]. Where there were no dwellings of men, God was the dwelling of His people.

Thou, O God, hast prepared of thy goodness for the poor. Within the guarded circle there was plenty for all; all were poor in themselves, yet there were no beggars in all the camp, for celestial fare was to be had for the gathering. We, too, still dwell within the circling protection of the Most High and we are enriched by grace; the covenant, the atonement, providence, and the Spirit's work within, making us ready for a fullness of the blessing of the Lord.

Psalm 68:11 *The Lord gave the word: great was the company of those that published it.*

EXPOSITION: *The Lord gave the word.* The enemy was near, and the silver trumpet from the tabernacle door was God's mouth to warn the camp; then was there hurrying to and fro, and a general telling of the news.

Great was the company of those that published it. The women ran from tent to tent and roused their lords to battle. The ten thousand maids of Israel, like good handmaids of the Lord, aroused the sleepers, called in the wanderers, and bade the valiant men to hasten to the fray. O for the zeal like that in the Church of today, so that, when the gospel is published, both men and women may eagerly spread the glad tidings of great joy.

Psalm 68:12 *Kings of armies did flee apace: and she that tarried at home divided the spoil.*

EXPOSITION: Verse 12. *Kings of armies did flee apace.* The lords of hosts fled before the Lord of Hosts. No sooner did the ark advance than the enemy turned his back: even the princely leaders stayed not, but took to flight. The rout was complete, the retreat hurried and disorderly—they "did flee."

And she that tarried at home divided the spoil. The women who had published the war cry shared the booty. The feeblest in Israel had a portion of the prey. Gallant warriors cast their spoils at the feet of the women and bade them array themselves in splendor, taking each one "a prize of diverse colors, of diverse colors of needlework on both sides."

Psalm 68:13 *Though ye have lien among the pots, yet shall ye be as the wings of a dove covered with silver, and her feathers with yellow gold.*

EXPOSITION: Verse 13. *Though ye have lien among the pots.* Of making many conjectures there is no end; but the sense seems to be, that from the lowest condition the Lord would lift up His people into joy, liberty, wealth, and beauty. Their enemies may have called them squatters among the pots—in allusion to their Egyptian slavery; they may have jested at them as scullions of Pharaoh's kitchen; but the Lord would avenge them and give them beauty for blackness, glory for grime.

Yet shall ye be as the wings of a dove covered with silver, and her feathers with yellow gold. The dove's wing flashed light like silver, and began to gleam with the radiance of "the pale, pure gold." The lovely, changeable colors of the dove might well image the mild, lustrous beauty of the nation, when arrayed in white holiday attire, bedecked with their gems, jewels, and ornaments of gold. God's saints have been in worse places than among the pots, but now they soar aloft into the heavenly places in Christ Jesus.

Psalm 68:14 *When the Almighty scattered kings in it, it was white as snow in Salmon.*

EXPOSITION: Verse 14. *When the almighty scattered*

kings in it, it was white as snow in Salmon. The victory was due to the Almighty arm alone; He scattered the haughty ones who came against His people, and He did it as easily as snow is driven from the bleak sides of Salmon.

Psalm 68:15 *The hill of God is as the hill of Bashan; an high hill as the hill of Bashan.*

EXPOSITION: Verse 15. Here the priests on the summit of the chosen hill begin to extol the Lord for His choice of Zion as His dwelling place.

The hill of God is as the hill of Bashan, that is to say, Bashan is an eminent mountain, far exceeding Zion in height. According to the Hebrew custom, every great or remarkable thing is thus designated. The more commendable idiom of the Hebrews speaks of the hill of God, the trees of the Lord, the river of God, etc.

An high hill as the hill of Bashan, it does not appear that Zion is compared with Bashan, but contrasted with it. Zion certainly was not a high hill comparatively; and it is here conceded that Bashan is a greater mount, but not so glorious, for the Lord in choosing Zion had exalted it above the loftier hills. The loftiness of nature is made as nothing before the Lord. He chooses as pleases Him, and, according to the counsel of His own will, He selects Zion, and passes by the proud, uplifted peaks of Bashan; thus does He make the base things of this world, and things that are despised, to become monuments of His grace and sovereignty.

Psalm 68:16 *Why leap ye, ye high hills? this is the hill which God desireth to dwell in; yea, the LORD will dwell in it for ever.*

EXPOSITION: Verse 16. *Why leap ye, ye high hills?*

Why are you moved to envy? Lift up yourselves, and even leap from your seats, you cannot reach the sublimity which Jehovah's presence has bestowed on the little hill of Moriah. *This is the hill which God desireth to dwell in.* Elohim makes Zion His abode, yea, Jehovah resides there. *Yea, the Lord will dwell in it for ever.* Spiritually the Lord abides eternally in Zion, His chosen Church, and it was Zion's glory to be typical thereof. What were Carmel and Sirion, with all their height, compared to Zion, the joy of the whole Earth! God's election is a patent of nobility. They are choice men whom God has chosen, and that place is superlatively honored which He honors with His presence.

Psalm 68:17 *The chariots of God are twenty thousand, even thousands of angels: the Lord is among them, as in Sinai, in the holy place.*

EXPOSITION: Verse 17. *The chariots of God are twenty thousand.* Other countries, which in the former verse were symbolically referred to as "high hills," gloried in their chariots of war; but Zion, though far more lowly, was stronger than they, for the omnipotence of God was to her as two myriads of chariots. *Even thousands of angels.* The Lord of Hosts could summon more forces into the field than all the petty lords who boasted in their armies; His horses of fire and chariots of fire would be more than a match for their fiery steeds and flashing cars. The original is grandly expressive: "the war chariots of Elohim are myriads, a thousand thousands." We read in Deuteronomy 33:2, of the Lord's coming *"with ten thousands of saints,"* or holy ones, and in Hebrews 12:22, we find upon mount Zion *"an innumerable company of angels,"* so that our worthy translators putting the texts together, inferred the angels, and the clause is so truthfully explanatory, that we have no fault to find with it.

The Lord is among them, as in Sinai, in the holy place, God is in Zion as the Commander-in-Chief of His countless hosts, and where He is, there is holiness. The throne of grace on Zion is as holy as the throne of justice on Sinai. The displays of His glory may not be as terrible under the new covenant as under the old; but they are even more marvelous if seen by the spiritual eye. Sinai has no excellency of glory beyond Zion; but rather 'it pales its light of law before the noontide splendors of Zion's grace and truth. The presence of God is the strength of the Church; all power is ours when God is ours. Twenty thousand chariots shall bear the gospel to the ends of the Earth; and myriads of agencies shall work for its success. Providence is on our side, and it "has servants everywhere."[86] There is no room for a shade of doubt or discouragement, but every reason for exultation and confidence.

> **Psalm 68:18** *Thou hast ascended on high, thou hast led captivity captive: thou hast received gifts for men; yea, for the rebellious also, that the* LORD *God might dwell among them.*

EXPOSITION: Verse 18. *Thou hast ascended on high.* The ark was conducted to the summit of Zion; God himself took possession of the high places of the Earth, being extolled and very high. The antitype of the ark, the Lord Jesus, has ascended into the heavens with signal marks of triumph. To do battle with our enemies, the Lord descended and left His throne; but now the fight is finished, He returns to His glory; high above all things He is now exalted.

Thou hast led captivity captive. A multitude of the sons

---

86. excerpt from a poem by J.J. Lynch based on Matthew 14:16

of men are the willing captives of Messiah's power. As great conquerors of old led whole nations into captivity, so Jesus leads forth from the territory of His foe a vast company as the trophies of His mighty grace. The Lord Jesus destroys His foes with their own weapons: He puts death to death, entombs the grave, and leads captivity captive.

Thou hast received gifts for men, Paul's rendering is the gospel one: Jesus has "received gifts for men," of which He makes plentiful distribution, enriching His Church with the priceless fruits of His ascension, such as apostles, evangelists, pastors, and teachers, and all their varied endowments. In Him, the man who received gifts for man, we are endowed with priceless treasures, and moved with gratitude, we return gifts to Him, yea, and we give Him ourselves, our all.

Yea, for the rebellious also: these gifts the rebels are permitted to share in; subdued by love, they are indulged with the benefits peculiar to the chosen. The original runs, "even the rebellious," or, "even from the rebellious," of which the sense is that rebels become captives to the Lord's power, and tributaries to His throne.

> Great King of grace my heart subdue,
> I would be led in triumph too;
> As willing captive to my Lord,
> To own the conquests of his word.[87]

That the Lord God might dwell among them. In the conquered territory, JAH Elohim would dwell as Lord of all, blessing with His condescending nearness those who were once His foes. When Canaan was conquered, and the fort of Zion carried by storm, then was there found a resting place for the ark of God; and so when the weapons of victorious grace have overcome the hearts of men, the Lord God, in all

---

87. from a hymn by Isaac Watts

the glory of His name, makes them to be His living temples. Moreover, the ascension of Jesus is the reason for the descent of the Lord God, the Holy Spirit. Because Jesus dwells with God, God dwells with men. Christ on high is the reason for the Spirit below. It was expedient that the Redeemer should rise, so the Comforter could come down.

> **Psalm 68:19** *Blessed be the Lord, who daily loadeth us with benefits, even the God of our salvation. Selah.*

EXPOSITION: **Verse 19.** *Blessed be the Lord.* At the mention of the presence of God among men the singers utter an earnest acclamation suggested by reverential love, and return blessings to Him who so plentifully blesses His people.

Who daily loadeth us with benefits. God's benefits are not few nor light, they are loads; neither are they intermittent, but they come "daily;" nor are they confined to one or two favorites, for all Israel can say, He loads us with benefits. Delitzsch[88] reads it, "He daily bears our burden;" and Alexander,[89] "Whoever lays a load upon us, the Mighty God is our salvation." If He himself burdens us with sorrow, He gives strength sufficient to sustain it; and if others endeavor to oppress us, there is no cause for fear, for the Lord will come to the rescue of His people.

Even the God of our salvation. A name most full of glory to Him, and consolation to us. A world of meaning is condensed into a few words. His yoke is easy, and His burden is light, therefore blessed be the Savior's name for evermore. All hail! Your are the blessed Prince of Peace! All your saved ones adore you and call you blessed.

---

88. J.F. Kark Keil and Franz Delitzsch co-authored a commentary on the Old Testament in 1861.

89. excerpt from an 1850 commentary on the psalms by Joseph Addison Alexander

Selah. Well may the strings need tuning; they have borne an unparalleled strain in this mighty song. Higher and yet higher, you men of music, lift up the strain. Dance before the ark, you maidens of Israel; bring forth the timbrel, and sing unto the Lord who has triumphed gloriously.

Psalm 68:20 *He that is our God is the God of salvation; and unto God the Lord belong the issues from death.*

EXPOSITION: Verse 20. *He that is our God is the God of salvation.* The Almighty who has entered into covenant with us is the source of our safety, and the author of our deliverances. As surely as He is our God He will save us. To be His is to be safe.

And unto God the Lord belong the issues from death. He has ways and means of rescuing His children from death: when they are at their wit's end, and see no way of escape, He can find a door of deliverance for them. He has set open the doors for all His people, and they shall enjoy triumphant issues from death. Jesus, our God, will save His people from their sins, and from all else besides, whether in life or death.

Psalm 68:21 *But God shall wound the head of his enemies, and the hairy scalp of such an one as goeth on still in his trespasses.*

EXPOSITION: Verse 21. *But God shall wound the head of his enemies.* He smites His foes on the crown of their pride. The seed of the woman crushes the serpent's head. There is no defense against the Lord; He can in a moment smite with utter destruction the lofty crests of His haughty foes.

And the hairy scalp of such a one as goeth on still in

his trespasses. He may glory in his outward appearance, and make his hair his pride, as Absalom did; but the Lord's sword shall find him out, and pour out his soul. He covers the head of His servants, but He crushes the head of His foes. At the second coming of the Lord Jesus, His enemies will find His judgments to be beyond terrible conception.

Psalm 68:22 *The Lord said, I will bring again from Bashan, I will bring my people again from the depths of the sea:*

EXPOSITION: **Verse 22.** *The Lord said, I will bring again from Bashan, I will bring my people again from the depths of the sea.* Though His foes might endeavor to escape, they would not be able. As there is no resisting Israel's God, so is there no escape from Him, neither the heights of Bashan nor the depths of the great sea can shelter from His eye of detection, and His hand of justice. The powers of evil may flee to the utmost ends of the Earth, but the Lord will arrest them, and lead them back in chains to adorn His triumph.

Psalm 68:23 *That thy foot may be dipped in the blood of thine enemies, and the tongue of thy dogs in the same.*

EXPOSITION: **Verse 23.** *That thy foot may be dipped in the blood of thine enemies.* Vengeance shall be awarded to the oppressed people and that most complete and terrible.

And the tongue of thy dogs in the same. So overwhelming should be the defeat of the foe that dogs should lick their blood. Terrible is the God of Israel when He comes forth as a man of war, and dreadful is even the Christ of God when He bares His arm to smite His enemies. Contemplate Revelation 19 and note the following:

And I saw heaven opened, and behold a white horse; and he that sat upon him was called Faithful and True, and in righteousness he doth judge and make war. His eyes were as a flame of fire, and on his head were many crowns; and he had a name written, that no man knew, but he himself. And he was clothed with a vesture dipped in blood; and his name is called The Word of God... And I saw an angel standing in the sun; and he cried with a loud voice, saying to all the fowls that fly in the midst of heaven, come and gather yourselves together unto the supper of the great God; that ye may eat the flesh of kings, and the flesh of captains, and the flesh of mighty men, and the flesh of horses, and of them that sit upon them, and the flesh of all men, both free and bond, both small and great. And I saw the beast, and the kings of the earth, and their armies, gathered together to make war against him that sat on the horse, and against his army. And the beast was taken, and with him the false prophet that wrought miracles before him, with which he deceived them that had the mark of the beast, and them that worshipped his image. These both were cast alive into a lake of fire burning with brimstone. And the remnant were slain with the sword of him that sat upon the horse, which sword proceeded out of his mouth: and all the fowls were filled with their flesh.

Psalm 68:24 *They have seen thy goings, O God; even the goings of my God, my King, in the sanctuary.*

EXPOSITION: **Verse 24.** *They have seen thy goings, O God.* In the song the marching of the Lord had been described; friends and foes had seen His goings forth with the ark and His people.

Even the goings of my God, my King, in the sanctuary. The splendid procession of the Ark, which symbolized the throne of the great King, was before the eyes of men and angels as it ascended to the holy place; and the psalmist points to it with exultation before he proceeds to describe it. All nature and providence are, as it were, a procession attending the great Lord in His visitations of this lower globe. Winter and summer, sun and moon, storm and calm, and all the varied glories of nature swell the pomp of the King of kings, of whose dominion there is no end.

Psalm 68:25 *The singers went before, the players on instruments followed after; among them were the damsels playing with timbrels.*

EXPOSITION: Verse 25. *The singers went before, the players on instruments followed after.* This was the order of the march, and God is to be worshipped evermore with due decorum. First the singers, and lastly the musicians, for the song must lead the music, and not the music drowning the singing. In the midst of the vocal and instrumental band, or all around them, were the maidens: *among them were the damsels playing with timbrels.* The procession depicted in this sublime song was one of joy, and every means was taken to express the delight of the nation in the Lord their God.

Psalm 68:26 *Bless ye God in the congregations, even the Lord, from the fountain of Israel.*

EXPOSITION: Verse 26. *Bless ye God in the congregations.* Let the assembled company magnify the God whose ark they followed. United praise is like the mingled perfume which Aaron made, it should all be presented unto God. He blesses us; let Him be blessed.

Even the Lord, from the fountain of Israel. A parallel passage to that in Deborah's song: *"They that are delivered from the noise of archers in the places of drawing water, there shall they rehearse the righteous acts of the Lord"* [Judges 5:11]. The seat of the ark would be the fountain of refreshing for all the tribes, and there they were to celebrate His praises. "Drink," says the old inscription, *"drink, weary traveller; drink and pray."*[90] Ezekiel saw an ever-growing stream flow from under the altar, and issue out from under the threshold of the sanctuary, and wherever it flowed it gave life: let as many as have quaffed this life giving stream glorify *the fountain of Israel.*

Psalm 68:27 *There is little Benjamin with their ruler, the princes of Judah and their council, the princes of Zebulun, and the princes of Naphtali.*

EXPOSITION: Verse 27. *There is little Benjamin with their ruler.* The tribe was small; having been greatly reduced in numbers, but it had the honor of including Zion within its territory. *"And of Benjamin he said, The beloved of the Lord shall dwell in safety by him; and the Lord shall cover him all the day long, and he shall dwell between his shoulders"* [Deuteronomy 33:12]. Little Benjamin had been Jacob's darling, and now the tribe is made to march first in the procession, and to dwell nearest to the holy place.

The princes of Judah and their council. Judah was a large and powerful tribe, not with one governor, like Benjamin, but with many princes "and their company," for so the margin

---

90. excerpt from an anecdote by Sir Walter Scott

has it. *"From thence is the shepherd, the stone of Israel"*, and the tribe was a quarry of stones wherewith to build up the nations: some such truth is hinted at in the Hebrew.

The princes of Zebulun, and the princes of Naphtali. Israel was there, as well as Judah; there was no schism among the people. The north sent a representative contingent as well as the south, and so the long procession set forth the hearty loyalty of all the tribes to their Lord and King. O happy day, when all believers shall be one around the ark of the Lord; striving for nothing but the glory of the God of grace.

Psalm 68:28 *Thy God hath commanded thy strength: strengthen, O God, that which thou hast wrought for us.*

EXPOSITION: Verse 28. *Thy God hath commanded thy strength.* His decree had ordained the nation strong, and His arm had made them so. This is a very rich though brief sentence, and, whether applied to an individual believer, or to the whole Church, it is full of consolation.

Strengthen, O God, that which thou hast wrought for us. We who have life should pray to have it more "abundantly;" if we have strength we should seek to be still more established. We expect God to bless His own work. He has never left any work unfinished yet, and He never will. "When we were without strength, in due time Christ died for the ungodly" [see Romans 5:6]; and now, being reconciled to God, we may look to Him to perfect that which concerns us, since He never forsakes the work of His own hands.

Psalm 68:29 *Because of thy temple at Jerusalem shall kings bring presents unto thee.*

EXPOSITION: Verse 29. *Because of thy temple at*

Jerusalem shall kings bring presents unto thee. So splendid was that edifice that the queen of far-off Sheba came with her gifts; and many neighboring princes, overawed by the wealth and power therein displayed, came with tribute to Israel's God. The Church of God, when truly spiritual, wins for her God the homage of the nations. In the latter day glory this truth shall be far more literally and largely verified.

Psalm 68:30 *Rebuke the company of spearmen, the multitude of the bulls, with the calves of the people, till every one submit himself with pieces of silver: scatter thou the people that delight in war.*

EXPOSITION: **Verse 30.** *Rebuke the company of spearmen;* speak to Egypt; let its growing power and jealousy be kept in order, by a word from you. Israel remembers her old enemy, already plotting the mischief, which would break out under Jeroboam, and begs for a rebuking word from her Omnipotent Friend. Antichrist also, that great red dragon, needs the effectual word of the Lord to rebuke its insolence.

The multitude of the bulls, the stronger foes; the proud, headstrong, rampant, fat, and roaring bulls, which sought to gore the chosen nation—these also need the Lord's rebuke, and they shall have it, too.

With the calves of the people. The poorer and baser sort are equally set on mischief, but the divine voice can control them; multitudes are as nothing to the Lord when He goes forth in power; whether bulls or calves, they are but cattle for the shambles when Omnipotence displays itself. The gospel, like the ark, has nothing to fear from great or small; it is a stone upon which every one that stumbles shall be broken.

Till every one submit himself with pieces of silver. The Lord is asked to subdue the enemies of Israel, till they rendered tribute in silver ingots. Blessed is that rebuke, which does not break but bend; for subjection to the Lord of hosts is liberty, and tribute to Him enriches him that pays it. Pieces of silver given to God are replaced with pieces of gold.

Scatter thou the people that delight in war. So that, notwithstanding the strong expression of Psalm 68:23, God's people were men of peace, and only desired the crushing of oppressive nations, that war might not occur again. Let the battles of peace be as fierce as they will; heap coals of fire on the heads of enemies, and slay their enmity thereby. That "they who take the sword should perish by the sword," is a just regulation for the establishment of quiet in the earth. [See Matthew 26:52.] Devoutly may we offer this prayer, and with equal devotion, we may bless God that it is sure to be answered, for *"he breaketh the bow, and cutteth the spear in sunder, he burneth the chariot in the fire"* [Psalm 46:9].

Psalm 68:31 *Princes shall come out of Egypt; Ethiopia shall soon stretch out her hands unto God.*

EXPOSITION: Verse 31. *Princes shall come out of Egypt.* Old foes shall be new friends. Solomon shall find a spouse in Pharaoh's house. Christ shall gather a people from the realm of sin. Great sinners shall yield themselves to the scepter of grace, and great men shall become good men, by coming to God.

Ethiopia shall soon stretch out her hands unto God. Cush shall hasten to present peace offerings. Poor Ethiopia, your hands have been long manacled and hardened by cruel toil, but millions of your sons have in their bondage found the liberty with which Christ made men free. Therefore, your cross, like the cross of Simon of Cyrene, has been Christ's Cross, and God has been your salvation. Hasten, O Lord, this day, when both the civilization and the barbarism of the Earth shall adore you, Egypt and Ethiopia blending with glad accord in your own time, good Lord.

Psalm 68:32 *Sing unto God, ye kingdoms of the earth; O sing praises unto the Lord; Selah*

EXPOSITION: Verse 32. *Sing unto God, ye kingdoms of the earth.* Glorious shall that song be in which whole empires join. Happy are men whose God is one who is consistently the object of joyous worship, for such are not the demons of the heathen. So sweet a thing is song that it ought to be all the Lord's; a secular concert seems almost a sacrilege, a licentious song is treason.

O sing praises unto the Lord. Again and again is God to be magnified; we have too much sinning against God, but cannot have too much singing to God.

Selah. Well may we rest now that our contemplations have reached the millennial glory. What heart will refuse to be lifted up by such a prospect!

Psalm 68:33 *To him that rideth upon the heavens of heavens, which were of old; lo, he doth send out his voice, and that a mighty voice.*

EXPOSITION: Verse 33. *To him that rideth upon the heavens of heavens, which were of old.* Before, He was described in His earthly manifestations, as marching through the desert; now, in His celestial glory, as riding in the heavens of the primeval ages. Long before this Heaven and Earth were made, the loftier abodes of the Deity stood fast; before men or angels were created, the splendors of the Great King were as great as now, and His triumphs as glorious. Our knowledge reaches but to a small fragment of the life of God, whose "goings forth were of old, even from everlasting" [see Psalm 90:2]. Well might the Jewish Church praise the eternal God, and well may we join therewith the adoration of the Great Firstborn:

> Ere sin was born, or Satan fell,[91]
> He led the host of morning stars.
> Thy generation who can tell?
> Or count the number of thy years?

Lo, he doth send out his voice, and that a mighty voice. To this hour, the voice of God is power. This gospel, which utters and reveals His Word, is *"the power of God unto salvation to every one that believeth"* [Romans 1:16]. Our voices are fitly called to praise Him whose voice spoke us into being, and gives us the effectual grace which secures our well-being.

Psalm 68:34 *Ascribe ye strength unto God: his excellency is over Israel, and his strength is in the clouds.*

EXPOSITION: Verse 34. *Ascribe ye strength unto God.* When even His voice rends the rocks and uproots the cedars, what cannot His hand do? His finger shakes the Earth; who can conceive the power of His arm? Let us never by our doubts or our daring defiance appear to deny power unto God; on the contrary, by yielding to Him and trusting in Him, let our hearts acknowledge His might. When we are reconciled to God, His omnipotence is an attribute of which we sing with delight.

His excellency is over Israel. The favored nation is protracted by His majesty; His greatness is to them goodness, His glory is their defense.

And his strength is in the clouds. He does not confine His power to the sons of men, but makes it like a canopy to

---

91. from a hymn written by Isaac Watts

cover the skies. Rain, snow, hail, and tempest are His artillery; He rules all nature with awe-inspiring majesty. Nothing is so high as to be above Him, or too low to be beneath Him; praise Him, then, in the highest.

> **Psalm 68:35** O God, thou art terrible out of thy holy places: the God of Israel is he that giveth strength and power unto his people. Blessed be God.

EXPOSITION: Verse 35. *O God, thou art terrible out of thy holy places.* You inspire awe and fear. Your saints obey with fear and trembling, and your enemies flee in dismay. From your threefold courts, and especially from the holy of holies, your majesty flashes forth and makes the sons of men prostrate themselves in awe.

The God of Israel is he that giveth strength and power unto his people. In this you, who are Israel's God by covenant, are terrible to your foes by making your people strong, so that one shall chase a thousand, and two put ten thousand to flight. All the power of Israel's warriors is derived from the Lord, the fountain of all might. He is strong, and makes strong; blessed are they who draw from His resources; they shall renew their strength. While the self-sufficient faint, the All-Sufficient One shall sustain the feeblest believer.

Blessed be God. A short but sweet conclusion. Let our souls say Amen to it, and yet again, Amen.

PSALM 69

PSALM 69:1–PSALM 69:36

Psalm 69:1 *Save me, O God; for the waters are come in unto my soul.*

EXPOSITION: Verse 1. *Save me, O God.* "He saved others, himself he cannot save" [see Matthew 27:42]. "*When he had offered up prayers and supplications with strong crying and tears unto him that was able to save him from death, and was heard in that he feared*" (Hebrews 5:7). Thus David had prayed, and here his Son and Lord utters the same cry. This is the second psalm which begins with a "Save me, O God," and the former (Psalm 54) is but a short summary of this more lengthened complaint. It is remarkable that such a scene of woe should be presented to us immediately after the jubilant ascension hymn of the last psalm, but this only shows how interwoven are the glories and the sorrows of our ever-blessed Redeemer. The head which now is crowned with glory is the same which wore the thorns; He to whom we pray, "Save us, O God," is the selfsame person who cried, "Save me, O God."

For the waters are come in unto my soul. Sorrows, deep, abounding, deadly, had penetrated His inner nature. Bodily anguish is not His first complaint; He begins not with the gall which embittered His lips, but with the mighty griefs which broke into His heart. "*A wounded spirit who can bear?*" [Proverbs 18:14]. Our Lord in this verse is seen before us as a Jonah, crying, "*The waters compassed me about, even to the soul*" [Jonah 2:5]. He was doing business for us on the great waters, at His Father's command; the stormy wind was lifting up the waves thereof, and He went down to the depths until His soul was melted because of trouble. In all this He has sympathy with us, and is able to help us when we, like Peter, beginning to sink, cry to Him, *"Lord, save, or we perish."* [See Matthew 8:25, 14:30.]

> **Psalm 69:2** *I sink in deep mire, where there is no standing: I am come into deep waters, where the floods overflow me.*

EXPOSITION: Verse 2. *I sink in deep mire.* In water one might swim, but in mud and mire all struggling is hopeless; the mire sucks down its victim.

Where there is no standing. Everything gave way under the Sufferer; he could not get foothold for support—this is a worse fate than drowning. Here our Lord pictures the close, clinging nature of His heart's woes. He *"began to be sorrowful, and very heavy"* [Matthew 26:37]. Sin is as mire for its filthiness, and the holy soul of the Savior must have loathed even that connection with it, though it was necessary for its expiation. His pure and sensitive nature seemed to sink in it, for it was not His element, He was not like us, born and acclimated to this great dismal swamp. Here our Redeemer became another Jeremiah, of whom it is recorded (Jeremiah 38:6) that his enemies cast him into a dungeon wherein *"was no water, but mire: so Jeremiah sunk in the mire."* Let our hearts feel the emotions, both of contrition and gratitude, as we see in this simile the deep humiliation of our Lord.

I am come into deep waters, where the floods overflow me. The sorrow gathers even greater force; He is as one cast into the sea, the waters go over His head. His sorrows were first within, then around, and now above Him. Our Lord was no fainthearted sentimentalist; His were real woes, and though He bore them heroically, yet they were terrible even to Him. His sufferings were unlike all others in degree, the waters were such as soaked into the soul; the mire was the mire of the abyss itself, and the floods were deep and overflowing. To us the promise is, *"the rivers shall not overflow thee"* s, but no such word of consolation was vouchsafed to Him. My soul, your Well-Beloved endured all this for you. Many waters could not quench His love, neither could the floods drown it; and, because of this, you have the rich benefit of that covenant assurance, *"as I have sworn that the waters of Noah should no more go over the earth; so have I sworn that I would not be wroth with thee, nor rebuke thee"* [Isaiah 54:9]. He stemmed the torrent of almighty wrath that we might forever rest in Jehovah's love.

Psalm 69:3 *I am weary of my crying: my throat is dried: mine eyes fail while I wait for my God.*

EXPOSITION: Verse 3. *I am weary of my crying.* Not of it, but by it, with it. He had prayed until He sweat great drops of blood, and well might physical weariness intervene.

My throat is dried, parched, and inflamed. Long pleading with awful fervor had scorched His throat as with flames of fire. Few, very few, of His saints follow their Lord in prayer so far as this. We are, it is to be feared, more likely to be hoarse with talking frivolities to men than by pleading with God; yet our sinful nature demands more prayer than His perfect humanity might seem to need. His prayers should shame us into fervor. Our Lord's supplications were salted with fire, they were hot with agony; and hence they weakened His system, and made Him "a weary man and full of woes."[92]

---

92. from Hymn 63 of *Hymnologia Christiana*.

Mine eyes fail while I wait for my God. He wanted in His direst distress nothing more than His God; that would be all in all to Him. Many of us know what watching and waiting mean; and we know something of the failing eye when hope is long deferred: but in all this Jesus bears the pain; no eyes ever failed as His did or for so deep a cause. No painter can ever depict those eyes; their pencils fail in every feature of His fair but marred countenance. Moreover they come short most of all when they venture to portray His eyes which were fountains of tears. He knew both how to pray and to watch, and He would have us learn the same. There are times when we should pray until the throat is dry, and watch until the eyes grow dim. Only then can we have fellowship with Him in His sufferings. What! Can we not watch with Him one hour? Does the flesh shrink back? O cruel flesh to be so tender of yourself, and so ungenerous to your Lord!

Psalm 69:4 *They that hate me without a cause are more than the hairs of mine head: they that would destroy me, being mine enemies wrongfully, are mighty: then I restored that which I took not away.*

EXPOSITION: **Verse 4.** *They that hate me.* Surprising sin that men should hate the altogether lovely one, truly it is added, *without a cause,* for there was no reason for this senseless enmity. He neither blasphemed God, nor injured man. As Samuel said: "*Whose ox have I taken? or whose ass have I taken? or whom have I defrauded? whom have I oppressed?*" [1 Samuel 12:3]. Even so might Jesus enquire. Besides, He had not only done us no evil, but He had bestowed countless and priceless benefits. Well might He demand, "For which of these works do ye stone me?" Yet from His cradle to His Cross, beginning with Herod and not ending with Judas, He had foes without number; and He justly said, *they are more than the hairs of mine head.* Both the civilians and the military, laics[93] and clerics, doctors and drunkards, princes and people, set themselves against the Lord's anointed. As in the Scripture Matthew 21:38, *"This is the heir, let us kill him that the inheritance may be ours,"* was the unanimous resolve of all the keepers of the Jewish vineyard; while the Gentiles outside the walls of the Garden of Gethsemane furnished the instruments for His murder, and actually did the deed. The hosts of Earth and hell, banded together, made up vast legions of antagonists, none of whom had any just ground for hating Him.

They that would destroy me, being mine enemies wrongfully, are mighty. It was bad that they were many, but worse that they were mighty. All the ecclesiastical and military powers of His country were arrayed against Him. The might of the Sanhedrin, the mob, and the Roman legions were combined in one for His utter destruction: *"Away with such a fellow from this earth; it is not fit that he should live,"* [Acts 22:22] was the shout of His ferocious foes. David's adversaries were on the throne when he was hiding in caverns, and our Lord's enemies were the great ones of the Earth; while He, of whom the world was not worthy, was reproached of men and despised of the people.

Then I restored that which I took not away. Though innocent, He was treated as guilty. Though David had no share in plots against Saul, yet he was held accountable for them. In reference to our Lord, it may be truly said that He restores what He took not away; for He gives back to the injured honor of God recompense, and to man his lost happiness, though the insult of the one and the fall of the other were neither of them, in any sense, His doings. Usually,

---

93. laypersons

when the ruler sins the people suffer, but here the proverb is reversed—the sheep go astray, and their wanderings are laid at the Shepherd's door.

Psalm 69:5 *O God, thou knowest my foolishness; and my sins are not hid from thee.*

EXPOSITION: Verse 5. *O God, thou knowest my foolishness.* David might well say this, but not David's Lord; unless it is understood as an appeal to God as to His freedom from the folly which men imputed to Him when they said He was mad. That which was foolishness to men was superlative wisdom before God.

And my sins are not hid from thee. They cannot be hid with any fig leaves of mine; only the covering which you will bring me can conceal their nakedness and mine. It ought to render confession easy, when we are assured that all is known already. He who can say, "You know my foolishness," is the only man who can add, 'But you know that I love you.'"

Psalm 69:6 *Let not them that wait on thee, O Lord God of hosts, be ashamed for my sake: let not those that seek thee be confounded for my sake, O God of Israel.*

EXPOSITION: Verse 6. *Let not them that wait on thee, O Lord God of hosts, be ashamed for my sake.* If He were deserted, others who were walking in the same path of faith would be discouraged and disappointed. Unbelievers are ready enough to catch at anything which may turn humble faith into ridicule, therefore, O God of all the armies of Israel, let not my case cause the enemy to blaspheme—such is the spirit of this verse.

Let not those that seek thee be confounded for my sake, O God of Israel. He appealed to the Lord of hosts by His power to help Him, and now to the God of Israel by His covenant faithfulness to come to the rescue. If the captain of the host fails, how will it fare with the rank and file? If David flees, what will his followers do? If the king of believers shall find His faith unrewarded, how will the feeble ones hold on their way? Our Lord's behavior during His sharpest agonies is no cause of shame to us; He wept, for He was man, but He murmured not, for He was sinless man; He cried, *"My Father, if it be possible, let this cup pass from me;"* for He was human, but He added, *"Nevertheless, not as I will, but as thou wilt,"* for His humanity was without taint of rebellion. [See Matthew 26:39.] In the depths of tribulation no repining word escaped Him, for there was no repining in His heart. The Lord of martyrs witnessed a good confession. He was strengthened in the hour of peril, and was more than a conqueror, as we also shall do, if we hold fast our confidence even to the end.

Psalm 69:7 *Because for thy sake I have borne reproach; shame hath covered my face.*

EXPOSITION: Verse 7. *Because for thy sake I have borne reproach.* Because He undertook to do the Father's will, and teach His truth, the people were angry; because He declared himself to be the Son of God, the priesthood raved. Reproach is at all times very cutting to a man of integrity, and it must have come with acute force upon one of so unsullied a character as our Lord; yet see, how He turns to His God, and finds His consolation in the fact that He is enduring all for His Father's sake.

Shame hath covered my face. They passed Him through the trial of cruel mocking, smeared His face with spittle, and covered His face with bruises, so that Pilate's "Ecce Homo"[94] called the world's attention to an unexampled spectacle of woe and shame. The stripping on the Cross must also have suffused the Redeemer's face with a modest blush, as He hung there exposed to the cruel gaze of a bawdy and offensive multitude. Ah, blessed Lord, it was our shame which you were made to bear! Nothing more deserves to be reproached and despised than sin, and lo, when you were made sin for us you were called to endure abuse and scorn. Blessed be your name it is over now, but we owe you more than heart can conceive for your amazing sacrificial stoop of love.

Psalm 69:8 *I am become a stranger unto my brethren, and an alien unto my mother's children.*

EXPOSITION: Verse 8. *I am become a stranger unto my brethren.* The Jews, His brethren in race rejected Him, His family, His brethren by blood were offended at Him, His disciples, His brethren in spirit forsook Him and fled; one of them sold Him, and another denied Him with oaths and cursings. Alas, my Lord, what loving pangs must have smitten your loving heart to be thus forsaken by those who should have loved you, defended you, and, if need be, died for you.

And an alien unto my mother's children. These were the nearest of relatives, the children of a father with many wives felt the tie of consanguinity[95] but loosely, but children of the same mother owned the band of love; yet our Lord found His nearest and dearest ones ashamed to own Him. As David's brethren envied Him, and spoke evil of Him, so our Lord's relatives by birth were jealous of Him, and His best beloved followers in the hour of His agony were afraid

---
94. "Behold the man."
95. blood kinship

to be known as having any connection with Him. These were sharp arrows of the mighty in the soul of Jesus, the tenderest of friends. May none of us ever act as if we were strangers to Him; never may we treat Him as if He were an alien to us: rather let us resolve to be crucified with Him, and may grace turn the resolve into fact.

> **Psalm 69:9** *For the zeal of thine house hath eaten me up; and the reproaches of them that reproached thee are fallen upon me.*

EXPOSITION: **Verse 9.** *For the zeal of thine house hath eaten me up.* His burning ardor, like the flame of a candle, fed on His strength and consumed it. His heart, like a sharp sword, cut through the scabbard. Some men are eaten up with lechery, others with covetousness, and a third class with pride, but the master passion with our great leader was the glory of God, jealousy for his name, and love to the divine family. When zeal eats us up, ungodly men seek to eat us up too, and this was preeminently the case with our Lord, because His holy jealousy was preeminent. With more than a seraph's fire He glowed, and consumed himself with His fervor.

And the reproaches of them that reproached thee have fallen upon me. Those who habitually blaspheme God now curse me instead. I have become the butt for arrows intended for the Lord himself. Thus the Great Mediator was, in this respect, a substitute for God as well as for man, He bore the reproaches aimed at the one, as well as the sins committed by the other.

> **Psalm 69:10** *When I wept, and chastened my soul with fasting, that was to my reproach.*

EXPOSITION: **Verse 10.** *When I wept, and chastened my soul with fasting, that was to my reproach.* Having resolved to hate him, everything he did was made a fresh reason for reviling. Our Savior wept much in secret for our sins, and no doubt His private soul chastenings on our behalf were very frequent. The emaciation which these exercises wrought in our Lord made Him appear nearly fifty years old when He was but little over thirty; this which was to his honor was used as a matter of reproach against Him.

Psalm 69:11 *I made sackcloth also my garment; and I became a proverb to them.*

EXPOSITION: **Verse 11.** *I made sackcloth also my garment.* This David did literally, but we have no reason to believe that Jesus did. In a spiritual sense He, as one filled with grief, was always a sackcloth wearer.

And I became a proverb to them. He was ridiculed as "the man of sorrows," quoted as "the acquaintance of grief." He might have said, "Here I and sorrow sit." This which should have won Him pity only earned Him new and more general scorn. To interweave one's name into a mocking proverb is the highest stretch of malice, and to insult one's acts of devotion is to add profanity to cruelty.

Psalm 69:12 *They that sit in the gate speak against me; and I was the song of the drunkards.*

EXPOSITION: **Verse 12.** *They that sit in the gate speak against me.* The ordinary gossips who meet at the city gates for idle talk make me their theme, the business men who resort there for trade forget their merchandise to slander me, and even the beggars who wait at men's doors for alms contribute their share of insult to the heap of infamy.

And I was the song of the drunkards. The ungodly know no merrier jest than that in which the name of the holy is traduced.[96] The character of the man of Nazareth was so far above the appreciation of the men of strength to mingle strong drink, it was so much out of their way and above their thoughts, that it is no wonder it seemed to them ridiculous, and therefore well adapted to create laughter over their cups. The saints are ever choice subjects for satire. Butler's *Hudibras*[97] owed more of its popularity to its irreligious banter than to any intrinsic cleverness.

> The byword of the passing throng,
> The ruler's scoff, the drunkard's song.

Psalm 69:13 *But as for me, my prayer is unto thee, O LORD, in an acceptable time: O God, in the multitude of thy mercy hear me, in the truth of thy salvation.*

EXPOSITION: Verse 13. *But as for me, my prayer is unto thee, O Lord.* He turned to Jehovah in prayer as being the most natural thing for the godly to do in their distress. To whom should a child turn but to his father. He did not answer them; like a sheep before her shearers He was dumb to them, but He opened his mouth unto the Lord His God, for He would hear and deliver.

In an acceptable time. It was a time of rejection with man, but of acceptance with God. Sin ruled on Earth, but grace reigned in Heaven. There is to each of us an accepted time, and woe to us if we suffer it to glide away unimproved.

---

96. spoken unfavorably about, slandered and maligned
97. A poem written by Samuel Butler that is a mock heroic narrative aimed at the Cromwellians and the Presbyterian Church.

God's time must be our time, or it will come to pass that, when time closes, we shall look in vain for space for repentance. Our Lord's prayers were well timed, and always met with acceptance.

O God, in the multitude of thy mercy hear me. Even the perfect one makes His appeal to the rich mercy of God, much more should we. To misery no attribute is sweeter than mercy, and when sorrows multiply, the multitude of mercy is much prized.

In the truth of thy salvation. Jehovah's faithfulness is a further mighty plea. His salvation is no fiction, no mockery, no changeable thing, therefore He is asked to manifest it, and make all men see His fidelity to His promise.

Psalm 69:14 *Deliver me out of the mire, and let me not sink: let me be delivered from them that hate me, and out of the deep waters.*

EXPOSITION: Verse 14. *Deliver me out of the mire and let me not sink.* He turns into prayer the very words of His complaint; and it is well, if, when we complain, we neither feel nor say anything which we should fear to utter before the Lord as a prayer. How strange it seems to hear such language from the Lord of glory. *Let me be delivered from them that hate me, and out of the deep waters.* Both from His foes, and the griefs which they caused Him, He seeks a rescue.

Psalm 69:15 *Let not the waterflood overflow me, neither let the deep swallow me up, and let not the pit shut her mouth upon me.*

EXPOSITION: Verse 15. *Let not the waterflood overflow me.* He was heard in that He feared.

Neither let the deep swallow me up. As Jonah came forth again, so let me also arise from the abyss of woe; here also our Lord was heard, and so shall we be. Death itself must disgorge us.

Let not the pit shut her mouth upon me. When a great stone was rolled over the well, or pit, used as a dungeon, the prisoner was altogether enclosed, and forgotten like one on the oubliettes[98] of the Bastille. He was baptized in agony but not drowned in it; the grave enclosed Him, but before she could close her mouth He had burst His prison. It is said that truth lies in a well, but it is assuredly an open well, for it walks abroad in power; and so our great Substitute in the pit of woe and death was yet the Conqueror of death and hell.

Psalm 69:16 *Hear me, O LORD; for thy lovingkindness is good: turn unto me according to the multitude of thy tender mercies.*

EXPOSITION: Verse 16. *Hear me, O Lord.* Do not refuse thy suppliant Son. It is to the covenant God, the ever-living Jehovah that He appeals with strong crying.

For thy lovingkindness is good. It has furnished sad souls much good cheer to take to pieces that grand Old Saxon word, which used here in our version, lovingkindness. Its composition is of two most sweet and fragrant things, fitted to inspire strength into the fainting, and make desolate hearts sing for joy.

Turn unto me according to the multitude of thy tender mercies. If the Lord does but turn the eye of pity, and the hand of power, the mourner's spirit revives. It is the gall of bitterness to be without the comfortable smile of God; in our Lord's case His grief culminated in "lama sabachthani," and

---

98. from the French, "oublier" (to forget): a dungeon with the only entrance or exit being a trip door in the ceiling

His bitterest cry was that in which He mourned an absent God. Observe how He dwells anew upon divine tenderness, and touches again that note of abundance, "*The multitude of thy tender mercies.*"

> **Psalm 69:17** *And hide not thy face from thy servant; for I am in trouble: hear me speedily.*

EXPOSITION: Verse 17. *And hide not thy face from thy servant.* A good servant desires the light of his master's countenance; that *servus servorum*,[99] who was also *rex regium*,[100] could not bear to lose the presence of His God. The more He loved His Father, the more severely He felt the hiding of His face.

For I am in trouble. If ever a man needs the comforting presence of God it is when he is in distress; and, being in distress, it is a reason to be pleaded with a merciful God why He should not desert us.

Hear me speedily. The case was urgent; delay was dangerous, nay deadly. Our Lord was the perfection of patience, yet He cried urgently for speedy mercy; and therein He gives us liberty to do the same, so long as we add, "nevertheless, not as I will, but as thou wilt."

> **Psalm 69:18** *Draw nigh unto my soul, and redeem it: deliver me because of mine enemies.*

EXPOSITION: Verse 18. *Draw nigh unto my soul.* The near approach of God is all the sufferer needs; one smile of Heaven will still the rage of hell.

And redeem it. It shall be redemption to me if you will appear to comfort me. This is a deeply spiritual prayer,

---
99. servant of the servants
100. king of kings

and one very suitable for a deserted soul. It is in renewed communion that we shall find redemption realized.

Deliver me because of mine enemies, lest they should, in their vaunting, blaspheme your name, and boast that you are not able to rescue those who put their trust in you. Jesus, in condescending to use such supplications, fulfils the request of His disciples: *"Lord, teach us to pray"* [Luke 11:1].

Psalm 69:19 *Thou hast known my reproach, and my shame, and my dishonour: mine adversaries are all before thee.*

Verse 19. *Thou hast known my reproach, and my shame, and my dishonour.* It is no novelty or secret, it has been long continued; you, O God, have seen it; and for you to see the innocent suffer is an assurance of help. Here are three words piled up to express the Redeemer's keen sense of the contempt poured upon Him; and His assurance that every form of malicious despite was observed of the Lord.

Mine adversaries are all before thee. The whole lewd and loud company is now present to your eye: Judas and his treachery; Herod and his cunning; Caiaphas and his counsel; Pilate and his vacillation; Jews, priests, people, rulers, and all you see and will judge.

Psalm 69:20 *Reproach hath broken my heart; and I am full of heaviness: and I looked for some to take pity, but there was none; and for comforters, but I found none.*

EXPOSITION: Verse 20. *Reproach hath broken my heart.* Our Lord died of a broken heart, and reproach had done the deed. Intense mental suffering arises from slander; and in the case of the sensitive nature of the immaculate

Son of Man, it sufficed to lacerate the heart until it broke. "Then burst his mighty heart."[101]

And I am full of heaviness. Calumny and insult bowed Him to the dust; He was sick at heart. The heaviness of our Lord in the Garden of Gethsemane is expressed by many forcible words in the four gospels, and each term goes to show that the agony was beyond measure great; He was filled with misery, like a vessel which is full to the brim.

And I looked for some to take pity, but I found none. "Deserted in His utmost need by those His former bounty fed."[102] Not one to say Him a kindly word, or drop a sympathetic tear. Among ten thousand foes there was not one who was touched by the spectacle of His misery; not one with a heart capable of humane feeling towards Him.

And for comforters, but I found none. His dearest ones had sought their own safety, and left their Lord alone. A sick man needs comforters, and a persecuted man needs sympathy; but our blessed Surety found neither on that dark and doleful night when the powers of darkness had their hour. A spirit like that of our Lord feels acutely desertion by beloved and trusted friends, and yearns for real sympathy. This may be seen in the story of Gethsemane—

> Backwards and forwards thrice he ran.[103]
> As if he sought some help from man;
> Or wished, at least, they would condole—
> It was all they could—his tortured soul.

---

101. excerpt from scene 2 of *Julius Caesar* by William Shakespeare
102. lines from the poem, "Alexander's Feast," by John Dryden
103. from verse 8 of a hymn by Joseph Hart titled "Come All Ye Chosen Saints of God"

What ever he sought for, there was none;
Our Captain fought the field alone.
Soon as the chief to battle led,
That moment every soldier fled.

Psalm 69:21 *They gave me also gall for my meat; and in my thirst they gave me vinegar to drink.*

EXPOSITION: **Verse 21.** *They gave me also gall for my meat.* This was the sole refreshment cruelty had prepared for Him. Others find pleasure in their food, but His taste was made to be an additional path of pain to Him.

And in my thirst they gave me vinegar to drink. A criminal's draught was offered to our innocent Lord, a bitter portion to our dying Master. Sorry entertainment had Earth for her King and Savior. How often have our sins filled the gall cup for our Redeemer? While we blame the Jews, let us not excuse ourselves.

Psalm 69:22 *Let their table become a snare before them: and that which should have been for their welfare, let it become a trap.*

EXPOSITION: From this point David and our Lord for awhile part company, if we accept the rendering of our version. The severe spirit of the law breathes out imprecations, while the tender heart of Jesus offers prayers for His murderers. The whole of these verses, however, may be viewed as predictions, and then they certainly refer to our Lord, for we find portions of them quoted in that manner by the Apostle Paul in Romans 11:9–10, and by Christ himself in Matthew 23:38.

Let their table become a snare before them. There they

laid snares, and there they shall find them. As birds and beasts are taken in a trap by means of baits for the appetite, so are men snared very often by their meats and drinks. Those who despise the upper springs of grace shall find the nether springs of worldly comfort prove their poison. The table is used, however, not alone for feeding, but for conversations, transacting business, counsel, amusement, and religious observance: to those who are the enemies of the Lord Jesus that table may, in all these respects, become a snare. This first plague is terrible, and the second is like unto it.

And that which should have been for their welfare, let it become a trap. This, if we follow the original closely, and the version of Paul in the Book of Romans, is a repetition of the former phrase; but we shall not err if we say that, to the rejecters of Christ, even those things which are calculated to work their spiritual and eternal good, become occasions for yet greater sin. They reject Christ, and are condemned for not believing on Him; they stumble on this stone, and are broken by it.

"Whom oils and balsams kill, what salve can cure?"[104]

Psalm 69:23 *Let their eyes be darkened, that they see not; and make their loins continually to shake.*

EXPOSITION: **Verse 23.** *Let their eyes be darkened, that they see not.* They shall wander in a darkness that may be felt. They have loved darkness rather than light, and in darkness they shall abide. Judicial blindness fell upon Israel after our Lord's death and their persecution of His apostles; they were blinded by the light which they would not accept. Eyes which see no beauty in the Lord Jesus, but flash wrath upon Him, may well grow yet dimmer, until death spiritual leads to death eternal.

---

104. from the poem, "The Church Porch," by George Herbert.

And make their loins continually to shake. Their conscience shall be so ill at ease that they shall continually quiver with fear; and their strength shall be utterly paralyzed, so that they cannot walk firmly, but shall totter at every step. See the terrifying, degrading, and enfeebling influence of unbelief. See also the retaliation of justice: those who will not see shall not see; those who would not walk in uprightness shall be unable to do so.

Psalm 69:24 *Pour out thine indignation upon them, and let thy wrathful anger take hold of them.*

EXPOSITION: Verse 24. *Pour out thine indignation upon them.* They deserve to be flooded with wrath, and they shall be; for upon all who rebel against the Savior, Christ the Lord, "the wrath is come to the uttermost" [See 1 Thessalonians 2:16]. God's indignation is no trifle; the anger of a holy, just, omnipotent, and infinite Being, is above all things to be dreaded; even a drop of it consumes, but to have it poured upon us is inconceivably dreadful. O God, who knows the power of your anger?

And let thy wrathful anger take hold of them. Grasping them, arresting them, abiding on them. God is not to be insulted with impunity, and His Son, our ever-gracious Savior, the best gift of infinite love, is not to be scorned and scoffed at for nothing. He that despised Moses' law died without mercy, but what shall be the *"sorer punishment"* reserved for those who have trodden underfoot the Son of God?

Psalm 69:25 *Let their habitation be desolate; and let none dwell in their tents.*

EXPOSITION: Verse 25. *Let their habitation be desolate; and let none dwell in their tents.* What occurs on a large scale to families and nations is often fulfilled in individuals, as was conspicuously the case with Judas, to whom Peter referred this prophecy, Acts 1:20. *"For it is written in the book of Psalms, let this habitation be desolate, and let no man dwell therein."* The fierce proclamation of Nebuchadnezzar,

"that every people, nation, and language, which speak anything amiss against the God of Shadrach, Meshach, and Abednego, shall be cut in pieces, and their houses shall be made a dunghill" [Daniel 3:29] is but an anticipation of that dread hour when the enemies of the Lord shall be broken in pieces, and perish out of the land.

Psalm 69:26 *For they persecute him whom thou hast smitten; and they talk to the grief of those whom thou hast wounded.*

EXPOSITION: **Verse 26.** *For they persecute him whom thou hast smitten.* Their merciless hearts invent fresh blows for Him who is *"smitten of God and afflicted"* [Isaiah 53:4].

And they talk to the grief of those whom thou hast wounded. They lay bare His wounds with their rough tongues. After this fashion the world still treats the members of Christ. "Report," say they, "and we will report it." If a godly man is a little down in estate, how glad they are to push him over altogether, and, meanwhile, to talk everywhere against him. God takes note of this, and will visit it upon the enemies of His children; He may allow them to act as a rod to his saints, but He will yet avenge His own elect:

"Thus saith the Lord of hosts; I am jealous for Jerusalem, and for Zion, with a great jealousy; and I am very sore displeased with the heathen that are at ease . . . for I was but a little displeased, and they helped forward the affliction" [Zechariah 1:14–15].

Psalm 69:27 *Add iniquity unto their iniquity: and let them not come into thy righteousness.*

EXPOSITION: Verse 27. *Add iniquity unto their iniquity: and let them not come into thy righteousness.* For men to be let alone to fill up the measure of their iniquity, is most equitable, but yet most awful. *And let them not come into your righteousness.* If they refuse it, and resist your gospel, let them shut themselves out of it.

> He that will not when he may,[105]
> When he would he shall have nay.

Those who choose evil shall have their choice. Men who hate divine mercy shall not have it forced upon them, but (unless sovereign grace interpose) shall be left to themselves to aggravate their guilt, and ensure their doom.

Psalm 69:28 *Let them be blotted out of the book of the living, and not be written with the righteous.*

EXPOSITION: Verse 28. *Let them be blotted out of the book of the living.* Judas first, and Pilate, and Herod, and Caiaphas, all in due time, were speedily wiped out of existence; their names only remain as bywords, but among the honored men who live after their departure they are not recorded.

And not be written with the righteous. This clause is parallel with the former, and shows that the inner meaning of being blotted out from the Book of Life is to have it made evident that the name was never written there at all. Man in his imperfect copy of God's Book of Life will have to make many corrections, both of insertion and erasure; but, as before the Lord, the record is forever fixed and unalterable. Beware,

---
105. English proverb by J. Heywood

O man, of despising Christ and His people, lest your soul should never partake in the righteousness of God, without which men are condemned already.

Psalm 69:29 *But I am poor and sorrowful: let thy salvation, O God, set me up on high.*

EXPOSITION: Verse 29. *But I am poor and sorrowful.* The psalmist was afflicted very much, but his faith was in God. The poor in spirit and mourners are both blessed under the gospel, so that here is a double reason for the Lord to smile on His suppliant. No man was ever poorer or more sorrowful than Jesus of Nazareth, yet His cry out of the depths was heard, and He was uplifted to the highest glory.

Let thy salvation, O God, set me up on high. How fully has this been answered in our great Master's case, He not only escaped His foes personally, but He has become the author of eternal salvation to all who obey Him, and this continues to glorify Him more and more. Lift up your heads, you who are sorrowful for your Lord is with you. You are trodden down today as the mire of the streets, but you shall ride upon the high places of the Earth before long; and even now you are raised up together, and made to sit together in the heavenlies in Christ Jesus. [see Ephesians 2:6].

Psalm 69:30 *I will praise the name of God with a song, and will magnify him with thanksgiving.*

EXPOSITION: Verse 30. *I will praise the name of God with a song.* He who sang after the Passover sings yet more joyously after the resurrection and ascension. He is, in very truth, "the sweet singer of Israel." He leads the eternal melodies, and all His saints join in chorus.

And will magnify him with thanksgiving. How sure was our Redeemer of ultimate victory, since He vows a song even while yet in the furnace. In us, also, faith foresees the happy issue forever increasing in volume, world without end. He alone could deliver and did deliver, and, therefore, to Him only be the praise.

> **Psalm 69:31** *This also shall please the* LORD *better than an ox or bullock that hath horns and hoofs.*

EXPOSITION: Verse 31. *This also shall please the Lord better than an ox or bullock that hath horns and hoofs.* No sacrifice is so acceptable to God, who is a Spirit, as that which is spiritual. He accepted bullocks under a dim and symbolical dispensation; but in such offerings, in themselves considered, He had no pleasure. *"Will I eat the flesh of bulls, or drink the blood of goats?"* [Psalm 50:13]. Here He puts dishonor upon mere outward offerings by speaking of the horns and hoofs, the offal of the victim. The *opus operatum*,[106] which our Ritualists think so much of, the Lord puffs at.

"Offer unto God thanksgiving" is the everlasting rubric of the true directory of worship. The depths of grief into which the suppliant had been plunged gave him all the richer an experience of divine power and grace in his salvation, and so qualified him to sing more sweetly "the song of loves." Such music is ever most acceptable to the infinite Jehovah.

> **Psalm 69:32** *The humble shall see this, and be glad: and your heart shall live that seek God.*

EXPOSITION: Verse 32. *The humble shall see this and be glad.* The standing consolation of the godly is the experience of their Lord, for as He is so are we also in this world; yea, moreover, His triumph has secured ours, and therefore, we may on the most solid grounds rejoice in Him. This gave our

---

106. "efficacy of the action"

great leader satisfaction as He foresaw the comforts which would flow to us from His conflict and conquest.

And your heart shall live that seek God. It would have been useless to seek if Jesus' victories had not cleared the way, and opened a door of hope; but, since the Breaker has gone up before us, and the King at the head of us, our hope is a living one, our faith is living, our love is living, and our renewed nature is full of a vitality which challenges the cold hand of death to damp it.

Psalm 69:33 *For the* LORD *heareth the poor, and despiseth not his prisoners.*

EXPOSITION: Verse 33. *For the Lord heareth the poor.* None can be brought lower than was the Nazarene, but see how highly He is exalted: descend into what depths we may, the prayer hearing God can bring us up again.

And despiseth not his prisoners. Poor men have their liberty, but these are bound; however, they are God's prisoners, and, therefore, prisoners of hope. The captive in the dungeon is the lowest and least esteemed of men, but the Lord sees not as man sees; the poor have the gospel preached to them, and the prisoners are loosed by His grace. Let all poor and needy ones hasten to seek His face, and to yield Him their love.

Psalm 69:34 *Let the heaven and earth praise him, the seas, and every thing that moveth therein.*

EXPOSITION: Verse 34. *Let the heaven and earth praise him, the seas, and every thing that moveth therein.* The writer had fathomed the deeps, and had ascended to the heights; and, therefore, calls on the whole range of creation to bless the Lord. Our Well-Beloved here excites us all to grateful adoration: who among us will hold back? God's love to Christ argues good to all forms of life; the exaltation of the Head brings good to the members, and to all in the least connected with Him. Glory be unto you, O Lord, for the sure and all including pledge of our Surety's triumph; we see in this the exaltation of all your poor and sorrowful ones, and our heart is glad.

Psalm 69:35 *For God will save Zion, and will build the cities of Judah: that they may dwell there, and have it in possession.*

EXPOSITION: Verse 35. *For God will save Zion, and will build the cities of Judah.* Poor, fallen Israel shall have a portion in the mercy of the Lord; but, above all, the Church, so dear to the heart of her glorious bridegroom, shall be revived and strengthened. It is the subject of cheering hope that better days are coming for the chosen people of God, and for this we would ever pray. O Zion, whatever other memories fade away, we cannot forget you.

That they may dwell there, and have it in possession. Whatever captivities may occur, or desolations be caused, the land of Canaan belongs to Israel by a covenant of salt, and they will surely repossess it; and this shall be a sign unto us, that through the atonement of the Christ of God, all the poor in spirit shall enjoy the mercies promised in the covenant of grace. The sure mercies of David shall be the heritage of all the seed.

Psalm 69:36 *The seed also of his servants shall inherit it: and they that love his name shall dwell therein.*

EXPOSITION: Verse 36. *The seed also of his servants shall inherit it.* Under this image, which, however, we dare not regard as a mere simile, but as having in itself a literal significance, we have set forth to us the enrichment of the saints, consequent upon the sorrow of their Lord. The termination of this psalm strongly recalls in us that of the twenty-second. The seeds lie near the Savior's heart, and their enjoyment of all promised good is the great concern of His disinterested soul. Because they are His Father's servants, therefore He rejoices in their welfare.

And they that love his name shall dwell therein. He has an eye to the Father's glory, for it is to His praise that those who love Him should attain, and forever enjoy, the utmost happiness. Thus a psalm, which began in the deep waters, ends in the city which has foundations. How gracious is the change. Hallelujah.

Psalm 70
Psalm 70:1–Psalm 70:5

Psalm 70:1 *Make haste, O God, to deliver me; make haste to help me, O LORD.*

EXPOSITION: Verse 1. *Make haste, O God, to deliver me; make haste to help me, O Lord.* It is not forbidden us, in hours of dire distress, to ask for speed on God's part in His coming to rescue us. As we have the words of this psalm twice in the letter, let them be doubly with us in spirit. It is most meet that we should day by day cry to God for deliverance and help; our frailty and our many dangers render this a perpetual necessity.

Psalm 70:2 *Let them be ashamed and confounded that seek after my soul: let them be turned backward, and put to confusion, that desire my hurt.*

EXPOSITION: Verse 2. *Let them be ashamed and confounded that seek after my soul: let them be turned backward, and put to confusion, that desire my hurt.* Turned back and driven back are merely the variations of the translators. When men labor to turn others back from the right road, it is God's retaliation to drive them back from the point they are aiming at.

Psalm 70:3 *Let them be turned back for a reward of their shame that say, Aha, aha.*

EXPOSITION: **Verse 3.** *Let them be turned back.* To be "turned back" may come to the same thing as to be "desolate;" disappointed malice is the nearest akin to desolation that can well be conceived.

For a reward of their shame that say, Aha, aha. They thought to shame the godly, but it was their shame, and shall be their shame forever

Psalm 70:4 *Let all those that seek thee rejoice and be glad in thee: and let such as love thy salvation say continually, Let God be magnified.*

EXPOSITION: **Verse 4.** *Let all those that seek thee rejoice and be glad in thee.* All true worshippers, though as yet in the humble ranks of seekers, shall have cause for joy. Even though the seeking commence in darkness, it shall bring light with it.

And let such as love thy salvation say continually, Let God be magnified. Those who have tasted divine grace, and are, therefore, wedded to it, are a somewhat more advanced race, and these shall not only feel joy, but shall with holy constancy and perseverance tell abroad their joy, and call upon men to glorify God.

Psalm 70:5 *But I am poor and needy: make haste unto me, O God: thou art my help and my deliverer; O Lord, make no tarrying.*

EXPOSITION: **Verse 5.** *But I am poor and needy.* Just the same plea as in the preceding psalm, Psalm 69:29: it seems to be a favorite argument with tried saints; evidently our poverty is our wealth, even as our weakness is our strength. May we learn well this riddle.

Make haste unto me, O God. This is written instead of

"*yet the Lord thinketh upon me,*" in Psalm 40: and there is a reason for the change, since the key note of the psalm frequently dictates its close. Psalm 40 sings of God's thoughts, and, therefore, ends therewith; but the peculiar note of Psalm 70 is "Make haste," and, therefore, so it concludes.

Thou art my help and my deliverer. My help in trouble, my deliverer out of it. O Lord, make no tarrying. Here is the name of "Jehovah" instead of "my God." I have presumed to close this recapitulatory exposition with an original hymn, suggested by the watchword of this psalm, "make haste":

> Make haste, O God, my soul to bless![107]
> My help and my deliverer thou;
> Make haste, for I am in deep distress,
> My case is urgent; help me now.
>
> Make haste, O God! make haste to save!
> For time is short, and death is nigh;
> Make haste ere yet I am in my grave,
> And with the lost forever lie.
>
> Make haste, for I am poor and low;
> And Satan mocks my prayers and tears;
> O God, in mercy be not slow,
> But snatch me from my horrid fears.
>
> Make haste, O God, and hear my cries;
> Then with the souls who seek thy face,
> And those who thy salvation prize,
> I will magnify thy matchless grace.

---

107. Hymn titled, "Make Hast, O My God, My Soul to Bless" by Charles Spurgeon, 1866

Psalm 71

Psalm 71:1–Psalm 71:24

Psalm 71:1 *In thee, O LORD, do I put my trust: let me never be put to confusion.*

EXPOSITION: Verse 1. *In thee, O Lord, do I put my trust.* Jehovah deserves our confidence; let Him have it all. God knows our faith, and yet He loves to hear us avow it; hence, the psalmist not only trusts in the Lord, but tells Him that he is so trusting.

Let me never be put to confusion. Confusion will silence me, and your cause will be put to shame. This verse is a good beginning for prayer; those who commence with trust shall conclude with joy.

Psalm 71:2 *Deliver me in thy righteousness, and cause me to escape: incline thine ear unto me, and save me.*

EXPOSITION: Verse 2. *Deliver me in thy righteousness, and cause me to escape.* Be true, O God, to your Word. I am taken as in a net, but you liberate me from the malice of my persecutors.

Incline thine ear unto me, and save me. Stoop to my feebleness, and hear my faint whispers; be gracious to my infirmities, and smile upon me.

Psalm 71:3 *Be thou my strong habitation, whereunto I may continually resort: thou hast given commandment to save me; for thou art my rock and my fortress.*

EXPOSITION: Verse 3. *Be thou my strong habitation.* Permit me to enter into you, and be as much at home as a man in his own house, and then allow me to remain in you as my settled abode.

Whereunto I may continually resort. Fast shut is this castle against all adversaries, its gates they cannot burst open; the drawbridge is up, the portcullis is down, the bars are fast in their places; but, there is a secret door, by which friends of the great Lord can enter at all hours of the day or night, as often as ever they please.

Thou hast given commandment to save me. Nature is charged to be tender with God's servants; Providence is ordered to work their good, and the forces of the invisible world are ordained as their guardians. While God's mandate shields us, no stones of the field can throw us down; while angels bear us up in their hands, neither can the beasts of the field devour us. David's God delivers us from their ferocity and Daniel's God puts them in awe of us.

For thou art my rock and my fortress. In God, we have all the security that nature furnishes the rock and builds the fortress could supply; He is the complete preserver of His people.

Psalm 71:4 *Deliver me, O my God, out of the hand of the wicked, out of the hand of the unrighteous and cruel man.*

EXPOSITION: Verse 4. *Deliver me, O my God, out of the hand of the wicked.* God is on the same side with us, and His own confederates, and He will not suffer the evil to triumph over the just. He who addresses such a prayer as this to Heaven does more injury to his enemies than if he had turned a battery of Armstrongs[108] upon them.

Out of the hand of the unrighteous and cruel man. Being wicked to God, they become unrighteous towards men, and cruel in their persecutions of the godly. Two hands are here mentioned: they grasp and they crush; they strike and they would slay if God did not prevent them; had they as many hands as Briareos,[109] the finger of God would more than match them.

Psalm 71:5 *For thou art my hope, O Lord God: thou art my trust from my youth.*

EXPOSITION: Verse 5. *For thou art my hope, O Lord God.* God, who gives us grace to hope in Him, will assuredly fulfill our hope, and, therefore, we may plead it in prayer. His name is "Jehovah, the hope of Israel" [see Jeremiah 17:13].

Thou art my trust from my youth. David had proved his faith by notable exploits when he was a youth and ruddy; it was to him a cheering recollection, and he felt persuaded that the God of his youth would not forsake him in his age. They are highly favored who can, like David, Samuel, Josiah, Timothy, and others say, *"Thou art my trust from my youth."*

Psalm 71:6 *By thee have I been holden up from the womb: thou art he that took me out of my mother's bowels: my praise shall be continually of thee.*

---

108. An Armstrong was a breech-loading heavy gun used in field battles.
109. a legendary giant in Greek mythology with one hundred hands and fifty heads, also called Aegeon

EXPOSITION: **Verse 6.** *By thee have I been holden up from the womb.* Before he was able to understand the power which preserved him, he was sustained by it. We do well to reflect upon divine goodness to us in childhood, for it is full of food for gratitude.

Thou art he that took me out of my mother's bowels. Even before conscious life, the care of God is over His chosen. She, whose life is preserved, should render thanks, and so should he whose life is given.

My praise shall be continually of thee. Where goodness has been unceasingly received, praise should unceasingly be offered. God is the circle where praise should begin, continue, and endlessly revolve, *"For in him we live, and move, and have our being"* [Acts 17:28].

Psalm 71:7 *I am as a wonder unto many; but thou art my strong refuge.*

EXPOSITION: **Verse 7.** *I am as a wonder unto many.* "To thousand eyes a mark and gaze am I."[110] The saints are men wondered at; often their dark side is gloomy even to amazement, while their bright side is glorious even to astonishment. Few understand us, many are surprised at us.

But thou art my strong refuge. Here is the answer to our riddle. If we are strong, it is in God; if we are safe, our refuge shelters us; if we are calm, our soul has found her stay in God. When faith is understood, and the grounds of her confidence seen, the believer is no longer a wonder; but the marvel is that so much unbelief remains among the sons of men.

---

110. from Psalm LXXI, *The Psalter,* or *Psalms of David, in English Verse,* by John Keble.

Psalm 71:8 *Let my mouth be filled with thy praise and with thy honour all the day.*

EXPOSITION: Verse 8. *Let my mouth be filled with thy praise and with thy honour all the day.* What a blessed mouthful! God's bread is always in our mouths, so should His praise be. He fills us with good; let us be also filled with gratitude.

Psalm 71:9 *Cast me not off in the time of old age; forsake me not when my strength faileth.*

EXPOSITION: Verse 9. *Cast me not off in the time of old age.* David was not tired of his Master, and his only fear was lest his Master should be tired of him, Old age robs us of personal beauty, and deprives us of strength for active service; but it does not lower us in the love and favor of God. An ungrateful country leaves its worn out defenders to starve upon a scanty pittance, but the pensioners of Heaven are satisfied with good things.

Forsake me not when my strength faileth. Bear with me, and endure my infirmities. To be forsaken of God is the worst of all conceivable ills, and if the believer can be but clear of that grievous fear, he is happy: no saintly heart need be under any apprehension upon this point.

Psalm 71:10 *For mine enemies speak against me; and they that lay wait for my soul take counsel together,*

EXPOSITION: Verse 10. *For mine enemies speak against me; and they that lay wait for my soul take counsel together.* The psalmist had enemies, and these were most malicious; seeking his utter destruction, they were very persevering, and staid long upon the watch; to this they added cunning, for they lay in ambush to surprise him, and take him at a disadvantage; and all this they did with the utmost unanimity and deliberation, neither spoiling their design by want of prudence, nor marring its accomplishment by a lack of unity. The Lord our God is our only and all sufficient resort from every form of persecution.

Psalm 71:11 *Saying, God hath forsaken him: persecute and take him; for there is none to deliver him.*

EXPOSITION: **Verse 11.** *Saying, God hath forsaken him.* O bitter taunt! There is no worse arrow in all the quivers of hell. Our Lord felt this barbed shaft, and it is no marvel if His disciples feel the same. Were this exclamation the truth, it would indeed be an ill day for us; but, glory be to God, it is a barefaced lie.

Persecute and take him. Let loose the dogs of persecution upon him, seize him, and worry him, *for there is none to deliver him.* O cowardly boasts of a braggart foe, how you do wound the soul of the believer and only when his faith cries to his Lord is he able to endure your cruelty.

Psalm 71:12 *O God, be not far from me: O my God, make haste for my help.*

EXPOSITION: **Verse 12.** *O God, be not far from me.* Nearness to God is our conscious security. A child in the dark is comforted by grasping its father's hand.

O my God, make haste for my help. To call God ours, as having entered into covenant with us, is a mighty plea in prayer, and a great stay to our faith. The cry of "make haste" has occurred many times in this portion of the psalms, and it was evoked by the sore pressure of affliction. Sharp sorrows soon put an end to procrastinating prayers.

Psalm 71:13 *Let them be confounded and consumed that are adversaries to my soul; let them be covered with reproach and dishonour that seek my hurt.*

EXPOSITION: Verse 13. *Let them be confounded and consumed that are adversaries to my soul.* It will be all this to them to see your servant preserved; their envy and malice, when disappointed, will fill them with life consuming bitterness. The defeat of their plans shall nonplus them; they shall be confounded as they enquire the reason for their overthrow. The men they seek to destroy seem so weak, and their cause so contemptible that they will be filled with amazement as they see them not only survive all opposition, but even surmount it.

Let them be covered with reproach and dishonour that seek my hurt. He would have their shame made visible to all eyes, by their wearing it in their blushes as a mantle. They would have made a laughingstock of the believer, if his God had forsaken him; therefore, let unbelief and atheism be made a public scoffing in their persons.

Psalm 71:14 *But I will hope continually, and will yet praise thee more and more.*

EXPOSITION: Verse 14. *But I will hope continually.* When I cannot rejoice in what I have, I will look forward to what shall be mine, and will still rejoice. We may always hope, for we always have grounds for it: we will always hope, for it is a never-failing consolation.

And will yet praise thee more and more. He was not slack in thanksgiving; in fact, no man was ever more diligent in it; yet he was not content with all his former praises, but vowed to become more and more a grateful worshipper.

Psalm 71:15 *My mouth shall shew forth thy righteousness and thy salvation all the day; for I know not the numbers thereof.*

EXPOSITION: Verse 15. *My mouth shall shew forth thy righteousness and thy salvation all the day.* We are to bear testimony as experience enables us, and not withhold from others that which we have tasted and handled. The faithfulness of God in saving us, in delivering us out of the hand of our enemies, and in fulfilling His promises, is to be everywhere proclaimed by those who have proved it in their own history. The preacher who should be confined to this one theme would never need seek another: it is the *medulla theologae*,[111] the very pith and marrow of revealed truth.

For I know not the numbers thereof. He knew the sweetness of it, the sureness, the glory, and the truth of it; but as to the full reckoning of its plenitude, variety, and sufficiency, he felt he could not reach to the height of the great argument. To creatures belong number and limit, to God and His grace there is neither. We may, therefore, continue to tell out His great salvation all day long, for the theme is utterly inexhaustible.

Psalm 71:16 *I will go in the strength of the Lord God: I will make mention of thy righteousness, even of thine only.*

EXPOSITION: Verse 16. *I will go in the strength of the Lord God: I will make mention of thy righteousness, even of thine only.* Man's righteousness is not fit to be mentioned—filthy rags are best hidden; neither is there any righteousness under Heaven, or in Heaven, comparable to the divine. As

---
111. the marrow of theology

God himself fills all space, and is, therefore, the only God, leaving no room for another, so God's righteousness, in Christ Jesus, fills the believer's soul, and He counts all other things but dross and dung "that he may win Christ, and be found in him, not having his own righteousness which is of the law, but the righteousness which is of God by faith." [See Philippians 3:8–9.] What would be the use of speaking upon any other righteousness to a dying man—and all are dying men? But; this is the true believer's immovable resolve: *I will make mention of thy righteousness, even of thine only.* Forever dedicated to you my Lord, be this poor, unworthy tongue, whose only glory shall be to love and glorify you.

Psalm 71:17 *O God, thou hast taught me from my youth: and hitherto have I declared thy wondrous works.*

EXPOSITION: Verse 17. *O God, thou hast taught me from my youth.* It was comfortable to the psalmist to remember that from his earliest days he had been the Lord's disciple. None are too young to be taught of God, and they make the most proficient scholars who begin early.

And hitherto have I declared thy wondrous works. He had learned to tell what he knew, he was a pupil teacher; he continued still learning and declaring, and did not renounce his first master. A sacred conservatism is much needed in these days, when men are giving up old lights for new. We mean both to learn and to teach the wonders of redeeming love, until we can discover something nobler or more soul-satisfying; for this reason we hope that our gray heads will be found in the same road as we have trodden, even from our beardless youth.

Psalm 71:18 *Now also when I am old and greyheaded, O God, forsake me not; until I have shewed thy strength unto this generation, and thy power to every one that is to come.*

EXPOSITION: Verse 18. *Now also when I am old and greyheaded, O God, forsake me not.* There is something touching in the sight of hair whitened with the snows of many a winter: the old and faithful soldier receives consideration from his king; the venerable servant is beloved by his master. When our infirmities multiply, we may, with confidence, expect enlarged privileges in the world of grace, to make up for our narrowing range in the field of nature.

Until I have shewed thy strength unto this generation. He desired to continue his testimony and complete it; he had respect to the young men and little children about him, and knowing the vast importance of training them in the fear of God, he longed to make them all acquainted with the power of God to support His people, that they also might be led to walk by faith. He had leaned on the almighty arm, and could speak experimentally of its all sufficiency, and longed to do so before life came to a close.

And thy power to every one that is to come. He would leave a record for unborn ages to read. Blessed are they who begin in youth to proclaim the name of the Lord, and cease not until their last hour brings their last word for their divine Master.

Psalm 71:19 *Thy righteousness also, O God, is very high, who hast done great things: O God, who is like unto thee!*

EXPOSITION: Verse 19. *Thy righteousness also, O God, is very high.* Very sublime, unsearchable, exalted, and glorious is the holy character of God, and His way of making men righteous. His plan of righteousness uplifts men from the gates of hell to the mansions of Heaven. It is a high doctrine gospel, gives a high experience, leads to high practice, and ends in high felicity.

Who hast done great things. Creation, providence, redemption, are all unique, and nothing can compare with them.

O God, who is like unto thee. As your works are so transcendent, so are you. You are without equal, or even second, and such are your works, and such, especially, your plan of justifying sinners by the righteousness which you have provided. Adoration is a fit frame of mind for the believer. When he draws near to God, he enters into a region where everything is surpassingly sublime; miracles of love abound on every hand, and marvels of mingled justice and grace. *O God, who is like unto thee!*

Psalm 71:20 *Thou, which hast shewed me great and sore troubles, shalt quicken me again, and shalt bring me up again from the depths of the earth.*

EXPOSITION: Verse 20. *Thou, which hast shewed me great and sore troubles, shalt quicken me again.* He has shown me many heavy and severe trials, and He will also show me many and precious mercies. He has almost killed me, He will speedily revive me; and though I have been almost dead and buried.

He will give me a resurrection, *and bring me up again from the depths of the Earth.* However low the Lord may permit us to sink, He will fix a limit to the descent, and in due time will bring us up again. It is safe to lean on Him, since He bears up the pillars both of Heaven and Earth.

Psalm 71:21 *Thou shalt increase my greatness, and comfort me on every side.*

EXPOSITION: Verse 21. *Thou shalt increase my greatness.* As a king, David grew in influence and power. God did great things for him, and by him, and this is all the greatness believers want. May we have faith in God, such as these words express.

And comfort me on every side. As we were surrounded with afflictions, so shall we be environed with consolations. From above, and from all around, light shall come to dispel our former gloom; the change shall be great, indeed, when the Lord returns to comfort us.

Psalm 71:22 *I will also praise thee with the psaltery, even thy truth, O my God: unto thee will I sing with the harp, O thou Holy One of Israel.*

EXPOSITION: Verse 22. *I will also praise thee with the psaltery.* David would give his best music, both vocal and instrumental, to the Best of Masters. His harp would not be silent, nor his voice.

Even thy truth, O my God. This is ever a most enchanting attribute—namely, the truth or faithfulness of our covenant God. On this we rest, and from it we draw streams of richest consolation. His promises are sure, His love unalterable, His veracity indisputable.

Unto thee will I sing with the harp, O thou Holy One of Israel. Here is a new name, and, as it were, a new song. The Holy One of Israel is at once a lofty and an endearing name, full of teaching. Let us resolve, by all means within our power, to honor Him.

Psalm 71:23 *My lips shall greatly rejoice when I sing unto thee; and my soul, which thou hast redeemed.*

EXPOSITION: Verse 23. *My lips shall greatly rejoice when I sing unto thee.* It shall be no weariness to me to praise you. It shall be a delightful recreation, a solace, a joy. The essence of song lies in the holy joy of the singer.

And my soul, which thou hast redeemed. Soul singing is the soul of singing. Until men are redeemed, they are like instruments out of tune; but when once the precious blood has set them at liberty, then are they fitted to magnify the Lord who bought them.

Psalm 71:24 *My tongue also shall talk of thy righteousness all the day long: for they are confounded, for they are brought unto shame, that seek my hurt.*

EXPOSITION: Verse 24. *My tongue also shall talk of thy righteousness all the day long.* I will talk to myself, and to you, my God, and to my fellow men: my theme shall be your way of justifying sinners, the glorious display of your righteousness and grace in your dear Son; and this most fresh and never to be exhausted subject shall be ever with me, from the rising of the sun to the going down of the same.

For they are confounded, for they are brought unto shame, that seek my hurt. Faith believes that she has her request, and she has it. She is the substance of things hoped for—a substance so real and tangible, that it sets the glad soul singing. Already sin, Satan, and the world are vanquished, and the victory is ours.

Sin, Satan, Death appear[112]
To harass and appal:
Yet since the gracious Lord is near,
Backward they go, and fall.

We meet them face to face,
Through Jesus' conquest blest;
March in the triumph of his grace,
Right onward to our rest.

---

112. from a hymn titled "More Than a Conqueror" by Samuel W. Gandy

Psalm 72
Psalm 72:1–Psalm 72:20

Psalm 72:1 *Give the king thy judgments, O God, and thy righteousness unto the king's son.*

EXPOSITION: **Verse 1.** *Give the king thy judgments, O God.* Israel was a theocracy, and the kings were but the viceroys of the greater King; hence the prayer that the new king might be enthroned by divine right, and then endowed with divine wisdom. Our glorious King in Zion has all judgment committed unto Him. He rules in the name of God over all lands. He is king *Dei gratia*[113] as well as by right of inheritance.

And thy righteousness unto the king's son. Our Lord has power and authority in himself, and also royal dignity given of His Father. He is the righteous king; in a word, He is "the Lord our righteousness." We are waiting until He shall be manifested among men as the ever-righteous Judge. May the Lord hasten on His own time the long looked-for day.

Psalm 72:2 *He shall judge thy people with righteousness, and thy poor with judgment.*

EXPOSITION: **Verse 2.** *He shall judge thy people with righteousness.* Clothed with divine authority, He shall use it on the behalf of the favored nation, for whom He shall show himself strong, that they be not misjudged, slandered,

---
113. by the grace of God

or in any way treated maliciously. What a consolation to feel that none can suffer wrong in Christ's kingdom: He sits upon the great white throne, unspotted by a single deed of injustice, or even mistake of judgment: reputations are safe enough with Him.

And thy poor with judgment. True wisdom is manifest in all the decisions of Zion's King. We do not always understand His doings, but they are always right. The sovereignty of God is a delightful theme to the poor in spirit; they love to see the Lord exalted, and have no quarrel with Him for exercising the prerogatives of His crown.

Psalm 72:3 *The mountains shall bring peace to the people, and the little hills, by righteousness.*

EXPOSITION: Verse 3. *The mountains shall bring peace to the people.* Where Jesus is there is peace, lasting, deep, eternal. Even those things which were once our dread lose all terror when Jesus is owned as monarch of the heart: death itself, that dark mountain, loses all its gloom. Trials and afflictions, when the Lord is with us, bring us an increase rather than a diminution of peace.

And the little hills, by righteousness. In a spiritual sense, peace is given to the heart by the righteousness of Christ; and all the powers and passions of the soul are filled with a holy calm, when the way of salvation, by a divine righteousness, is revealed. "Then do we go forth with joy, and are led forth with peace; the mountains and the hills break forth before us into singing." [See Isaiah 55:12.]

Psalm 72:4 *He shall judge the poor of the people, he shall save the children of the needy, and shall break in pieces the oppressor.*

EXPOSITION: **Verse 4.** *He shall judge the poor of the people.* He will do them justice, yea, and blessed be His name, more than justice, for He will delight to do them good.

He shall save the children of the needy. Happy are God's poor and needy ones; they are safe under the wing of the Prince of Peace, for He will save them from all their enemies.

And shall break in pieces the oppressor. He is strong to smite the foes of His people. Sin, Satan, and all our enemies must be crushed by the iron rod of King Jesus. We have, therefore, no cause to fear; but abundant reason to sing–

> All hail the power of Jesus' name![114]
> Let angels prostrate fall,
> Bring forth the royal diadem,
> And crown him lord of all.

Psalm 72:5 *They shall fear thee as long as the sun and moon endure, throughout all generations.*

EXPOSITION: **Verse 5.** *They shall fear thee as long as the sun and moon endure.* Where Jesus reigns in power men must render obeisance of some sort. His kingdom is no house of cards, or dynasty of days; it is as lasting as the lights of Heaven

Throughout all generations shall the throne of the Redeemer stand. As long as there are men on earth Christ shall have a throne among them. Even at this hour we have before us the tokens of His dominion which have not been overturned, though the mightiest of empires have gone like visions of the night. We see on the shore of time the wrecks of the Caesars, the relics of the Moguls, and the last remnants

---

114. from hymn titled, "All Hail The Power of Jesus Name," by Edward Perronet

of the Ottomans.[115] Charlemagne, Maximilian, Napoleon, how they flit like shadows before us! They were and are not; but Jesus forever is. As for the houses of Hohenzollern,[116] Guelph,[117] or Hapsburg,[118] they have their hour; but the Son of David has all hours and ages as His own.

Psalm 72:6 *He shall come down like rain upon the mown grass: as showers that water the earth.*

EXPOSITION: Verse 6. *He shall come down like rain upon the mown grass.* Blessings upon His gentle sway! He with mild, benignant influence softly refreshes the weary and wounded among men, and makes them spring up into newness of life. Pastures mown with the scythe, or shorn by the teeth of cattle, present, as it were, so many bleeding stems of grass, but when the rain falls it is balm to all these wounds, and it renews the verdure and beauty of the field; fit image of the visits and benedictions of *"the consolation of Israel"* [Luke 2:25]. My soul, how well it is for you to be brought low, and to be even as the meadows eaten bare and trodden down by cattle, for then to you shall the Lord have respect; He shall remember your misery, and with His own most precious love restore you to more than your

---

115. The Ottoman Empire, created by Turkish tribes in Asia Minor, was one of the most powerful states in the world in the 15th and 16th century until 1922, when it was replaced by the Turkish Republic.
116. The Hohenzollern dynasty was the ruling house of Brandenburg-Prussia (1415–1918) and imperial Germany (1871—1918).
117. The House of Guelph was a European dynasty that included many German and British monarchs from the 11th to 20th centuries, and Emperor Ivan VI of Russia in the 18th century.
118. House of Hapsburg, also called House of Austria, was one of the principal sovereign dynasties of Europe from the 15th to the 20th century.

former glory. Welcome Jesus, you true Bien-aimé,[119] the Well-Beloved, thou art far more than Titus ever was—the Delight of Mankind.

As showers that water the earth. Each crystal drop of rain tells of heavenly mercy, which forgets not the parched plains: Jesus is all grace, all that He does is love, and His presence among men is joy. We need to preach Him more, for no shower can so refresh the nations. Philosophic preaching mocks men as with a dust shower, but the gospel meets the case of fallen humanity, and happiness flourishes beneath its genial power. Come down, O Lord, upon my soul, and my heart shall blossom with thy praise—

> He shall come down as still and light[120]
> As scattered drops on genial field;
> And in his time who loves the right,
> Freely shall bloom, sweet peace her harvest yield.

Psalm 72:7 *In his days shall the righteous flourish; and abundance of peace so long as the moon endureth.*

EXPOSITION: Verse 7. *In his days shall the righteous flourish.* Beneath the deadly Upas[121] of unrighteous rule no honest principles can be developed, and good men can scarcely live; but where truth and uprightness are on the throne, the best of men prosper most. In the gentle Jesus the godly find a happy shelter.

And abundance of peace so long as the moon endureth. Where Jesus reigns He is known as the true Melchizedek,

---

119. French for "beloved"
120. stanza of hymn by Isaac Watts, "Psalm LXXII," as found in the hymnal titled *Hymns of the Church Universal,* collected by J. and E.A. Rylands
121. a tropical Asian tree from which is collected an arrow poison

king both of righteousness and peace. Peace based upon right is sure to be lasting, but no other will be. The peace which Jesus brings is not superficial or short-lived; it is abundant in its depth and duration. Let all hearts and voices welcome the King of nations; Jesus the Good, the Great, the Just, the Ever-Blessed.

Psalm 72:8 *He shall have dominion also from sea to sea, and from the river unto the ends of the earth.*

EXPOSITION: Verse 8. *He shall have dominion also from sea to sea.* Widespread shall be the rule of Messiah; only the land's end shall end His territory: to the Ultima Thule[122] shall His scepter be extended. Jesus shall be Ruler of all mankind.

And from the river unto the ends of the earth. Start where you will, by any river you choose, and Messiah's kingdom shall reach on to the utmost bounds of the round world. We are encouraged by such a passage as this to look for the Savior's universal reign; whether before or after His personal advent we leave for the discussion of others. In this psalm, at least, we see a personal monarch, and He is the central figure, the focus of all the glory; not His servant, but himself do we see possessing the dominion and dispensing the government. Personal pronouns referring to our great King are constantly occurring in this psalm; He has dominion and kings fall down before Him, and serve Him; for He delivers, He spares, He saves, He lives, and daily He is praised.

Psalm 72:9 *They that dwell in the wilderness shall bow before him; and his enemies shall lick the dust.*

---

122. the northernmost part of the habitable ancient world

Psalm 72

EXPOSITION: Verse 9. *They that dwell in the wilderness shall bow before him.* Unconquered by arms, they shall be subdued by love. Wild and lawless as they have been, they shall gladly wear His easy yoke; then shall their deserts be made glad, yea, they shall rejoice and blossom as the rose.

And his enemies shall lick the dust. If they will not be His friends, they shall be utterly broken and humbled. Those who will not joyfully bow to such a prince richly merit to be hurled down and laid prostrate; the dust is too good for them, since they trampled on the blood of Christ.

Psalm 72:10 *The kings of Tarshish and of the isles shall bring presents: the kings of Sheba and Seba shall offer gifts.*

EXPOSITION: Verse 10. *The kings of Tarshish and of the isles shall bring presents.* Trade shall be made subservient to the purposes of mediatorial rule; merchant princes, both far and near, shall joyfully contribute of their wealth to His throne. Seafaring places are good centers from which to spread the gospel; and seafaring men often make earnest heralds of the Cross.

The kings of Sheba and Seba shall offer gifts. Foreign princes from inland regions, as yet unexplored, shall own the all-embracing monarchy of the King of kings; they shall be prompt to pay their reverential tribute. Religious offerings shall they bring, for their King is their God. Their freewill offering is all Christ and His Church desire; they want no forced levies and distraints,[123] let all men give of their own free will, kings as well as commoners.

---

123. property seizures

Psalm 72:11 *Yea, all kings shall fall down before him: all nations shall serve him.*

EXPOSITION: Verse 11. *Yea, all kings shall fall down before him.* Personally they shall pay their reverence, however mighty they may be. No matter how high their state, how ancient their dynasty, or far off their realms, they shall willingly accept Him as their Imperial Lord.

All nations shall serve him. The people shall be as obedient as the governors. The extent of the mediatorial rule is set forth by the two far-reaching *alls*, all kings, and all nations: we see not as yet all things put under Him, but since we see Jesus crowned with glory and honor in Heaven, we are altogether without doubt as to His universal monarchy on Earth. It is not to be imagined that an Alexander or a Caesar shall have wider sway than the Son of God. "Every knee shall bow to him, and every tongue shall confess that Jesus Christ is Lord, to the glory of God the Father" [see Romans 14:11]. Hasten it, O Lord, in your own time.

Psalm 72:12 *For he shall deliver the needy when he crieth; the poor also, and him that hath no helper.*

EXPOSITION: Verse 12. *For he shall deliver the needy.* Here is an excellent reason for man's submission to the Lord Christ; it is not because they dread His overwhelming power, but because they are won over by His just and condescending rule. Who would not fear so good a Prince, who makes the needy His peculiar care, and pledges himself to be their deliverer in times of need?

When he crieth. A child's cry touches a father's heart, and our King is the Father of His people. If we can do no more than cry it will bring omnipotence to our aid

The poor also, and him that hath no helper. The proverb

says, "God helps those that help themselves,"[124] but it is yet truer that Jesus helps those who cannot help themselves, nor find help in others. All helpless ones are under the especial care of Zion's compassionate King; let them hasten to put themselves in fellowship with Him. Let them look to Him, for He is looking for them.

Psalm 72:13 *He shall spare the poor and needy, and shall save the souls of the needy.*

EXPOSITION: **Verse 13.** *He shall spare the poor and needy.* His pity shall be manifested to them; He will not allow their trials to overwhelm them

And shall save the souls of the needy. His is the dominion of souls, a spiritual and not a worldly empire; and the needy, the consciously unworthy and weak, shall find that He will give them His salvation. Jesus calls not the righteous, but sinners to repentance. We ought to be anxious to be among these needy ones whom the Great King so highly favors.

Psalm 72:14 *He shall redeem their soul from deceit and violence: and precious shall their blood be in his sight.*

EXPOSITION: **Verse 14.** *He shall redeem their soul from deceit and violence.* These two things are the weapons with which the poor are assailed: both law and no law are employed to fleece them. The fox and the lion are combined against Christ's lambs, but the Shepherd will defeat them, and rescue the defenseless from their teeth.

And precious shall their blood be in his sight. He will not throw away His subjects in needless wars as tyrants

---
124. Often-quoted phrase not in the Bible, often attributed to Benjamin Franklin and quoted in *Poor Richard's Almanac*.

have done, but will take every means for preserving the humblest of them. Jesus, though He gave His own blood, is very cautious of the blood of His servants, and if they must die for Him as martyrs, He loves their memory, and counts their lives as His precious things.

> **Psalm 72:15** *And he shall live, and to him shall be given of the gold of Sheba: prayer also shall be made for him continually; and daily shall he be praised.*

EXPOSITION: **Verse 15.** *And he shall live.* Vive le Roi! O King![125] Live forever! He was slain, but is risen and ever lives.

And to him shall be given of the gold of Sheba. These are coronation gifts of the richest kind, cheerfully presented at His throne. How gladly would we give Him all that we have and are, and count the tribute far too small. We may rejoice that Christ's cause will not stand still for want of funds; the silver and the gold are His, and if they are not to be found at home, far-off lands shall hasten to make up the deficit. God help us to have more faith and more generosity.

Prayer also shall be made for Him continually. May all blessings be upon His head; all His people desire that His cause may prosper, therefore do they hourly cry, *"Thy kingdom come"* [Matthew 6:10]. Prayer for Jesus is a very sweet idea, and one which should be forevermore lovingly carried out; for the Church is Christ's body, and the truth is His scepter; therefore we pray for Him when we plead for these.

And daily shall he be praised. As he will perpetually show himself to be worthy of honor, so shall He be incessantly praised:

---

125. French for "Long live the King"

> For him shall constant prayer be made,[126]
> And praises throng to crown his head;
> His name, like sweet perfume, shall rise
> With every morning's sacrifice.

Psalm 72:16 *There shall be an handful of corn in the earth upon the top of the mountains; the fruit thereof shall shake like Lebanon: and they of the city shall flourish like grass of the earth.*

EXPOSITION: **Verse 16.** *There shall be an handful of corn in the earth upon the top of the mountains.* What a blessing that there is a handful; *"except the Lord of hosts had left unto us a very small remnant we should have been as Sodom, and we should have been like unto Gomorrah"* [Isaiah 1:9], but now the faithful are a living seed, and shall multiply in the land.

The fruit thereof shall shake like Lebanon. The harvest shall be so great that the wind shall rustle through it, and sound like the cedars upon Lebanon:

> Like Lebanon, by soft winds fanned,[127]
> Rustles the golden harvest far and wide.

God's Church is no insignificant thing; its beginnings are small, but its increase is of the most astonishing kind. As Lebanon is conspicuous and celebrated, so shall the Church be.

And they of the city shall flourish like grass of the earth. We need not fear for the cause of truth in the land; it is in good hands, where the pleasure of the Lord is sure to prosper. *"Fear not, little flock; for it is your Father's good pleasure to give you the kingdom"* [Luke 12:32].

---

126. from the hymn, "Jesus Shall Reign Where'er the Sun," by Isaac Watts
127. from the hymn, "Psalm LXXII," by John Keble.

Psalm 72:17 *His name shall endure for ever: his name shall be continued as long as the sun: and men shall be blessed in him: all nations shall call him blessed.*

EXPOSITION: Verse 17. *His name shall endure for ever.* In its saving power, as the rallying point of believers, and as renowned and glorified, His name shall remain forever the same.

His name shall be continued as long as the sun. While time is measured out by days, Jesus shall be glorious among men.

And men shall be blessed in him. He himself shall be Earth's greatest blessing; when men wish to bless others they shall bless in His name.

All nations shall call him blessed. The grateful nations shall echo His benedictions, and wish Him happy who has made them happy. Not only shall some glorify the Lord, but all; no land shall remain in heathenism; all nations shall delight to do Him honor.

Psalm 72:18–19 *Blessed be the* LORD *God, the God of Israel, who only doeth wondrous things. And blessed be his glorious name for ever: and let the whole earth be filled with his glory; amen, and Amen.*

EXPOSITION: Verses 18–19. *Blessed be the Lord God, the God of Israel, who only doeth wondrous things.* As Quesnel[128] well observes, thwese verses explain themselves. They call rather for profound gratitude, and emotion of heart, than for an exercise of the understanding; they are rather to be used for adoration than for exposition. *And blessed be his glorious name for ever: and let the whole earth be filled*

---

128. Pasquier Quesnel (1634–1719), a French theologian and author of a devotional commentary on the New Testament.

with his glory. It is, and ever will be, the acme of our desires, and the climax of our prayers, to behold Jesus exalted King of kings and Lord of lords. For so bright a consummation our heart yearns daily, and we cry *Amen, and Amen.*

Psalm 72:20 *The prayers of David the son of Jesse are ended.*

EXPOSITION: Verse 20. *The prayers of David the son of Jesse are ended.* What more could he ask? He has climbed the summit of the mount of God; he desires nothing more. With this upon his lips, He is content to die. He strips himself of his own royalty and becomes only the "son of Jesse," thrice happy to subside into nothing before the crowned Messiah. Before his believing eye the reign of Jesus, like the sun, filled all around with light, and the holy soul of the man after God's own heart exulted in it, and sung his "Nunc dimittis"[129]—*"Lord, now lettest thou thy servant depart in peace, according to thy word, for mine eyes have seen thy salvation!"* [Luke 2:29]. We, too, will cease from all petitioning if it be granted to us to see the Day of the Lord. Our blissful spirits will then have nothing further to do but forever to praise the Lord our God.

---

129. "Now you may dismiss," the opening words of Simeon's song of praise upon seeing the infant Jesus in the Temple

PSALM 73
PSALM 73:1–PSALM 73:28

Psalm 73:1 *Truly God is good to Israel, even to such as are of a clean heart.*

EXPOSITION: Verse 1. *Truly God is good to Israel.* He only is good, nothing else but good to His own covenanted ones. He cannot act unjustly or unkindly to them; His goodness to them is beyond dispute, and without mixture.

Even to such as are of a clean heart. These are the true Israel, not the ceremonially clean but the really so; those who are clean in the inward parts, pure in the vital mainspring of action. To such He is, and must be, goodness itself. O my God, however perplexed I may be, let me never think ill of you. If I cannot understand you, let me never cease to believe in you. It must be so, it cannot be otherwise, you are good to those whom you have made good; and where you have renewed the heart you will not leave it to its enemies.

Psalm 73:2 *But as for me, my feet were almost gone; my steps had well nigh slipped.*

EXPOSITION: Verse 2. Here begins the narrative of a great soul battle, a spiritual marathon, and a hard and well-fought field, in which the half-defeated became in the end wholly victorious.

But as for me The Lord is good to His saints, but as for me, am I one of them? Can I expect to share His grace? Yes, I do share it; but I have acted an unworthy part, very unlike one who is truly pure in heart.

My feet were almost gone. Errors of heart and head soon affect the conduct. When men doubt the righteousness of God, their own integrity begins to waver.

My steps had well nigh slipped. Asaph could make no progress in the good road; his feet ran away from under him like those of a man on a sheet of ice. How ought we to watch the inner man, since it has so forcible an effect upon the outward character.

Psalm 73:3 *For I was envious at the foolish, when I saw the prosperity of the wicked.*

EXPOSITION: Verse 3. *For I was envious at the foolish.* "The foolish" is the generic title of all the wicked: they are beyond all others fools, and he must be a fool who envies. It is a pitiful thing that an heir of Heaven should have to confess "I was envious," but worse still that he should have to put it, "I was envious at the foolish." Yet this acknowledgment is, we fear, due from most of us.

When I saw the prosperity of the wicked. His eye was fixed too much on one thing; he saw their present, and forgot their future, saw their outward display, and overlooked their soul's discomfort. All things considered, Dives[130] had more cause to envy Lazarus than Lazarus to be envious of Dives.

Psalm 73:4 *For there are no bands in their death: but their strength is firm.*

EXPOSITION: Verse 4. *For there are no bands in their death.* The notion is still prevalent that a quiet death means a happy hereafter. The psalmist had observed that the very

---

130. traditional name of the rich man in Jesus' parable about of the beggar Lazarus (Luke 16:19–31)

reverse is true. Careless persons become case-hardened, and continue presumptuously secure, even to the last. Some are startled at the approach of judgment, but many more have received a strong delusion to believe a lie.

Their strength is firm. What do they care for death? Frequently they are brazen and insolent, and can vent defiant blasphemies even on their last couch. Let the righteous die as they may, let my last end be like theirs.

Psalm 73:5 *They are not in trouble as other men; neither are they plagued like other men.*

EXPOSITION: Verse 5. *They are not in trouble as other men.* The prosperous wicked escape the killing toils which afflict the mass of mankind; their bread comes to them without care, their wine without stint. Ordinary domestic and personal troubles do not appear to molest them.

Neither are they plagued like other men. Fierce trials do not arise to assail them: they do not smart under the divine rod. If earthly good were of much value, the Lord would not give so large a measure of it to those who have least of His love.

Psalm 73:6 *Therefore pride compasseth them about as a chain; violence covereth them as a garment.*

EXPOSITION: Verse 6. *Therefore pride compasseth them about as a chain.* They are as great in their own esteem as if they were aldermen[131] of the New Jerusalem; they want no other ornament than their own pomposity.

Violence covereth them as a garment. In their boastful arrogance they array themselves; they wear the livery of the devil, and are fond of it.

---
131. members of a legislative municipal body

Psalm 73:7 *Their eyes stand out with fatness: they have more than heart could wish.*

EXPOSITION: **Verse 7.** *Their eyes stand out with fatness.* In cases of obesity the eyes usually appear to be enclosed in fat, but sometimes they protrude; in either case the countenance is changed, loses its human form, and is assimilated to that of fatted swine.

They have more than heart could wish. The heart is beyond measure gluttonous, and yet in the case of certain ungodly millionaires, who have rivaled Sardanapalus[132] both in lust and luxury, it has seemed as if their wishes were exceeded, and their meat surpassed their appetite.

Psalm 73:8 *They are corrupt, and speak wickedly concerning oppression: they speak loftily.*

EXPOSITION: **Verse 8.** *They are corrupt.* They rot above ground; their heart and life are depraved. *And speak wickedly concerning oppression.* The reek of the sepulcher rises through their mouths; the nature of the soul is revealed in the speech. *They speak loftily.* Their high heads, like tall chimneys, vomit black smoke. They are Sir Oracle[133] in every case; they speak as from the judges' bench, and expect all the world to stand in awe of them.

Psalm 73:9 *They set their mouth against the heavens, and their tongue walketh through the earth.*

EXPOSITION: **Verse 9.** *They set their mouth against*

---

132. Assyrian emperor-king known for his self-indulgent, luxurious lifestyle
133. the name of a player in Shakespeare's play, *The Merchant of Venice*, act 1, scene 1, applied to all "oracles" who feel they are divinely inspired

the heavens. Against God himself they aim their blasphemies. Yet they might let God alone, for their pride will make them enemies enough without their defying Him.

And their tongue walketh through the earth. When these men's tongues are out for a walk, they who meet them are unhappy, for it is impossible altogether to avoid them, both on land and sea they make their voyages. They waylay men in the king's highway, but they are able to hunt across country, too. Their whip has a long lash, and reaches both high and low.

Psalm 73:10 *Therefore his people return hither: and waters of a full cup are wrung out to them.*

EXPOSITION: Verse 10. *Therefore his people return hither.* God's people are driven to fly to His throne for shelter. The saints come again, and again, to their Lord, laden with complaints on account of the persecutions they endure from these proud and graceless men.

And waters of a full cup are wrung out to them. Though beloved of God, they have to drain the bitter cup; their sorrows are as full as the wicked man's prosperity. The medicine cup is not for rebels, but for those whom Jehovah Rophi[134] loves.

Psalm 73:11 *And they say, How doth God know? and is there knowledge in the most High?*

EXPOSITION: Verse 11. *And they say, How doth God know?* Thus dare the ungodly speak. They flatter themselves that their oppressions and persecutions are unobserved of Heaven. So they console themselves if judgments are threatened.

Is there knowledge in the Most High? Well were they

---

134. "the Lord who heals"

called foolish. This is a solecism[135] in language, a madness of thought. How could such language flow from their lips, even under the most depressing perplexities?

Psalm 73:12 *Behold, these are the ungodly, who prosper in the world; they increase in riches.*

EXPOSITION: Verse 12. *Behold, these are the ungodly, who prosper in the world.* Look! See! Consider! They deserve to be hung in chains, they are worthy to be chased from the world, and yet the world becomes all their own.

They increase in riches or strength. Both wealth and health are their dowry. Lord, how is this? Your poor servants, who become yet poorer, and groan under their burdens, are made to wonder at your mysterious ways.

Psalm 73:13 *Verily I have cleansed my heart in vain, and washed my hands in innocency.*

EXPOSITION: Verse 13. *Verily I have cleansed my heart in vain.* Poor Asaph![136] He questions the value of holiness when its wages are paid in the coin of affliction. In the presence of temporal circumstances, the pure in heart may seem to have cleansed themselves altogether in vain, but we must not judge after the sight of the eyes.

And washed my hands in innocency. Asaph had been as careful of his hands as of his heart; he had guarded his outer as well as his inner life, and it was a bitter thought that all of this was useless, and left him in even a worse condition than foul-handed, black-hearted worldlings. It smelled too strong of a lie to be tolerated long in the good man's soul; hence, in a verse or two, we see his mind turning in another direction.

---

135. a tactless act or blunder
136. writer of this psalm

Psalm 73:14 *For all the day long have I been plagued, and chastened every morning.*

EXPOSITION: **Verse 14.** *For all the day long have I been plagued.* He was smitten from the moment he woke to the time he went to bed. *And chastened every morning.* The downcast seer was in a muse and a maze. The affairs of mankind appeared to him to be in a fearful tangle; how could it be permitted by a just ruler that things should be so turned upside down, and the whole course of justice dislocated.

Psalm 73:15 *If I say, I will speak thus; behold, I should offend against the generation of thy children.*

EXPOSITION: **Verse 15.** *If I say, I will speak thus.* From such a man as the psalmist, the utterance which his discontent suggested would have been a heavy blow and deep discouragement to the whole brotherhood. He dared not, therefore, come to such a resolution, but paused, and would not decide to declare his feelings. It was well, for in his case second thoughts were by far the best.

I should offend against the generation of thy children. I would scandalize them, grieve them, and perhaps cause them to offend also. We ought to look at the consequences of our speech to all others, and especially to the Church of God. Expressions which convey the impression that the Lord acts unjustly or unkindly, especially if they fall from the lips of men of known character and experience, are as dangerous as firebrands among stubble; they are used for blasphemous purposes by the ill-disposed; and the timid and trembling are sure to be cast down thereby, and to find reason for yet deeper distress of soul.

Psalm 73:16 *When I thought to know this, it was too painful for me;*

EXPOSITION: Verse 16. *When I thought to know this, it was too painful for me.* The thought of scandalizing the family of God he could not bear, and yet his inward thoughts seethed and fermented, and caused an intolerable anguish within. A smothered grief is hard to endure. The triumph of conscience which compels us to keep the wolf hidden beneath our own garments, does not forbid its gnawing at our vitals. Those who know Asaph's dilemma will pity him as none others can.

Psalm 73:17 *Until I went into the sanctuary of God; then understood I their end.*

EXPOSITION: Verse 17. *Until I went into the sanctuary of God.* His mind entered the eternity where God dwells as in a holy place, he left the things of sense for the things invisible, his heart gazed within the veil, and he stood where the thrice holy God stands. Thus he shifted his point of view, and apparent disorder resolved itself into harmony.

Then understood I their end. He had seen too little to be able to judge; a wider view changed his judgment; he saw with his mind's enlightened eye the future of the wicked, and his soul was in debate no longer as to the happiness of their condition

Psalm 73:18 *Surely thou didst set them in slippery places: thou castedst them down into destruction.*

EXPOSITION: Verse 18. The psalmist's sorrow had culminated, not in the fact that the ungodly prospered, but that God had arranged it so.

Surely thou didst set them in slippery places. Their position was dangerous, and, therefore, God did not set His friends there but His foes alone. He chose, in infinite love, a rougher but safer standing for His own beloved.

Thou castedst them down into destruction. The same hand which led them up to their Tarpeian[137] rock, hurled them down from it. They were but elevated by judicial arrangement for the fuller execution of their doom. The ascent to the fatal gallows of Haman was an essential ingredient in the terror of the sentence—*"hang him thereon"* [see Esther 7:9]. If the wicked had not been raised so high they could not have fallen so low.

Psalm 73:19 *How are they brought into desolation, as in a moment! they are utterly consumed with terrors.*

EXPOSITION: **Verse 19.** *How are they brought into desolation, as in a moment!* This is an exclamation of godly wonder at the suddenness and completeness of the sinners' overthrow.

They are utterly consumed with terrors. They have neither root nor branch left. They cease to exist among the sons of men, and, in the other world, there is nothing left of their former glory The momentary glory of the graceless is in a moment effaced, their loftiness is consumer in an instant.

Psalm 73:20 *As a dream when one awaketh; so, O Lord, when thou awakest, thou shalt despise their image.*

EXPOSITION: **Verse 20.** *As a dream when one awaketh; so, O Lord, when thou awakest, thou shalt despise*

---

137. a rock of peak of the Capitoline Hill in Rome from which condemned criminals were hurled to their death

their image. When God awakes to judgment, they who despise Him shall be despised; they are already "such stuff as dreams are made on,"[138] but then the baseless fabric shall not leave a wreck behind. Lord, leave us not to the madness which covets unsubstantial wealth, and ever teach us your own true wisdom.

Psalm 73:21 *Thus my heart was grieved, and I was pricked in my reins.*

EXPOSITION: Verse 21. *Thus my heart was grieved.* It was a deep-seated sorrow, and one which penetrated his inmost being. His spirit had become embittered; he had judged in a harsh, crabbed, surly manner. He had become atrabilious,[139] full of black bile, melancholy, and choleric; he had poisoned his own life at the fountainhead, and made all its streams to be bitter as gall.

And I was pricked in my reins. He was as full of pain as a man afflicted with renal disease; he had pierced himself through with many sorrows; his hard thoughts were like so many calculi[140] in his kidneys; he was utterly wretched and woebegone, and all through his own reflections. O miserable philosophy, which stretches the mind on the rack, and breaks it on the wheel! O blessed faith, which drives away the inquisitors, and sets the captives free!

Psalm 73:22 *So foolish was I, and ignorant: I was as a beast before thee.*

EXPOSITION: Verse 22. *So foolish was I.* Though a saint of God, he had acted as if he had been one of the fools

---
138. excerpt from Shakespeare's play, *The Tempest*, act 4, scene 1
139. ill-natured
140. kidney stones

whom God abhors. Had he not even envied them—and what is that but to aspire to be like them? The wisest of men have enough folly in them to ruin them unless grace prevents.

And ignorant. He did not know how sufficiently to express his sense of his own fatuity.[141]

I was as a beast before thee. Even in God's presence he had been brutish, and worse than a beast. It was but an evidence of his true wisdom that he was so deeply conscious of his own folly. We see how bitterly good men bewail mental wanderings; they make no excuses for themselves, but set their sins in the pillory[142], and cast the vilest reproaches upon them. O for grace to detest the very appearance of evil!

Psalm 73:23 *Nevertheless I am continually with thee: thou hast holden me by my right hand.*

EXPOSITION: Verse 23. *Nevertheless I am continually with thee.* He does not give up his faith, though he confesses his folly. Sin may distress us, and yet we may be in communion with God. It is sin beloved and delighted in which separates us from the Lord, but when we bewail it heartily, the Lord will not withdraw from us. Our double nature, as it always causes conflict, so it is a continuous paradox: the flesh allies us with the brutes, and the spirit affiliates us to God.

Thou hast holden me by my right hand. With love you embrace me, with honor you ennoble me, and with power you uphold me. This verse contains the two precious mercies of communion and upholding, and as they were both given to one who confessed himself a fool, we also may hope to enjoy them.

---

141. absurdity
142. a wooden framework designed to hold offenders in public humiliation

Psalm 73:24 *Thou shalt guide me with thy counsel, and afterward receive me to glory.*

EXPOSITION: Verse 24. *Thou shalt guide me with thy counsel.* I am done with choosing my own way, and trying to pick a path amid the jungle of reason. The end of our own wisdom is the beginning of our being wise. With Him is counsel, and when we come to him, we are sure to be led rightly.

And afterward. "Afterward!" Blessed word. We can cheerfully put up with the present, when we foresee the future. What is around us just now is of small consequence, compared with afterward.

Receive me to glory. Take me up into your splendor of joy. Your guidance shall conduct me to this matchless terminus. Glory shall I have, and you yourself will admit me into it. As Enoch was not, for God took him, so all the saints are taken—received up into glory.

Psalm 73:25 *Whom have I in heaven but thee? and there is none upon earth that I desire beside thee.*

EXPOSITION: Verse 25. *Whom have I in heaven but thee?* He felt that his God was better to him than all the wealth, health, honor, and peace, which he had so much envied in the worldling. Yes, He was not only better than all on Earth, but more excellent than all in Heaven. He bade all things else go, that he might be filled with his God.

And there is none upon earth that I desire beside thee. No longer would his wishes ramble, no other object would tempt them to stray; henceforth, the Ever-Living One would be his all in all.

Psalm 73:26 *My flesh and my heart faileth: but God is the strength of my heart, and my portion for ever.*

EXPOSITION: Verse 26. *My flesh and my heart faileth.* They had failed him already, and he had almost fallen. *But God is the strength of my heart, and my portion for ever.* His God would not fail him, either as protection or a joy. We shall do well to follow his example. There is nothing desirable save God; let us, then, desire only Him. All other things must pass away; let our hearts abide in Him, who alone abides forever.

Psalm 73:27 *For, lo, they that are far from thee shall perish: thou hast destroyed all them that go a whoring from thee.*

EXPOSITION: Verse 27. *For, lo, they that are far from thee shall perish.* We must be near God to live; to be far off by wicked works is death.

Thou hast destroyed all them that go a whoring from thee. If we pretend to be the Lord's servants, we must remember that He is a jealous God, and requires spiritual chastity from all His people. We read examples of this in Israel's history; may we never create fresh instances in our own persons.

Psalm 73:28 *But it is good for me to draw near to God: I have put my trust in the Lord God, that I may declare all thy works.*

EXPOSITION: Verse 28. *But it is good for me to draw near to God.* The greater our nearness to God, the less we are affected by the attractions and distractions of Earth. Access into the most holy place is a great privilege, and a cure for a multitude of ills. It is good for all saints, it is good for me in particular; it is always good, and always will be good for me to approach the greatest good, the source of all good, even God himself.

I have put my trust in the Lord God. He dwells upon the glorious name of the Lord Jehovah, and avows it as the basis of his faith. Faith is wisdom; it is the key of enigmas, the clue of mazes, and the pole star of pathless seas. Trust and you will know.

That I may declare all thy works. He who believes shall understand, and so be able to teach. He who is ready to believe the goodness of God shall always see fresh goodness to believe in, and he who is willing to declare the works of God shall never be silent for lack of wonders to declare.

Psalm 74
Psalm 74:1–Psalm 74:23

Psalm 74:1 O God, why hast thou cast us off for ever? why doth thine anger smoke against the sheep of thy pasture?

EXPOSITION: Verse 1. *O God, why hast thou cast us off for ever?* To cast us off at all was hard, but when you do so for so long a time desert your people it is an evil beyond all endurance—the very chief of woes and abyss of misery. God is never weary of His people so as to abhor them, and even when His anger is turned against them, it is but for a small moment, and with a view to their eternal good. Grief in its distraction asks strange questions and surmises impossible terrors. It is a wonder of grace that the Lord has not long ago put us away as men lay aside cast off garments, *"but he hateth putting away"*, and will still be patient with His chosen.

Why doth thine anger smoke against the sheep of thy pasture? It is a terrible thing when the anger of God smokes, but it is an infinite mercy that it does not break into a devouring flame. It is good to pray the Lord to remove every sign of His wrath, for it is to those who are truly the Lord's sheep a most painful thing to be the objects of His displeasure.

Psalm 74:2 *Remember thy congregation, which thou hast purchased of old; the rod of thine inheritance, which thou hast redeemed; this mount Zion, wherein thou hast dwelt.*

EXPOSITION: Verse 2. *Remember thy congregation, which thou hast purchased of old.* The Church is no new purchase of the Lord; from before the world's foundation the chosen were regarded as redeemed by the Lamb slain; shall ancient love die out, and the eternal purpose become frustrate? The Lord would have His people remember the Paschal Lamb, the bloodstained lintel, and the overthrow of Egypt; and will He forget all this himself? Let us put Him in remembrance, let us plead together the woes of Calvary, and the covenant of which they are the seal, are the security of the saints.

The rod of thine inheritance, which thou hast redeemed. The Lord's portion is His people—will He lose His inheritance? His Church is His Kingdom, over which He stretches the rod of sovereignty; will He allow His possessions to be torn from Him? No man will willingly lose his inheritance, and no prince will relinquish his dominions; therefore we believe that the King of kings will hold His own, and maintain His rights against all comers.

This mount Zion, wherein thou hast dwelt. The Lord's having made Zion the especial center of His worship, and place of His manifestation, is yet another plea for the preservation of Jerusalem. It may be well to note that this psalm was evidently written with a view to the temple upon Zion, and not to the tabernacle which was there in David's time, and was a mere tent; but the destructions here bewailed were exercised upon the carved work of a substantial structure. Those who had seen the glory of God in Solomon's peerless temple might well mourn in bitterness, when the Lord allowed His enemies to make an utter ruin of that matchless edifice.

Psalm 74:3 *Lift up thy feet unto the perpetual desolations; even all that the enemy hath done wickedly in the sanctuary.*

EXPOSITION: **Verse 3.** *Lift up thy feet unto the perpetual desolations.* This is another argument with God. Would Jehovah sit still and see His own land made a wilderness, His own palace a desolation? Until He should arise, and draw near, the desolation would remain; only His presence could cure the evil, therefore is He entreated to hasten with uplifted feet for the deliverance of His people.

Even all that the enemy hath done wickedly in the sanctuary. Every stone in the ruined temple appealed to the Lord; on all sides were the marks of impious spoilers, the holiest places bore evidence of their malicious wickedness. Faith finds pleas in the worst circumstances; she uses even the fallen stones of her desolate palaces, and assails with them the gates of Heaven, casting them forth with the great engine of prayer.

Psalm 74:4 *Thine enemies roar in the midst of thy congregations; they set up their ensigns for signs.*

EXPOSITION: **Verse 4.** *Thine enemies roar in the midst of thy congregations.* Where your people sang like angels, these barbarians roar like beasts. When your saints come together for worship, these cruel men attack them with all the fury of lions. When hypocrites abound in the Church, and pollute her worship, the case is parallel to that before us; Lord save us from so severe a trial.

They set up their ensigns for signs. Idolatrous emblems used in war were set up over God's altar, as an insulting token of victory, and of contempt for the vanquished and their God. Papists,[143] Arians,[144] and the modern school of

---

143. Roman Catholics
144. followers of the beliefs of the fourth-century Arius, who preached that Jesus was not truly divine

Neologians,[145] have, in their day, set up their ensigns for signs. As a Jew felt a holy horror when he saw an idolatrous emblem set up in the holy place, even so do we when in a Protestant church we see the fooleries of Rome, and when from pulpits, once occupied by men of God, we hear philosophy and vain deceit.

> **Psalm 74:5** *A man was famous according as he had lifted up axes upon the thick trees.*

EXPOSITION: **Verse 5.** *A man was famous according as he had lifted up axes upon the thick trees.* In the olden times our sires dealt sturdy blows against the forests of error, and labored hard to lay the axe at the root of the trees; but, unfortunately their sons appear to be quite as diligent to destroy the truth and to overthrow all that their fathers built up. O for the good old times again! O for an hour of Luther's hatchet, or Calvin's mighty axe!

> **Psalm 74:6** *But now they break down the carved work thereof at once with axes and hammers.*

EXPOSITION: **Verse 6.** *But now they break down the carved work thereof at once with axes and hammers.* In these days men are using axes and sledgehammers against the gospel and the Church. Glorious truths, far more exquisite than the goodliest carving, are caviled over and smashed by the blows of modern criticism.

Truths which have upheld the afflicted and cheered the dying are smitten by pretentious Goths, who would be accounted learned, but know not the first principals of the truth.

---

145. proponents of new doctrines

Psalm 74:7 *They have cast fire into thy sanctuary, they have defiled by casting down the dwelling place of thy name to the ground.*

EXPOSITION: **Verse 7.** *They have cast fire into thy sanctuary.* To this day the enmity of the human heart is quite as great as ever; and, if providence did not restrain, the saints would still be as fuel for the flames. *They have defiled by casting down the dwelling place of thy name to the ground.* They made a heap of the temple, and left not one stone upon another. Yet, even if they could wreak their will upon the cause of Christ, they are not able to destroy it, it would survive their blows and fires; the Lord would hold them still like dogs on a leash, and in the end frustrate all their designs.

Psalm 74:8 *They said in their hearts, Let us destroy them together: they have burned up all the synagogues of God in the land.*

EXPOSITION: **Verse 8.** *They said in their hearts, Let us destroy them together.* Extirpation was the desire of Haman, and the aim of many another tyrant; not a remnant of the people of God would have been left if oppressors could have had their way. Pharaoh's policy to stamp out the nation has been a precedent for others, yet the Jews survive, and will: the bush though burning has not been consumed. Even thus the Church of Christ has gone through baptism of blood and fire, but it is all the brighter for them.

They have burned up all the synagogues of God in the land. Here is no allusion to places called synagogues, but to assemblies; and as no assemblies for worship here held in but one place, the ruin of the temple was the destruction of all the holy gatherings, and so in effect all the meeting places were destroyed. How happy are we that we can meet for worship in any place we choose, and none dare molest us.

> **Psalm 74:9** *We see not our signs: there is no more any prophet: neither is there among us any that knoweth how long.*

EXPOSITION: Verse 9. *We see not our signs.* Alas, poor Israel! We, too, as believers, know what it is to lose our evidences and grope in darkness; and too often do our churches also miss the tokens of the Redeemer's presence, and their lamps remain untrimmed. Sad complaint of a people under a cloud!

There is no more any prophet. Prophecy was suspended. No inspiring psalm or consoling promise fell from bard or seer. It is to be feared, that with all the ministers now existing, there is yet a dearth of men whose hearts and tongues are touched with the celestial fire.

Neither is there any among us that knoweth how long. Blessed be God, He has not left His Church in these days to be so deplorably destitute of cheering words; let us pray that He never may. Contempt of the Word is very common, and may well provoke the Lord to withdraw it from us; may His long-suffering endure the strain, and His mercy afford us still the Word of Life.

> **Psalm 74:10** *O God, how long shall the adversary reproach? Shall the enemy blaspheme thy name for ever?*

EXPOSITION: Verse 10. *O God, how long shall the adversary reproach.* God has His reasons for delay, and His seasons for action, and in the end it shall be seen that He *"is not slack concerning His promise"* [2 Peter 3:9].

Shall the enemy blaspheme thy name for ever? Is there to be no end to all this sacrilege and cursing? Yes, it shall all be ended, but not by and by. There is a time for the sinner to rage, and a time in which patience bears with him; yet it is but a time, and then, ah, then!

Psalm 74:11 *Why withdrawest thou thy hand, even thy right hand? pluck it out of thy bosom.*

EXPOSITION: Verse 11. *Why withdrawest thou thy hand, even thy right hand? The kingdom of heaven suffereth violence*, and he who learns the art shall surely prevail with God by its means. [See Matthew 11:12.] It is fit that we should enquire why the work of grace goes on so slowly, and the enemy has so much power over men: the inquiry may suggest practical reflections of unbounded value.

> Why dost thou from the conflict stay?
> Why do thy chariot wheels delay?
>
> Lift up thyself, hell's kingdom shake,
> Arm of the Lord, awake, awake.[146]

Pluck it out of thy bosom. When God seems to fold His arms we must not fold ours, but rather renew our entreaties that He would again put His hand to the work. The heart of God is always moved by such entreaties. When we bring forth out strong reasons, then He will bring forth His choice mercies.

Psalm 74:12 *For God is my King of old, working salvation in the midst of the earth.*

---

146. from the hymn, "Awake, O Arm of the Lord," by Henry March.

Spurgeon on the Psalms

EXPOSITION: Verse 12. *For God is my King of old.* How consoling is this avowal! Israel in holy loyalty acknowledges her King, and claims to have been His possession from of old, and thence she derives a plea for defense and deliverance.

Working salvation in the midst of the earth. From the most remote period of Israel's history the Lord had worked out for her many salvations; especially at the Red Sea, the very heart of the world was astonished by His wonders of deliverance. Each past miracle of grace assures us that He who has begun to deliver will continue to redeem us from all evil. His deeds of old were public and wrought in the teeth of His foes, they were no delusions or make-believes; and, therefore, in all our perils we look for true and manifest assistance, and we shall surely receive it.

Psalm 74:13 *Thou didst divide the sea by thy strength: thou brakest the heads of the dragons in the waters.*

EXPOSITION: Verse 13. *Thou didst divide the sea by thy strength.* Infinite power split the Red Sea in twain. Israel delighted to rehearse this famous act of the Lord.

Thou brakest the heads of the dragons in the waters. That old dragon Pharaoh was utterly broken, and Egypt herself had the head of her power and pomp broken with an almighty blow. Even thus is that old dragon broken by Him, who, came to bruise the serpent's head, and the sea of wrath no longer rolls before us; we pass through it dry-shod. Our faith as to the present is revived by glad memories of the past.

Psalm 74:14 *Thou brakest the heads of leviathan in pieces, and gavest him to be meat to the people inhabiting the wilderness.*

EXPOSITION: Verse 14. *Thou brakest the heads of leviathan in pieces.* It is the Lord who has done it all. The mighty dragon of Egypt was utterly slain, and his proud heads broken in pieces.

And gavest him to be meat to the people inhabiting the wilderness. Not only did the wild beasts feed upon the carcasses of the Egyptians, but the dwellers along the shores stripped the bodies and enriched themselves with the spoil. Let us not give way to fear; hydra-headed evils shall be slain, and monstrous difficulties shall be overcome, and all things shall work our lasting good.

Psalm 74:15 *Thou didst cleave the fountain and the flood: thou driedst up mighty rivers.*

EXPOSITION: Verse 15. *Thou didst cleave the fountain and the flood.* Jordan was divided by Jehovah's power; the Lord is able to repeat His miracles, what He did with a sea, He can do with a river; lesser difficulties shall be removed as well as greater ones.

Thou driedst up mighty rivers, rivers which were permanent, and not like the transient torrents of the land, were dried up for awhile; the Jordan itself, being such, was laid dry for a season.

Psalm 74:16 *The day is thine, the night also is thine: thou hast prepared the light and the sun.*

EXPOSITION: Verse 16. *The day is thine, the night also is thine.* You are not restricted by times and seasons. Our prosperity comes from you, and our adversity is ordained by you. You rule in the darkness, and one glance of your eye kindles it into day. Lord, be not slack to keep your Word, but rise for the help of your people.

Thou hast prepared the light and the sun. Both light and the light bearer are of God. Our help, and the instrument of it, are both in His hand. There is no limit to His power; may He be pleased to display it and make His people glad, letting His sacred preparations of mercy ripen, saying, *"Let there be light"* and light shall at once dispel our gloom.

Psalm 74:17 *Thou hast set all the borders of the earth: thou hast made summer and winter.*

EXPOSITION: Verse 17. *Thou hast set all the borders of the earth.* Land and sea receive their boundaries from Him. Continents and islands are mapped by His hand. It will be well when all our "-ologies" are tinctured with "theology," and the Creator is seen at work amid His universe. The argument of our text is that He who bounds the sea can restrain His foes; and He who guards the borders of the dry land can also protect His chosen.

Thou hast made summer and winter. The God of nature is the God of grace; and we may argue from the revolving seasons that sorrow is not meant to rule the year, the flowers of hope will blossom, and ruddy fruits of joy will yet ripen.

Psalm 74:18 *Remember this, that the enemy hath reproached, O LORD, and that the foolish people have blasphemed thy name.*

EXPOSITION: Verse 18. *Remember this, that the enemy hath reproached, O Lord.* Against you, the ever-glorious Maker of all things, have they spoken, your honor have they assailed, and defied even you. This is forcible pleading indeed, and reminds us of Moses and Hezekiah in their intercessions: *"What wilt thou do unto thy great name?"* *"It may be that the Lord thy God will hear the words of Rabshakeh, who* *hath reproached the living God"* [Joshua 7:9, 2 Kings 19:4]. Jehovah is a jealous God, and will surely glorify His own name; here our hope finds foothold.

And that the foolish people have blasphemed thy name. The meanness of the enemy is here pleaded. Sinners are fools, and shall fools be allowed to insult the Lord and oppress His people; shall the abject ones curse the Lord and defy Him to His face? When error grows too bold its day is near, and its fall certain.

> **Psalm 74:19** *O deliver not the soul of thy turtledove unto the multitude of the wicked: forget not the congregation of thy poor for ever.*

EXPOSITION: Verse 19. *O deliver not the soul of thy turtledove unto the multitude of the wicked.* Your poor Church is weak and defenseless as a dove, but yet her adversaries cannot touch her without your permission; do not give them leave to devour her, consign her not to the merciless fangs of her foes. Thus may we each plead, and with good hope of prevailing, for the Lord is very pitiful and full of compassion.

Forget not the congregation of thy poor for ever. They look to you for everything, for they are very poor, and they are your poor, and there is a company of them, collected by yourself; do not turn your back on them for long, do not appear strange unto them, but let their poverty plead with you; turn unto them, and visit your afflicted.

> **Psalm 74:20** *Have respect unto the covenant: for the dark places of the earth are full of the habitations of cruelty.*

EXPOSITION: Verse 20. *Have respect unto the covenant.* Here is the master key—Heaven's gate must open to this. *"God* is not a man that He should lie"* [Numbers 23:19]; His covenant He will not break, nor alter the thing that has gone forth out of His lips. What a grand word it is! Reader, do you know how to cry *"Have respect unto the covenant"*?

For the dark places of the Earth are full of the habitations of cruelty. Darkness is the fit hour for beasts of prey, and ignorance the natural dwelling place of cruelty. Has not the Lord declared that the whole Earth shall be filled with His glory? How can this be if He always permits cruelty to riot in dark places? Surely, He must arise, and end the days of wrong, the era of oppression.

Psalm 74:21 *O let not the oppressed return ashamed: let the poor and needy praise thy name.*

EXPOSITION: Verse 21. *O let not the oppressed return ashamed.* Though broken and crushed, they come to you with confidence; allow them to not be disappointed, for then they will be ashamed of their hope.

Let the poor and needy praise thy name. It is not the way of the Lord to allow any of those who trust in Him to be put to shame; for His Word is, *"He shall call upon me, and I will deliver him, and he shall glorify me"* [Psalm 91:15].

Psalm 74:22 *Arise, O God, plead thine own cause: remember how the foolish man reproacheth thee daily.*

EXPOSITION: Verse 22. *Arise, O God, plead thine own cause.* Answer the taunts of the profane by arguments which shall annihilate both the blasphemy and the blasphemer. Long has the fight been trembling in the balance; one glance of His eyes, one word from His lip, and the banners of victory shall be borne on the breeze.

Remember how the foolish man reproacheth thee daily.

The Lord is begged to remember that He is himself reproached and that by a mere man—that man is a fool, and He is also reminded that these foul reproaches are incessant and repeated with every revolving day. It is bravely done when faith can pluck pleas out of the dragon's mouth and out of the blasphemies of fools find arguments with God.

Psalm 74:23 *Forget not the voice of thine enemies: the tumult of those that rise up against thee increaseth continually.*

EXPOSITION: Verse 23. *Forget not the voice of thine enemies.* If the cries of your children are too feeble to be heard, be pleased to note the loud voices of your foes and silence their profanities forever.

The tumult of those that rise up against thee increaseth continually. The ungodly clamor against you and your people, their blasphemies are loud and incessant, they defy you, even you, and because you reply not they laugh you to scorn. May the Church never cease to plead with you until judgment shall be executed, and the Lord avenged upon Antichrist.

Psalm 75
Psalm 75:1–Psalm 75:10

Psalm 75:1 *Unto thee, O God, do we give thanks, unto thee do we give thanks: for that thy name is near thy wondrous works declare.*

EXPOSITION: Verse 1. *Unto thee, O God, do we give thanks.* Not to ourselves, for we were helpless, but to Elohim who heard our cry, and replied to the taunt of our foes. As the smiling flowers gratefully reflect in their lovely colors the various constituents of the solar ray, so should gratitude spring up in our hearts after the smiles of God's providence.

Unto thee do we give thanks. We should praise God again and again. For infinite goodness there should be measureless thanks. Faith promises redoubled praise for greatly needed and signal deliverances.

For that thy name is near thy wondrous works declare. God is at hand to answer and do wonders—we adore the present Deity. Glory be unto the Lord, whose perpetual deeds of grace and majesty are the sure tokens of His being with us always, even unto the ends of the world.

Psalm 75:2 *When I shall receive the congregation I will judge uprightly.*

EXPOSITION: Verse 2. *When I shall receive the congregation I will judge uprightly.* This is generally believed to be the voice of God, who will, when He accepts His people, mount His judgment seat and avenge their cause in righteousness.

> God never is before his time,[147]
> He never is too late.

He determines the period of interposition, and when that arrives swift His blows and sure are His deliverances. Let the appointed assize come, O Jesus, and sit on your throne to judge the world in equity.

Psalm 75:3 *The earth and all the inhabitants thereof are dissolved: I bear up the pillars of it. Selah.*

EXPOSITION: **Verse 3.** *The earth and all the inhabitants thereof are dissolved.* When anarchy is abroad, and tyrants are in power, everything is unloosed, dissolution threatens all things, the solid mountains of government melt as wax; but even then the Lord upholds and sustains the right.

I bear up the pillars of it. Hence, there is no real cause for fear. In the day of the Lord's appearing a general melting will take place, but in that day our covenant God will be the sure support of our confidence.

> How can I sink with such a prop[148]
> As my eternal God,
> Who bears the earth's huge pillars up,
> And spreads the heavens abroad.

Selah. Here may the music pause while the sublime vision passes before our view; a world dissolved and an immutable God uplifting all His people above the terrible commotion.

Psalm 75:4 *I said unto the fools, Deal not foolishly: and to the wicked, Lift not up the horn:*

---

147. from hymn #417 by Thomas T. Lynch in *Psalms and Hymns for Public, Social, and Private Worship* (1858).
148. from the hymn, "How Can I Sink With Such a Prop" by Isaac Watts.

EXPOSITION: Verse 4. *I said unto the fools, Deal not foolishly.* How calm is He, how quiet are His words, yet how divine the rebuke. If the wicked were not insane, they would even now hear in their consciences the still small voice bidding them cease from evil, and forbear their pride.

And to the wicked, Lift not up the horn. He bids the ungodly stay their haughtiness. In dignified majesty He rebukes the inane glories of the wicked, who beyond measure exalt themselves in the day of their fancied power.

Psalm 75:5 *Lift not up your horn on high: speak not with a stiff neck.*

EXPOSITION: Verse 5. *Lift not up your horn on high.* A word from God soon abases the lofty. I pray God that all proud men would obey the word here given them; for, if they do not, He will take effectual means to secure obedience, and then woe will come upon them, such as shall break their horns and roll their glory in the mire forever.

Speak not with a stiff neck. Impudence is madness before God. The outstretched neck of insolent pride is sure to provoke His axe. Silence, you silly boaster! Silence! or God will answer you. Be hushed, you vainglorious prater, or vengeance shall silence you to your eternal confusion.

Psalm 75:6 *For promotion cometh neither from the east, nor from the west, nor from the south.*

EXPOSITION: Verse 6. *For promotion cometh neither from the east, nor from the west, nor from the south.* Though deliverance is hopeless from all points of the compass, yet God can work it for His people; and though judgment comes neither from the rising or the setting of the sun, nor from the wilderness of mountains, yet come it will, for the Lord reigns. The foolish dream that He is not, but He is near even now, and on the way to bring in His hand that cup of spiced wine of vengeance, one draught of which shall stagger all His foes.

Psalm 75:7 *But God is the judge: he putteth down one, and setteth up another.*

EXPOSITION: **Verse 7.** *But God is the judge.* Even now He is actually judging. His seat is not vacant; His authority is not abdicated; the Lord reigns evermore.

He putteth down one, and setteth up another. Empires rise and fall at His bidding. A dungeon here and there a throne, His will assigns. Assyria yields to Babylon, and Babylon to the Medes. Kings are but puppets in His hand; they serve His purpose when they rise and when they fall. A certain author has issued a work called *Historic Ninepins*, (Timbs),[149] a fit name of scorn for all the great ones of the Earth. God only is; all power belongs to Him; all else is shadow, coming and going, unsubstantial, misty, dreamlike.

Psalm 75:8 *For in the hand of the LORD there is a cup, and the wine is red; it is full of mixture; and he poureth out of the same: but the dregs thereof, all the wicked of the earth shall wring them out, and drink them.*

EXPOSITION: **Verse 8.** *For in the hand of the Lord there is a cup.* The punishment of the wicked is prepared, God himself holds it in readiness; He has collected and concocted woes most dread, and in the chalice of His wrath He holds it. They who scoffed at His feast of love; shall be dragged to His table of justice, and made to drink their due deserts.

---

149. John Timbs (1801–1875) an English author and antiquarian

And the wine is red. The retribution is terrible, it is blood for blood, foaming vengeance for foaming malice. The very color of divine wrath is terrible; what must the taste be? *It is full of mixture.* Spices of anger, justice, and incensed mercy are there. Their misdeeds, their blasphemies, their persecutions have strengthened the liquor as with potent drugs;

> Mingled, strong, and mantling high;[150]
> Behold the wrath divine.

Ten thousand woes are burning in the depths of that fiery cup, which to the brim is filled with indignation.

And he poureth out of the same. The full cup must be quaffed, the wicked cannot refuse the terrible draught, for God himself pours it out for them and into them. Vain are their cries and entreaties.

But the dregs thereof, all the wicked of the earth shall wring them out, and drink them. Even to the bitter end must wrath proceed. They must drink on and on forever, even to the bottom where lie the lees of deep damnation; these they must suck up, and still must they drain the cup. Oh happy they who drink the cup of godly sorrow, and the cup of salvation: these, though now despised, will then be envied by the very men who trod them underfoot.

Psalm 75:9 *But I will declare for ever; I will sing praises to the God of Jacob.*

EXPOSITION: Verse 9. *But I will declare for ever.* Thus will the saints occupy themselves with rehearsing Jehovah's praises, while their foes are drunk with the wine of wrath. They shall chant while the others roar in anguish, and justly so, for the former psalm informed us that such had been the

---

150. from *The Psalter* or *Psalms of David in English Verse,* John Keble, 1839

case on Earth—*"thine enemies roar in the sanctuary,"*—the place where the chosen praised the Lord. [See Psalm 74:4.]

I will sing praises to the God of Jacob. The covenant God, who delivered Jacob from a thousand afflictions, our soul shall magnify. He has kept His covenant which He made with the patriarch, and has redeemed His seed, therefore we will spread abroad His fame world without end.

Psalm 75:10 *All the horns of the wicked also will I cut off; but the horns of the righteous shall be exalted.*

EXPOSITION: Verse 10. *All the horns of the wicked also will I cut off.* Power and liberty being restored to Israel, she begins again to execute justice, by abasing the godless who had gloried in the reign of oppression. Their power and pomp are to be smitten down. Men wore horns in those days as a part of their state, and these, both literally and figuratively, were to be lopped off; for since God abhors the proud, His Church will not tolerate them any longer.

But the horns of the righteous shall be exalted. In a rightly ordered society, good men are counted great men, virtue confers true rank, and grace is more esteemed than gold. Being saved from unrighteous domination, the chief among the chosen people here promises to rectify the errors which had crept into the commonwealth, and after the example of the Lord himself, to abase the haughty and elevate the humble. This memorable ode may be sung in times of great depression, when prayer has performed her errand at the mercy seat, and when faith is watching for speedy deliverance. It is a song of the second advent, concerning the nearness of the Judge with the cup of wrath.

Psalm 76
Psalm 76:1–Psalm 76:12

Psalm 76:1 *In Judah is God known: his name is great in Israel.*

EXPOSITION: Verse 1. *In Judah is God known.* If unknown in all the world beside, He has so revealed himself to His people by His deeds of grace, that He is no unknown God to them.

His name is great in Israel. Although Judah and Israel were unhappily divided politically, yet the godly of both nations were agreed concerning Jehovah their God; and truly whatever schisms may mar the visible church, the saints always "appear as one" in magnifying the Lord their God.

Psalm 76:2 *In Salem also is his tabernacle, and his dwelling place in Zion.*

EXPOSITION: Verse 2. *In Salem also is his tabernacle.* In the peaceful city He dwells, and the peace is perpetuated, because there His sacred tent is pitched. The Church of God is the place where the Lord abides and He is to her the Lord and giver of peace.

And his dwelling place in Zion. Upon the chosen hill was the palace of Israel's Lord. It is the glory of the Church that the Redeemer inhabits her by His Holy Spirit. Immanuel, God with us, finds a home among His people, who then shall work us ill?

Psalm 76:3 *There brake he the arrows of the bow, the shield, and the sword, and the battle. Selah.*

EXPOSITION: Verse 3. *There brake he the arrows of the bow.* Without leaving His tranquil abode, He sent forth His word and snapped the arrows of His enemies before they could shoot them. The idea is sublime, and marks the ease, completeness, and rapidity of the divine action.

The shield, and the sword, and the battle. Death bearing bolts and life preserving armor were alike of no avail when the Breaker sent forth His word of power. In the spiritual conflicts of this and every age, the same will be seen; no weapon that is formed against the Church shall prosper, and every tongue that rises against her in judgment, she shall condemn.

Psalm 76:4 *Thou art more glorious and excellent than the mountains of prey.*

EXPOSITION: Verse 4. *Thou art more glorious and excellent than the mountains of prey.* Far more is Jehovah to be extolled than all the invading powers which sought to oppress His people, though they were for power and greatness comparable to mountains. But the Lord is glorious in holiness, and His terrible deeds are done in justice for the defense of the weak and the deliverance of the enslaved. Mere power may be glorious, but it is not excellent: when we behold the mighty acts of the Lord, we see a perfect blending of the two qualities.

Psalm 76:5 *The stouthearted are spoiled, they have slept their sleep: and none of the men of might have found their hands.*

EXPOSITION: Verse 5. *The stouthearted are spoiled.* They came to spoil, and lo they are spoiled themselves! Their stout hearts are cold in death, the angel of the pestilence has dried up their lifeblood, and their very heart is taken from them. *They have slept their sleep.* Their last sleep—the sleep of death. *And none of the men of might have found their hands.* Their arms are palsied; they cannot lift a finger, for the rigor of death has stiffened them. Thus shall you fight for us, and in the hour of peril overthrow the enemies of your gospel. Therefore in you will we trust and not be afraid.

Psalm 76:6 *At thy rebuke, O God of Jacob, both the chariot and horse are cast into a dead sleep.*

EXPOSITION: Verse 6. *At thy rebuke.* A word accomplished all; there was no need of a single blow.

O God of Jacob. God of your wrestling people, who again like their father supplant their enemy; God of the covenant and the promise, you have in this gracious character fought for your elect nation.

Both the chariot and horse are cast into a dead sleep. They will neither neigh nor rattle again; still are the tramping of the horses and the crash of the cars; the cavalry no more creates its din. Thus can the Lord send a judicial sleep over the enemies of the Church, a premonition of the second death, and this He can do when they are in the zenith of power; and, as they imagine, in the very act of blotting out the remembrance of His people. The world's Rabshakehs[151] can write terrible letters, but the Lord answers not with pen and ink, but with rebukes, which bear death in every syllable.

---

151. Rabshakeh was one of the officers sent by Sennacherib, the king of Assyria, to demand the surrender of Jerusalem, which was under siege by the Assyrian army.

Psalm 76:7 *Thou, even thou, art to be feared: and who may stand in thy sight when once thou art angry?*

EXPOSITION: Verse 7. *Thou, even thou, art to be feared.* Not Sennacherib, nor Nisroch his god, but Jehovah alone, who with a silent rebuke had withered all the monarch's host.

> Fear him, ye saints, and then ye shall
> Have nothing else to fear.[152]

The fear of man is a snare, but the fear of God is a great virtue, and has great power for good over the human mind. God is to be feared profoundly, continually, and alone. Let all worship be to Him only.

And who may stand in thy sight when once thou art angry? Who indeed? The angels fell when their rebellion provoked His justice; Adam lost his place in Paradise in the same manner; Pharaoh and other proud monarchs passed away at His frown. How blest are they who are sheltered in the atonement of Jesus, and hence have no cause to fear the righteous anger of the Judge of all the Earth.

Psalm 76:8 *Thou didst cause judgment to be heard from heaven; the earth feared, and was still,*

EXPOSITION: Verse 8. *Thou didst cause judgment to be heard from heaven.* So complete an overthrow was evidently a judgment from Heaven; those who saw it not, yet heard the report of it, and said, "This is the finger of God."

The earth feared and was still. All nations trembled at the tidings, and sat in humbled awe. How readily can Jehovah command an audience! It may be that in the latter days He will, by some such miracles of power in the realms

---

152. from the hymn, "Through All the Changing Scenes of Life," by Nahum Tate and Nicholas Bradley (1698)

of grace, constrain all Earth's inhabitants to attend to the gospel, and submit to the reign of His all glorious Son. So be it, good Lord.

Psalm 76:9 *When God arose to judgment, to save all the meek of the earth. Selah.*

EXPOSITION: Verse 9. *When God arose to judgment.* Men were hushed when He ascended the judgment seat and actively carried out the decrees of justice. When God is still the people are in tumult; when He arises they are still as a stone.

To save all the meek of the earth. "Blessed are the meek: for they shall inherit the earth" [Matthew 5:5]. They have little enough of it now, but their avenger is strong and He will surely save them. He who saves His people is the same God who overthrows their enemies; He is as omnipotent to save as to destroy. Glory be unto His name.

Psalm 76:10 *Surely the wrath of man shall praise thee: the remainder of wrath shalt thou restrain.*

EXPOSITION: Verse 10. *Surely the wrath of man shall praise thee.* It shall not only be overcome but rendered subservient to thy glory. Man with his breath of threatening is but blowing the trumpet of the Lord's eternal fame. Furious winds often drive vessels the more swiftly into port. The devil blows the fire and melts the iron, and then the Lord fashions it for His own purposes. Let men and devils rage as they may, they cannot do otherwise than subserve the divine purposes.

The remainder of wrath shalt thou restrain. Malice is tethered and cannot break its bounds. The verse clearly teaches that even the most rampant evil is under the control of the Lord, and will in the end be overruled for His praise.

Psalm 76:11 *Vow, and pay unto the* LORD *your God: let all that be round about him bring presents unto him that ought to be feared.*

EXPOSITION: Verse 11. *Vow, and pay unto the Lord your God.* To vow or not is a matter of choice, but to discharge our vows is our mandatory duty. He who would defraud God, his own God, is a wretch indeed. He keeps his promises; let not His people fail in theirs. He is their faithful God and deserves to have a faithful people.

Let all that be round about him bring presents unto him that ought to be feared. Let surrounding nations submit to the only living God, let His own people with alacrity present their offerings, and let His priests and Levites be leaders in the sacred sacrifice.

Psalm 76:12 *He shall cut off the spirit of princes: he is terrible to the kings of the earth.*

EXPOSITION: Verse 12. *He shall cut off the spirit of princes.* Their courage, skill, and life are in His hands, and He can remove them as a gardener cuts off a slip from a plant. None are great in His hand. Caesars and Napoleons fall under His power as the boughs of the tree beneath the woodman's axe.

He is terrible to the kings of the earth. While they are terrible to others, He is terrible to them. If they oppose themselves to His people, He will make short work of them; they shall perish before the terror of His arm, *"for the Lord is a man of war: the Lord is his name"* [Exodus 15:3]. Rejoice before Him all you who adore the God of Jacob.

Psalm 77

Psalm 77:1–Psalm 77:20

Psalm 77:1 *I cried unto God with my voice, even unto God with my voice; and he gave ear unto me.*

EXPOSITION: Verse 1. *I cried unto God with my voice.* This psalm has much sadness in it, but we may be sure it will end well, for it begins with prayer, and prayer never has an ill issue. Sometimes the soul feels compelled to use the voice, for thus it finds a freer vent for its agony. It is a comfort to hear the alarm bell ringing when the house is invaded by thieves.

Even unto God with my voice. If once sufficed not, he cried again. He needed an answer, he expected one, he was eager to have it soon, therefore he cried again and again, and with his voice too, for the sound helped his earnestness.

And he gave ear unto me. Importunity prevailed. The gate opened to the steady knock. It shall be so with us in our hour of trial, the God of grace will hear us in due season.

Psalm 77:2 *In the day of my trouble I sought the Lord: my sore ran in the night, and ceased not: my soul refused to be comforted.*

EXPOSITION: Verse 2. *In the day of my trouble I sought the Lord.* All day long his distress drove him to his God, so that when night came he continued still in the same search. God had hidden His face from His servant; therefore the first care of the troubled saint was to seek his Lord again.

This was going to the root of the matter and removing the main impediment first. Diseases and tribulations are easily enough endured when God is found of us, but without Him they crush us to the ground.

My sore ran in the night, and ceased not. As by day so by night his trouble was on him and his prayer continued.

My soul refused to be comforted. As a sick man turns away even from the most nourishing food, so did he. It is impossible to comfort those who refuse to be comforted. You may bring them to the waters of the promise, but who shall make them drink if they will not do so

Psalm 77:3 *I remembered God, and was troubled: I complained, and my spirit was overwhelmed. Selah.*

EXPOSITION: Verse 3. *I remembered God, and was troubled.* He who is the wellspring of delight to faith becomes an object of dread to the psalmist's distracted heart. He is wretched indeed whose memories of the Ever-Blessed prove distressing to him; yet the best of men know the depth of this abyss.

I complained, and my spirit was overwhelmed. His inward disquietudes did not fall asleep as soon as they were expressed, but rather they returned upon him, and leaped over him like raging billows of an angry sea. It was not his body alone which smarted, but his noblest nature writhed in pain; his life itself seemed crushed into the ground. It is in such a case that death is coveted as a relief, for life becomes an intolerable burden. With no spirit left in us to sustain our infirmity, our case becomes forlorn; like man in a tangle of briars who is stripped of his clothes, every hook of the thorns becomes a lancet, and we bleed with ten thousand wounds. Alas, my God, the writer of this exposition well knows what your servant Asaph meant, for his soul is familiar with the way of grief. Deep glens and lonely caves of soul depressions, my spirit knows full well your awful glooms!

Selah. Let the song go softly; this is no merry dance for the swift feet of the daughters of music, pause awhile, and let sorrow take breath between her sighs.

Psalm 77:4 *Thou holdest mine eyes waking: I am so troubled that I cannot speak.*

EXPOSITION: Verse 4. *Thou holdest mine eyes waking.* Sleep is a great comforter, but it forsakes the sorrowful, and then their sorrow deepens and eats into the soul. If God holds the eyes waking, what anodyne shall give us rest? How much we owe to Him who gives His beloved sleep!

I am so troubled that I cannot speak. Words fail the man whose heart fails him. He had cried to God but he could not speak to man, what a mercy it is that if we can do the first, we need not despair though the second should be quite out of our power. Sleepless and speechless Asaph was reduced to great extremities, and yet he rallied, and even so shall we.

Psalm 77:5 *I have considered the days of old, the years of ancient times.*

EXPOSITION: Verse 5. *I have considered the days of old, the years of ancient times.* If no good was in the present, memory then ransacked the past to find consolation. It is our duty to search for comfort, in quiet contemplation topics may occur to us which will prove to be the means of raising our spirits. There is scarcely any theme more likely to prove consolatory than that which deals with the years of the old. Yet it seems that even this consideration created depression rather than delight in the good man's soul, for he contrasted his own mournful condition with all that was bright in the venerable experiences of ancient saints, and complained. Sad calamity of a jaundiced mind, to see through a veiled mist.

> **Psalm 77:6** *I call to remembrance my song in the night: I commune with mine own heart: and my spirit made diligent search.*

EXPOSITION: Verse 6. *I call to remembrance my song in the night.* At other times his spirit had a song for the darkest hour, but now he could only recall the strain as a departed memory. Where is the harp which once thrilled sympathetically to the touch of those joyful fingers? My tongue, have you forgotten to praise? Have you no skill except in mournful ditties? Ah me, how sadly fallen am I! How lamentable that I, who like the nightingale could charm the night, am now fit comrade for the hooting owl.

I commune with mine own heart. He did not cease from introspection, for he was resolved to find the bottom of his sorrow, and trace it to its fountainhead. He made sure work of it by talking not with his mind only, but with his inmost heart; it was heart work with him. He was no idler, no melancholy trifler; he was up and at it, resolutely resolved that he would not tamely die of despair, but would fight for his hope to the last moment of life.

And my spirit made diligent search. He ransacked his experience, his memory, his intellect, his whole nature, his entire self, either to find comfort or to discover the reason why it was denied him. That man will not die by the hand of the enemy who has enough force of soul remaining to struggle in this fashion.

> **Psalm 77:7** *Will the Lord cast off for ever? and will he be favourable no more?*

EXPOSITION: Verse 7. *Wilt the Lord cast off forever?* This was one of the matters he enquired into. He painfully knew that the Lord might leave His people for a season, but his fear was that the time might be prolonged and have no close; eagerly, therefore, he asked, will the Lord utterly and finally reject those who are His own, and suffer them to be the objects of His contemptuous reprobation, His everlasting castoffs? This he was persuaded could not be. No instance in the years of ancient times led him to fear that such could be the case.

And will he be favourable no more? Would He be favorable again? Would spring never follow the long and dreary winter? The questions are suggested by fear, but they are also the cure for fear. It is a blessed thing to have grace enough to look such questions in the face, for their answer is self-evident and eminently fitted to cheer the heart.

Psalm 77:8 *Is his mercy clean gone for ever? doth his promise fail for evermore?*

EXPOSITION: Verse 8. *Is his mercy clean gone for ever?* If He has no love for His elect, has He not still His mercy left? Has that dried up? Has He no pity for the sorrowful?

Doth his promise fail for evermore? His word is pledged to those who plead with Him; is that become of none effect? Shall it be said that from one generation to another the Lord's word has fallen to the ground; whereas in the past He kept His covenant to all generations of them that fear Him? It is a wise thing thus to put unbelief through the catechism. Each one of the questions is a dart aimed at the very heart of despair. Thus have we also in our days of darkness done battle for life itself.

Psalm 77:9 *Hath God forgotten to be gracious? hath he in anger shut up his tender mercies? Selah.*

EXPOSITION: **Verse 9.** *Hath God forgotten to be gracious?* Has El, the Mighty One, become great in everything but grace? Does He know how to afflict, but not how to uphold? Can He forget anything? Above all, can He forget to exercise that attribute which lies nearest to His essence, for He is love?

Hath he in anger shut up his tender mercies? Are the pipes of goodness choked up so that love can no more flow through them? Do the bowels of Jehovah no longer yearn towards His own beloved children? Thus with cord after cord unbelief is smitten and driven out of the soul; it raises questions and we will meet it with questions: it makes us think and act ridiculously, and we will heap scorn upon it. The argument of this passage assumes very much the form of a *reductio ad absurdam*.[153] Strip it naked, and mistrust is a monstrous piece of folly.

Selah. Here rest awhile, for the battle of questions needs a lull.

Psalm 77:10 *And I said, This is my infirmity: but I will remember the years of the right hand of the most High.*

EXPOSITION: **Verse 10.** *And I said, This is my infirmity.* He has won the day, he talks reasonably now, and surveys the field with a cooler mind. He confesses that unbelief is an infirmity, a weakness, a folly, a sin. He may also be understood to mean, "this is my appointed sorrow," I will bear it without complaint. When we perceive that our affliction is meted out by the Lord, and is the ordained portion of our cup, we become reconciled to it, and no longer rebel against the inevitable. Why should we not be content if it be the

---

153. carrying something to an absurd extreme

Lord's will? What He arranges it is not for us to cavil at. *But I will remember the years of the right hand of the most High.* Here a good deal is supplied by our translators, and they make the sense to be that the psalmist would console himself by remembering the goodness of God to himself and others of his people in times gone by: but the original seems to consist only of the words, "the years of the right hand of the most High," and to express the idea that his long continued affliction, reaching through several years, was allotted to him by the Sovereign Lord of all. It is well when a consideration of the divine goodness and greatness silences all complaining, and creates a childlike acquiescence.

Psalm 77:11 *I will remember the works of the LORD: surely I will remember thy wonders of old.*

EXPOSITION: Verse 11. *I will remember the works of the Lord.* Fly back my soul, away from present turmoil, to the grandeurs of history, the sublime deeds of Jehovah, the Lord of Hosts; for He is the same and is ready even now to defend His servants as in days of old.

Surely I will remember thy wonders of old. Whatever else may glide into oblivion, the marvelous works of the Lord in the ancient days must not be suffered to be forgotten. Memory is a fit handmaid for faith. When faith has its seven years of famine, memory like Joseph in Egypt opens her granaries.

Psalm 77:12 *I will meditate also of all thy work, and talk of thy doings.*

EXPOSITION: Verse 12. *I will meditate also of all thy work.* Sweet work to enter into Jehovah's work of grace, and there to lie down and ruminate, every thought being absorbed in the one precious subject.

And talk of thy doings. It is good that the overflow of the mouth should indicate the good matter which fills the heart. Meditation makes rich talking; it is to be lamented that so much of the conversation of professors is utterly barren, because they take no time for contemplation. A meditative man should be a talker; otherwise he is a mental miser, a mill which grinds corn only for the miller. The subject of our meditation should be choice, and then our task will be edifying; if we meditate on folly and affect to speak wisdom, our double-mindedness will soon be known unto all men. Holy talk following upon meditation has a consoling power in it for ourselves as well as for those who listen, hence its value in the connection in which we find it in this passage.

Psalm 77:13 *Thy way, O God, is in the sanctuary: who is so great a God as our God?*

EXPOSITION: Verse 13. *Thy way, O God, is in the sanctuary,* or in holiness. In the holy place we understand our God, and rest assured that all His ways are just and right. When we cannot trace His way, because it is "in the sea," it is a rich consolation that we can trust it, for it is in holiness. We must have fellowship with holiness if we would understand "the ways of God to man." He who would be wise must worship. The pure in heart shall see God, and pure worship is the way to the philosophy of providence.

Who is so great a God as our God? In Him the good and the great are blended. He surpasses in both. None can for a moment be compared with the mighty One of Israel.

Psalm 77:14 *Thou art the God that doest wonders: thou hast declared thy strength among the people.*

EXPOSITION: **Verse 14.** *Thou art the God that doest wonders.* He alone is Almighty. The false gods are surrounded with the pretence of wonders, but He really works them. It is His peculiar prerogative to work marvels; it is no new or strange thing with Him, it is according to His wont and use. Herein is renewed reason for holy confidence. It would be a great wonder if we did not trust the wonder-working God.

Thou hast declared thy strength among the people. Not only Israel, but Egypt, Bashan, Edom, Philistia, and all the nations have seen Jehovah's power. It was no secret in the olden time and to this day it is published abroad. God's providence and grace are both full of displays of His power; He is in the latter peculiarly conspicuous as "mighty to save." Who will not be strong in faith when there is so strong an arm to lean upon? Shall our trust be doubtful when His power is beyond all question? My soul, see to it that these considerations banish your mistrusts.

Psalm 77:15 *Thou hast with thine arm redeemed thy people, the sons of Jacob and Joseph. Selah.*

EXPOSITION: **Verse 15.** *Thou hast with thine arm redeemed thy people, the sons of Jacob and Joseph.* All Israel, the two tribes of Joseph as well as those which sprang from the other sons of Jacob, were brought out of Egypt by a display of divine power, which is here ascribed not to the hand but to the arm of the Lord, because it was the fullness of His might. Ancient believers were in the constant habit of referring to the wonders of the Red Sea, and we also can unite with them, taking care to add the song of the Lamb to that of Moses, the servant of God. The comfort derivable from such a meditation is obvious and abundant, for He who brought up His people from the house of bondage will continue to redeem and deliver until we come into the promised rest.

Selah. Here we have another pause preparatory to a final burst of song.

Psalm 77:16 *The waters saw thee, O God, the waters saw thee; they were afraid: the depths also were troubled.*

EXPOSITION: **Verse 16.** *The waters saw thee, O God, the waters saw thee; they were afraid.* As if conscious of its Maker's presence, the sea was ready to flee from before His face. The conception is highly poetical; the psalmist has the scene before his mind's eye, and describes it gloriously. The water saw its God, but man refuses to discern Him; it was afraid, but proud sinners are rebellious and fear not the Lord.

The depths also were troubled. To their heart the floods were made afraid. Quiet caves of the sea, far down in the abyss, were moved with fear; and the lowest channels were left bare, as the water rushed away from its place, in terror of the God of Israel.

Psalm 77:17 *The clouds poured out water: the skies sent out a sound: thine arrows also went abroad.*

EXPOSITION: **Verse 17.** *The clouds poured out water.* Obedient to the Lord, the lower region of the atmosphere yielded its aid to overthrow the Egyptian host. The cloudy chariots of Heaven hurried forward to discharge their floods.

The skies sent out a sound. From the loftier aerial regions thundered the dread artillery of the Lord of Hosts. Peal on peal the skies sounded over the heads of the routed enemies, confusing their minds and adding to their horror.

Thine arrows also went abroad. Lightning flew like bolts from the bow of God. Swiftly, hither and thither, went the red tongues of flame, on helm and shield they gleamed; now with blue bale fires revealing the innermost caverns of the hungry sea which waited to swallow up the pride of Mizraim.[154] Behold, how all the creatures wait upon their God, and show themselves strong to overthrow His enemies.

Psalm 77:18 *The voice of thy thunder was in the heaven: the lightnings lightened the world: the earth trembled and shook.*

EXPOSITION: Verse 18. *The voice of thy thunder was in the heaven,* or in the whirlwind. Rushing on with terrific swiftness and bearing all before it, the storm was as a chariot driven furiously, and a voice was heard (even thy voice, O Lord!) out of the fiery car, even as when a mighty man in battle urges forward his charger, and shouts to it aloud. All Heaven resounded with the Voice of the Lord.

The lightnings lightened the world. The entire globe shone in the blaze of Jehovah's lightning. No need for other light amid the battle of that terrible night, every wave gleamed in the fire flashes, and the shore was lit up with the blaze. How pale were men's faces in that hour, when all around the fire leaped from sea to shore, from crag to hill, from mountain to star, till the whole universe was illuminated in honor of Jehovah's triumph.

The earth trembled and shook. It quaked and quaked again. Sympathetic with the sea, the solid shore forgot its quiescence and heaved in dread. How dreadful are you, O God, when you come forth in your majesty to humble your arrogant adversaries.

---

154. referring to the land of Egypt

Psalm 77:19 *Thy way is in the sea, and thy path in the great waters, and thy footsteps are not known.*

EXPOSITION: **Verse 19.** *Thy way is in the sea.* Far down in secret channels of the deep is your roadway; when you will you can make a sea a highway for your glorious march.

And thy path in the great waters. There, where the billows surge and swell, you still walk; Lord of each crested wave.

And thy footsteps are not known. None can follow your tracks by foot or eye. You are alone in your glory, and your ways are hidden from mortal ken. Your purposes you will accomplish, but the means are often concealed, yea, they need no concealing, for they are in themselves too vast and mysterious for human understanding. Glory be to you, O Jehovah.

Psalm 77:20 *Thou leddest thy people like a flock by the hand of Moses and Aaron.*

EXPOSITION: **Verse 20.** *Thou leddest thy people like a flock by the hand of Moses and Aaron.* What a transition from tempest to peace, from wrath to love. Quietly as a flock Israel was guided on, by human agency which veiled the excessive glory of the divine presence. The smiter of Egypt was the Shepherd of Israel. He drove His foes before Him, but went before His people. Heaven and Earth fought on His side against the sons of Ham, but they were equally subservient to the interests of the sons of Jacob. Therefore, with devout joy and full of consolation, we close this psalm; the song of one who forgot how to speak and yet learned to sing far more sweetly than his fellows.

Psalm 78
Psalm 78:1–Psalm 78:72

Psalm 78:1 *Give ear, O my people, to my law: incline your ears to the words of my mouth.*

EXPOSITION: Verse 1. *Give ear, O my people, to my law.* The inspired bard calls on his countrymen to give heed to his patriotic teaching. We naturally expect God's chosen nation to be first in hearkening to His voice. When God gives His truth a tongue, and sends forth His messengers trained to declare His word with power, it is the least we can do to give them our ears and the earnest obedience of our hearts. Shall God speak, and His children refuse to hear? His teaching has the force of law; let us yield both ear *and heart to it.*

Incline your ears to the words of my mouth. Give earnest attention; bow your stiff necks, lean forward to catch every syllable. We are at this day, as readers of the sacred records, bound to study them deeply, exploring their meaning, and laboring to practice their teaching. As the officer of an army commences his drill by calling for "Attention," even so every trained soldier of Christ is called upon to give ear to His words. Men lend their ears to music, how much more then should they listen to the harmonies of the gospel; they sit enthralled in the presence of an orator, how much rather should they yield to the eloquence of Heaven.

Psalm 78:2 *I will open my mouth in a parable: I will utter dark sayings of old:*

EXPOSITION: Verse 2. *I will open my mouth in a parable.* Analogies are not only to be imagined, but are intended by God to be traced between the story of Israel and the lives of believers. Israel was ordained to be a type; the tribes and their marching are living allegories traced by the hand of an all wise providence. Unspiritual persons may sneer about fancies and mysticisms, but Paul spake well when he said in Galatians 4:24 *"which things are an allegory,"* and Asaph in the present case spoke to the point when he called his narrative "a parable." That such was his meaning is clear from the quotation,

> All these things spake Jesus unto the multitude in parables; and without a parable spake he not unto them: that it might be fulfilled which was spoken by the prophet, saying, I will open my mouth in parables; I will utter things which have been kept secret from the foundation of the world. (Matthew 13:34–35)

I will utter dark sayings of old; enigmas of antiquity, riddles of long ago. The mind of the poet prophet was so full of ancient lore that he poured it forth in a copious stream of song, while beneath the gushing flood lay pearls and gems of spiritual truth, capable of enriching those who could dive into the depths and bring them up. The letter of this song is precious, but the inner sense is beyond all price. Whereas the first verse called for attention, the second justifies the demand by hinting that the outer sense conceals an inner and hidden meaning, which only the thoughtful will be able to perceive.

Psalm 78:3 *Which we have heard and known, and our fathers have told us.*

EXPOSITION: Verse 3. *Which we have heard and known, and our fathers have told us.* Tradition was of the utmost service to the people of God in the olden time, before the more sure word of prophecy had become complete and generally accessible. The receipt of truth from the lips of others laid the instructed believer under solemn obligation to pass on the truth to the next generation. Truth, endeared to us by its fond associations with godly parents and venerable friends, deserves of us our best exertions to preserve and propagate it. Our fathers told us, we hear them, and we know personally what they taught; it remains for us in our turn to hand it on. Blessed be God we have now the less mutable testimony of written revelation, but this by no means lessens our obligation to instruct our children in divine truth by word of mouth: rather, with such a gracious help, we ought to teach them far more fully the things of God. Dr. Doddridge[155] owed much to the Dutch tiles and his mother's explanations of the Bible narratives. The more of parental teaching the better; ministers and Sabbath school teachers were never meant to be substitutes for mother's tears and father's prayers.

> **Psalm 78:4** *We will not hide them from their children, shewing to the generation to come the praises of the* LORD, *and his strength, and his wonderful works that he hath done.*

EXPOSITION: Verse 4. *We will not hide them from their children.* Our negligent silence shall not deprive our own and our father's offspring of the precious truth of God,

---

155. Philip Doddridge (1702–1751) was an English Non-conformist leader, educator and hymn-writer. When he was too young to read, his mother taught him Bible stories using the pictures on the Dutch chimney-tiles.

it would be shameful indeed if we did so.

Shewing to the generation to come the praises of the Lord. We will look forward to future generations, and endeavor to provide for their godly education. It is the duty of the Church of God to maintain, in fullest vigor, every agency intended for the religious education of the young; to them we must look for the Church of the future, and as we sow towards them so shall we reap. Children are to be taught to magnify the Lord; they ought to be well informed as to His wonderful doings in ages past, and should be made to know *his strength, and his wonderful works that he hath done.*

The best education is education in the best things. The first lesson for a child should be concerning his mother's God. Teach him what you will; if he learns not the fear of the Lord, he will perish for lack of knowledge. Grammar is poor food for the soul if it is not flavored with grace. Every satchel should have a Bible in it. The world may teach secular knowledge alone, it is all she has a heart to know, but the Church must not deal so with her offspring; she should look well to every Timothy, and see to it that from a child he knows the Holy Scriptures. Around the fireside fathers should repeat not only the Bible records, but the deeds of the martyrs and reformers, and moreover the dealings of the Lord with themselves both in providence and grace. We dare not follow the vain and vicious traditions of the apostate church of Rome, neither would we compare the fallible record of the best human memories with the infallible written Word. Yet would we gladly see oral tradition practiced by every Christian in his family, and children taught cheerfully by word of mouth by their own mothers and fathers, as well as by the printed pages of what they too often regard as dull, dry task books. What happy hours and pleasant evenings have children had at their parents' knees as they have listened to some "sweet story of old." Reader, if you have children, do not fail in this duty.

Psalm 78:5 *For he established a testimony in Jacob, and appointed a law in Israel, which he commanded our fathers, that they should make them known to their children:*

EXPOSITION: Verse 5. *For he established a testimony in Jacob.* The favored nation existed for the very purpose of maintaining God's truth in the midst of surrounding idolatry. Theirs were the oracles; they were the conservators and guardians of the truth.

And appointed a law in Israel, which he commanded our fathers, that they should make them known to their children. The testimony for the true God was to be transmitted from generation to generation by the careful instruction of succeeding families. We have the command for this oral transmission very frequently given in the Pentateuch, and it may suffice to quote one instance from Deuteronomy 6:7: "*And thou shalt teach them diligently unto thy children, and shalt talk of them when thou sittest in thine house, and when thou walkest by the way, and when thou liest down, and when thou risest up.*" Reader, if you are a parent, have you conscientiously discharged this duty?

Psalm 78:6 *That the generation to come might know them, even the children which should be born; who should arise and declare them to their children:*

EXPOSITION: Verse 6. *That the generation to come might know them, even the children which should be born.* As far on as our brief life allows us to arrange, we must industriously provide for the godly nurture of youth. The narratives, commands, and doctrines of the Word of God are not worn out; they are calculated to exert an influence as long as our race shall exist.

Who should arise and declare them to their children. The one object aimed at is transmission; the testimony is only given that it may be passed on to succeeding generations.

Psalm 78:7 *That they might set their hope in God, and not forget the works of God, but keep his commandments:*

EXPOSITION: **Verse 7.** *That they might set their hope in God.* Faith comes by hearing. Those who know the name of the Lord will set their hope in Him, and that they may be led to do so is the main end of all spiritual teaching.

And not forget the works of God. Grace cures bad memories; those who soon forget the merciful works of the Lord have need of teaching; they need to learn the divine art of holy memory.

But keep his commandments. Those who forget God's works are sure to fail in their own. He who does not keep God's love in memory is not likely to remember His law. The design of teaching is practical; holiness towards God is the end we aim at, and not the filling of the head with speculative notions.

Psalm 78:8 *And might not be as their fathers, a stubborn and rebellious generation; a generation that set not their heart aright, and whose spirit was not stedfast with God.*

EXPOSITION: **Verse 8.** *And might not be as their fathers, a stubborn and rebellious generation.* There was room for improvement. Fathers stubborn in their own way, and rebellious against God's way, are sorry examples for their children; and it is earnestly desired that better instruction may bring forth a better race. It is common in some regions for men to count their family custom as the very best rule; but disobedience is not to be excused because it is hereditary. The leprosy was none the less loathsome because it had been long in the family. If our fathers were rebellious we must be better than they were, or else we shall perish as they did.

A generation that set not their heart aright. They had no decision for righteousness and truth. In them there was no preparedness, or willingness of heart, to entertain the Savior; neither judgments, nor mercies could bind their affections to their God; they were fickle as the winds, and changeful as the waves.

And whose spirit was not stedfast with God. The tribes in the wilderness were constant only in their inconstancy; there was no depending upon them. It was, indeed, needful that their descendants should be warned, so that they might not blindly imitate them. How blessed it would be if each age improved upon its predecessor; but, it is to be feared that decline is more general than progress, and too often the heirs of true saints are far more rebellious than even their fathers were in their unregeneracy. May the reading of this patriotic and divine song move many to labor after the elevation of themselves and their posterity.

Psalm 78:9 *The children of Ephraim, being armed, and carrying bows, turned back in the day of battle.*

EXPOSITION: Verse 9. *The children of Ephraim, being armed, and carrying bows, turned back in the day of battle.* Well-equipped and furnished with the best weapons of the times, the leading tribe failed in faith and courage and retreated before the foe. There were several particular instances of this, but probably the psalmist refers to the general failure of Ephraim to lead the tribes to the conquest of Canaan. How often have we also, although supplied with every gracious weapon, failed to wage successful war against our sins, we have marched onward gallantly enough until the testing hour has come, and then "in the day of battle "we have proved false to good resolutions and holy obligations. How altogether vain is unregenerate man! Array him in the best that nature and grace can supply, he still remains a helpless coward in the holy war, so long as he lacks a loyal faith in his God.

Psalm 78:10 *They kept not the covenant of God, and refused to walk in his law;*

EXPOSITION: **Verse 10.** *They kept not the covenant of God.* Vows and promises were broken, idols were set up, and the living God was forsaken. They were brought out of Egypt in order to be a people separated unto the Lord, but they fell into the sins of other nations, and did not maintain a pure testimony for the one only true God.

And refused to walk in his law. They gave way to fornication, and idolatry, and other violations of the Decalogue,[156] and were often in a state of rebellion against the benign theocracy under which they lived. They had pledged themselves at Sinai to keep the law, and then they willfully disobeyed it, and so became covenant breakers.

Psalm 78:11 *And forgat his works, and his wonders that he had shewed them.*

EXPOSITION: **Verse 11.** *And forgat his works, and his wonders that he had shewed them.* Had they remembered them they would have been filled with gratitude and inspired with holy awe: but the memory of God's mercies to them was as soon effaced as if written upon water. Scarcely could

---

156. the Ten Commandments

one generation retain the sense of the divine presence in miraculous power, the succeeding race needed a renewal of the extraordinary manifestations, and even then was not satisfied without many displays thereof. Ere we condemn them, let us repent of our own wicked forgetfulness, and confess the many occasions upon which we also have been unmindful of past favors.

Psalm 78:12 *Marvellous things did he in the sight of their fathers, in the land of Egypt, in the field of Zoan.*

EXPOSITION: Verse 12. *Marvellous things did he in the sight of their fathers, in the land of Egypt, in the field of Zoan.* Egypt, here called the field of Zoan, was the scene of marvelous things which were done in open day in the sight of Israel. These were extraordinary, upon a vast scale, astounding, indisputable, and such as ought to have rendered it impossible for an Israelite to be disloyal to Jehovah, Israel's God.

Psalm 78:13 *He divided the sea, and caused them to pass through; and he made the waters to stand as an heap.*

EXPOSITION: Verse 13. *He divided the sea, and caused them to pass through.* A double wonder, for when the waters were divided the bottom of the sea would naturally be in a very unfit state for the passage of so vast a host as that of Israel; it would in fact have been impassable, had not the Lord made the road for His people. Who else has ever led a nation through a sea? Yet the Lord has done this full often for His saints in providential deliverances, making a highway for them where nothing short of an almighty arm could have done so.

And he made the waters to stand as an heap. He forbade a drop to fall upon His chosen; they felt no spray from the crystal walls on either hand. Fire will descend and water stands upright at the bidding of the Lord of all. The nature of creatures is not their own intrinsically, but is retained or altered at the will of Him who first created them. The Lord can cause those evils which threaten to overwhelm us to suspend their ordinary actions, and become innocuous to us.

Psalm 78:14 *In the daytime also he led them with a cloud, and all the night with a light of fire.*

EXPOSITION: Verse 14. *In the daytime also he led them with a cloud.* He did it all. He alone. He brought them into the wilderness, and He led them through it; it is not the Lord's manner to begin a work, and then cease from it while it is incomplete. The cloud both led and shadowed the tribes. It was by day a vast sun-screen, rendering the fierce heat of the sun and the glare of the desert sand bearable.

And all the night with a light of fire. So constant was the care of the Great Shepherd that all night and every night the token of His presence was with His people. That cloud which was a shade by day was as a sun by night. Even thus the grace which cools and calms our joys soothes and solaces our sorrows. What a mercy to have a light of fire with us amid the lonely horrors of the wilderness of affliction. Our God has been all this to us, and shall we prove unfaithful to Him? We have felt Him to be both shade and light, according as our changing circumstances have required.

Psalm 78:15 *He clave the rocks in the wilderness, and gave them drink as out of the great depths.*

EXPOSITION: **Verse 15.** *He clave the rocks in the wilderness.* Moses was the instrument, but the Lord did it all. Twice He made the flint a gushing rill. What can He not do?

And gave them drink as out of the great depths—as though it gushed from Earth's innermost reservoirs. The streams were so fresh, so copious, so constant, that they seemed to well up from the Earth's primeval fountains, and to leap at once from *"the deep which coucheth beneath"* [Deuteronomy 33:13]. Here was a divine supply for Israel's urgent need, and such a one as ought to have held them forever in unwavering fidelity to their wonderworking God.

Psalm 78:16 *He brought streams also out of the rock, and caused waters to run down like rivers.*

EXPOSITION: **Verse 16.** *He brought streams also out of the rock, and caused waters to run down like rivers.* The supply of water was as plenteous in quantity as it was miraculous in origin. Torrents, not driblets, came from the rocks. Streams followed the camp; the supply was not for an hour or a day. This was a marvel of goodness. If we contemplate the abounding of divine grace, we shall be lost in admiration. Mighty rivers of love have flowed for us in the wilderness. Alas, great God! Our return has not been commensurate with that, but far otherwise.

Psalm 78:17 *And they sinned yet more against him by provoking the most High in the wilderness.*

EXPOSITION: **Verse 17.** *And they sinned yet more against him.* Outdoing their former sins, going into greater deeps of evil: the more they had the more loudly they clamored for more, and murmured because they had not every luxury that pampered appetites could desire. It was bad enough to mistrust their God for necessaries, but to revolt against Him in a greedy rage for superfluities was far worse. Ever is it the nature of the disease of sin to proceed from bad to worse; men never weary of sinning, but rather increase their speed in the race of iniquity. In the case before us the goodness of God was abused into a reason for greater sin. Had not the Lord been so good they would not have been so bad. If He had wrought fewer miracles before, they would not have been so inexcusable in their unbelief, so wanton in their idolatry.

By provoking the most High in the wilderness. Although they were in a position of obvious dependence upon God for everything, being in a desert where the soil could yield them no support, yet they were graceless enough to provoke their benefactor. At one time they provoked His jealousy by their hankering after false gods, later they excited His wrath by their challenges of His power, their slanders against His love, and their rebellions against His will. He was all bounty of love, and they all superfluity of naughtiness. They were favored above all nations, and yet none were more ill-favored. For them the heavens dropped manna, and they returned murmurs; the rocks gave them rivers, and they replied with floods of wickedness. Herein, as in a mirror, we see ourselves. Israel in the wilderness acted out, as in a drama, all the story of man's conduct toward His God.

Psalm 78:18 *And they tempted God in their heart by asking meat for their lust.*

EXPOSITION: **Verse 18.** *And they tempted God in their heart.* He was not tempted, for He cannot be tempted by any, but they acted in a manner calculated to tempt Him, and it always just to charge that upon men which is the obvious tendency of their conduct. Christ cannot die again, and yet many crucify Him afresh, because such would be the legitimate result of their behavior if its effects were not prevented by other forces. The sinners in the wilderness would have had the Lord change His wise proceedings to humor their whims, hence they are said to tempt Him. *By asking meat for their lust.* Would they have God become purveyor for their greediness? Was there nothing for it but that He must give them whatever their diseased appetites might crave? The sin began in their hearts, but it soon reached their tongues. What they at first silently wished for, they soon loudly demanded with menaces, insinuations, and upbraiding.

Psalm 78:19 *Yea, they spake against God; they said, Can God furnish a table in the wilderness?*

EXPOSITION: Verse 19. From this verse we learn that unbelief of God is a slander against Him. *Yea, they spake against God.* But how? The answer is, *They said, Can God furnish a table in the wilderness?* To question the ability of one, who is manifestly Almighty, is to speak against Him. These people were base enough to say that although their God had given them bread and water, yet He could not properly order or furnish a table. He could give them coarse food, but could not prepare a feast properly arranged, so they were ungrateful enough to declare. As if the manna was a mere makeshift, and the flowing rock stream a temporary expedient, they asked to have a regularly furnished table, such as they had been accustomed to in Egypt. Alas, how have we also quarreled with our mercies, and querulously pined for some imaginary good, counting our actual enjoyments to be nothing because they did not happen to be exactly conformed to our foolish fancies. They who will not be content will speak against providence even when it daily loads them with benefits.

Psalm 78:20 *Behold, he smote the rock, that the waters gushed out, and the streams overflowed; can he give bread also? can he provide flesh for his people?*

EXPOSITION: **Verse 20.** *Behold, he smote the rock, that the waters gushed out, and the streams overflowed.* They admit what He had done, and yet, with superabundant folly and insolence, demand further proofs of His omnipotence.

Can he give bread also? can he provide flesh for his people? As if the manna were nothing, as if animal food alone was true nourishment for men. If they had argued, "can he not give flesh?" the argument would have been reasonable, but they ran into insanity; when, having seen many marvels of omnipotence, they dared to insinuate that other things were beyond the divine power. Yet, in this also, we have imitated their senseless conduct. Each new difficulty has excited fresh incredulity. We are still fools and slow of heart to believe our God, and this is a fault to be bemoaned with deepest penitence. For this cause the Lord is often wroth with us and chastens us sorely; for unbelief has in it a degree of provocation of the highest kind.

Psalm 78:21 *Therefore the* LORD *heard this, and was wroth: so a fire was kindled against Jacob, and anger also came up against Israel;*

EXPOSITION: **Verse 21.** *Therefore the Lord heard this, and was wroth.* He was not indifferent to what they said. He dwelt among them in the holy place, and, therefore, they insulted Him to His face. He did not hear a report of it, but the language itself came into His ears.

So a fire was kindled against Jacob. The fire of His anger which was also attended with literal burnings.

And anger also came up against Israel. Whether He

viewed them in the lower or higher light, as Jacob or as Israel, He was angry with them: even as mere men they ought to have believed Him; and as chosen tribes, their wicked unbelief was without excuse. The Lord does well to be angry at so ungrateful, gratuitous and dastardly an insult as the questioning of His power.

> **Psalm 78:22** *Because they believed not in God, and trusted not in his salvation:*

EXPOSITION: Verse 22. *Because they believed not in God, and trusted not in his salvation.* This is the master sin, the crying sin. Like Jeroboam, the son of Nebat, it sins and makes Israel to sin; it is in itself evil and the parent of evils. It was this sin that shut Israel out of Canaan, and it shuts myriads out of Heaven. God is ready to save, combining power with willingness, but rebellious man will not trust His Savior, and therefore is condemned already. In the text it appears as if all Israel's other sins were as nothing compared with this; this is the peculiar spot which the Lord points at, the special provocation that angered Him. From this let every unbeliever learn to tremble more at his unbelief than at anything else. If he is no fornicator, or thief, or liar, let him reflect that it is quite enough to condemn him if he trusts not in God's salvation.

> **Psalm 78:23** *Though he had commanded the clouds from above, and opened the doors of heaven,*

EXPOSITION: Verse 23. *Though he had commanded the clouds from above.* Such a marvel ought to have rendered unbelief impossible: when clouds become granaries, seeing should be believing, and doubts should dissolve.

And opened the doors of heaven. The great storehouse

doors were set wide open, and the corn of Heaven poured out in heaps. Those who would not believe in such a case were hardened indeed; and yet our own position is very similar, for the Lord has wrought for us great deliverances, quite as memorable and undeniable, and yet suspicions and forebodings haunt us. He might have shut the gates of hell upon us, instead He has opened the doors of Heaven; shall we not both believe in Him and magnify Him for this?

> **Psalm 78:24** *And had rained down manna upon them to eat, and had given them of the corn of heaven.*

EXPOSITION: **Verse 24.** *And had rained down manna upon them to eat.* There was so much of it, the skies poured with food, the clouds burst with provender. It was fit food, proper not for looking at but for eating; they could eat it as they gathered it. Mysterious though it was, so that they called it manna, or "what is it?" yet it was eminently adapted for human nourishment; and it was both abundant and adapted, also it was available! They had not far to fetch it, it was near them, and they had only to gather it up. O Lord Jesus, you blessed manna of Heaven, how all this agrees with you! We will even now feed on you as our spiritual meat, and will pray you to chase away all wicked unbelief from us. Our fathers ate manna and doubted; we feed upon you and are filled with assurance.

And had given them of the corn of heaven. It was all a gift without money and without price. Food which dropped from above, and was of the best quality, so as to be called heavenly corn, was freely granted them. The manna was round, like a coriander seed, and hence was rightly called corn; it did not rise from the ground, but descended from the clouds, and hence the words of the verse are literally accurate.

The point to be noted is that this wonder of wonders left the beholders, and the feasters, as prone as ever to mistrust their Lord.

Psalm 78:25 *Man did eat angels' food: he sent them meat to the full.*

EXPOSITION: Verse 25. *Man did eat angel's food.* The delicacies of kings were outdone, for the dainties of angels were supplied. Bread of the mighty ones fell on feeble man. Those who are lower than the angels fared as well. It was not for the priests, or the princes, that the manna fell; but for all the nation, for every man, woman, and child in the camp: and there was sufficient for them all, for *He sent them meat to the full.* God's banquets are never stinted; He gives the best diet, and plenty of it. Gospel provisions deserve every praise that we can heap upon them; they are free, full, and preeminent; they are of God's preparing, sending, and bestowing. He is well fed whom God feeds; heaven's meat is nourishing and plentiful. If we have ever fed upon Jesus we have tasted better than angel's food; for

> Never did angels taste above[157]
> Redeeming grace and dying love.

It will be our wisdom to eat to the full of it, for God has so sent it that we are not distressed in Him, but in our own bowels. Happy pilgrims who in the desert have their meat sent from the Lord's own palace above; let them eat abundantly of the celestial banquet, and magnify the all sufficient grace which supplies all their needs, *"according to His riches in glory, by Christ Jesus"* [Philippians 4:19].

---

157. from the hymn, "Far from my Thoughts," by Isaac Watts

Psalm 78:26 *He caused an east wind to blow in the heaven: and by his power he brought in the south wind.*

EXPOSITION: Verse 26. *He caused an east wind to blow in the heaven.* He is Lord Paramount, above the prince of the power of the air: storms arise and tempests blow at his command. Winds sleep till God arouses them, and then, like Samuel, each one answers, "Here am I, for thou didst call me."

And by his power he brought in the south wind. Either these winds followed each other, and so blew the birds in the desired direction, or else they combined to form a southeast wind; in either case they fulfilled the design of the Lord, and illustrated His supreme and universal power. If one wind will not serve, another shall; and if need be, they shall both blow at once. We speak of fickle winds, but their obedience to their Lord is such that they deserve a better word. If we ourselves were half as obedient as the winds, we should be far superior to what we are now.

Psalm 78:27 *He rained flesh also upon them as dust, and feathered fowls like as the sand of the sea:*

EXPOSITION: Verse 27. *He rained flesh also upon them as dust.* First He rained bread and then flesh, when He might have rained fire and brimstone. The words indicate the speed, and the abundance of the descending quails.

And feathered fowls like as the sand of the sea; there was no counting them. By a remarkable providence, if not by miracle, enormous numbers of migratory birds were caused to alight around the tents of the tribes. It was, however, a doubtful blessing, as easily acquired and super abounding riches generally are. Lord, save us from meat which is seasoned with divine wrath.

Psalm 78:28 *And he let it fall in the midst of their camp, round about their habitations.*

EXPOSITION: Verse 28. *And he let it fall in the midst of their camp.* They had no journey to make; they had clamored for flesh, and it almost flew into their mouths, *round about their habitations.* This made them glad for the moment, but they knew not that mercies can be sent in anger, for then they would have trembled at sight of the good things which they had lusted after.

Psalm 78:29 *So they did eat, and were well filled: for he gave them their own desire;*

EXPOSITION: Verse 29. *So they did eat, and were well filled.* They greedily devoured the birds, even to repletion. The Lord showed them that He could *"provide flesh for his people"* [v. 20], even enough and to spare. He also showed them that when lust wins its desire it is disappointed, and by the way of satiety arrive at distaste. First the food satiates, then it nauseates.

For he gave them their own desire. They were filled with their own ways. The flesh meat was unhealthy for them, but as they cried for it they had it, and a curse with it. O my God, deny me my most urgent prayers sooner than answer them in displeasure. Better to hunger and thirst after righteousness than to be well filled with sin's dainties.

Psalm 78:30–31 *They were not estranged from their lust. But while their meat was yet in their mouths, the wrath of God came upon them, and slew the fattest of them, and smote down the chosen men of Israel.*

EXPOSITION: Verse 30–31. *They were not estranged from their lust.* Lust grows upon that which it feeds on. If sick of too much flesh, yet men grow not weary of lust, they change the object, and go on lusting still. When one sin is proved to be bitterness, men do not desist, but pursue another iniquity. If, like Jehu, they turn from Baal, they fall to worshipping the calves of Bethel.

But while their meat was yet in their mouths, before they could digest their coveted meat, it turned to their destruction.

The wrath of God came upon them before they could swallow their first meal of flesh. Short was the pleasure, sudden was the doom. The festival ended in a funeral *and slew the fattest of them, and smote down the chosen men of Israel.* Perhaps these were the ringleaders in the lusting; they are first in the punishment. God's justice has no respect of persons, the strong and the valiant fall as well as the weak and the small. What they ate on Earth they digested in hell, as many have done since. How soon they died, though they felt not the edge of the sword! How terrible was the havoc, though not amid the din of battle! My soul, see here the danger of gratified passions; they are the janitors of hell. When the Lord's people hunger God loves them; Lazarus is His beloved, though He pines upon crumbs; but when He fattens the wicked He abhors them; Dives[158] is hated of Heaven when he fares sumptuously every day. We must never dare to judge men's happiness by their tables; the heart is the place to look at. The poorest starveling believer is more to be envied than the most full fleshed of the favorites of the world. Better to be God's dog than the devil's darling. *They were not estranged from their lust.*

---

158. The rich man in the parable in Luke 16

Psalm 78:32 *For all this they sinned still, and believed not for his wondrous works.*

EXPOSITION: Verse 32. *For all this they sinned still.* Judgments moved them no more than mercies. They defied the wrath of God. Though death was in the cup of their iniquity, yet they would not put it away, but continued to quaff it as if it were a healthful potion. How truly might these words be applied to ungodly men who have been often afflicted, laid upon a sick bed, broken in spirit, and impoverished in estate, and yet have persevered in their evil ways, unmoved by terrors, unswayed by threatenings.

And believed not for his wondrous works. Their unbelief was chronic and incurable. Miracles both of mercy and judgment were unavailing. They might be made to wonder, but they could not be taught to believe. Continuance in sin and unbelief go together. Had they believed they would not have sinned, had they not have been blinded by sin they would have believed. There is a reflex action between faith and character. How can the lover of sin believe? How, on the other hand, can the unbeliever cease from sin? God's ways with us in providence are in themselves both convincing and converting, but unrenewed nature refuses to be either convicted or converted by them.

Psalm 78:33 *Therefore their days did he consume in vanity, and their years in trouble.*

EXPOSITION: Verse 33. *Therefore their days did he consume in vanity.* Apart from faith life is vanity. To wander up and down in the wilderness was a vain thing indeed, when unbelief had shut them out of the Promised Land. It was right that those who would not live to answer the divine purpose by believing and obeying their God should be made to live to no purpose, and to die before their time, unsatisfied, unblessed. Those who wasted their days in sin had little cause to wonder when the Lord cut short their lives, and swore that they would never enter the rest which they had despised.

And their years in trouble. Weary marches were their trouble, and to come to no resting place was their vanity. Innumerable graves were left all along the track of Israel, and if any ask, "Who slew all these?" the answer must be, *"They could not enter in because of unbelief"* [Hebrews 3:19]. Doubtless much of the vexation and failure of many lives results from their being sapped by unbelief, and honeycombed by evil passions. None live so fruitlessly and so wretchedly as those who allow sense and sight to override faith, and their reason and appetite to domineer over their fear of God. Our days go fast enough according to the ordinary lapse of time, but the Lord can make them rust away at a bitterer rate, until we feel as if sorrow actually ate out the heart of our life, and like a canker devoured our existence. Such was the punishment of rebellious Israel, the Lord grant it may not be ours.

> **Psalm 78:34** *When he slew them, then they sought him: and they returned and enquired early after God.*

EXPOSITION: Verse 34. *When he slew them, then they sought him.* Like whipped curs, they licked their Master's feet. They obeyed only so long as they felt the whip about their loins. Hard are the hearts which only death can move. While thousands died around them, the people of Israel became suddenly religious, and returned to the tabernacle door, like sheep that run in a mass while the black dog drives them, but scatter and wander when the shepherd whistles him off.

And they returned and enquired early after God. They

could not be too zealous; they were in hot haste to prove their loyalty to their divine King. "The devil was sick and the devil a monk would be."[159] Who would not be pious while the plague is abroad? Doors, which were never so sanctified before, put on the white cross then. Even reprobates send for the minister when they lie dying. Thus sinners pay involuntary homage to the power of right and the supremacy of God, but their hypocritical homage is of small value in the sight of the Great Judge.

> **Psalm 78:35** *And they remembered that God was their rock, and the high God their redeemer.*

EXPOSITION: Verse 35. And they remember that God was their rock. Sharp strokes awoke their sleepy memories. Reflection followed infliction. They were led to see that all their dependence must be placed upon their God; for He alone had been their shelter, their foundation, their fountain of supply, and their unchangeable friend. What could have made them forget this? Was it that their stomachs were so full of flesh that they had no space for ruminating upon spiritual things?

And the high God their redeemer. They had forgotten this also. The high hand and outstretched arm which redeemed them out of bondage had both faded from their mental vision. Alas, poor man, how readily you forget your God! Shame on you, ungrateful worm, to have no sense of favors a few days after they have been received. Will nothing make you keep in memory the mercy of your God except the utter withdrawal of it?

---

159. old proverb. (When sickness comes, even the devil is quick to put on piety.)

Psalm 78:36 *Nevertheless they did flatter him with their mouth, and they lied unto him with their tongues.*

EXPOSITION: Verse 36. *Nevertheless they did flatter him with their mouth.* Bad were they at their best. False on their knees, liars in their prayers. Mouth worship must be very detestable to God when dissociated from the heart: other kings love flattery, but the King of kings abhors it. Since the sharpest afflictions only extort from carnal men a feigned submission to God, there is proof positive that the heart is desperately set on mischief, and that sin is ingrained in our very nature. If you beat a tiger with many stripes you cannot turn him into a sheep. The devil cannot be whipped out of human nature, though another devil, namely, hypocrisy may be whipped into it. Piety produced by the damps of sorrow and the heats of terror is of mushroom growth; it is rapid in its springing up—*"they enquired early after God"* [v. 34]—but but it is a mere unsubstantial fungus of unabiding excitement.

And they lied unto him with their tongues. Their godly speech was cant,[160] their praise mere wind, their prayer a fraud. Their skin-deep repentance was a film too thin to conceal the deadly wound of sin. This teaches us to place small reliance upon professions of repentance made by dying men, or upon such even when the basis is evidently slavish fear, and nothing more. Any thief will whine out repentance if he thinks the judge will thereby be moved to let him go scot free.

Psalm 78:37 *For their heart was not right with him, neither were they stedfast in his covenant.*

EXPOSITION: Verse 37. *For their heart was not right*

---
160. insincere expression of enthusiasm for high principles

with him. There was no depth in their repentance, it was not heart work. They were fickle as a weathervane, every wind turned them, and their mind was not settled upon God. *Neither were they stedfast in his covenant.* Their promises were no sooner made than broken, as if only made in mockery. Good resolutions called at their hearts as men do at inns; they tarried awhile, and then took their leave. They were hot today for holiness, but cold towards it tomorrow. Variable as the hues of the dolphin, they changed from reverence to rebellion, from thankfulness to murmuring. One day they gave their gold to build a tabernacle for Jehovah, and the next they plucked off their earrings to make a golden calf. Surely the heart is a chameleon. Proteus[161] had not so many changes. As in the ague[162] we both burn and freeze, so do inconstant natures in their religion.

Psalm 78:38 *But he, being full of compassion, forgave their iniquity, and destroyed them not: yea, many a time turned he his anger away, and did not stir up all his wrath.*

EXPOSITION: Verse 38. *But he, being full of compassion, forgave their iniquity, and destroyed them not.* Though they were full of flattery, He was full of mercy, and for this cause he had pity on them. Not because of their pitiful and hypocritical pretensions to penitence, but because of His own real compassion for them He overlooked their provocations.

Yea, many a time turned he his anger away. When he had grown angry with them he withdrew his displeasure. Even unto seventy times seven did he forgive their offences. He

---
161. mythological Greek god sometimes referred to as "the god of elusive sea change" (Homer's "Old Man of the Sea")
162. an illness characterized by alternating chills and fever

was slow, very slow, to anger. The sword was uplifted and flashed in midair, but it was sheathed again, and the nation yet lived. Though not mentioned in the text, we know from the history that a mediator interposed, the man Moses stood in the gap; even so at this hour the Lord Jesus pleads for sinners, and averts the divine wrath. Many a barren tree is left standing because the dresser of the vineyard cries "let it alone this year also."

And did not stir up all his wrath. Had he done so they must have perished in a moment. When His wrath is kindled only a little, men are burned up as chaff; but if He were to let loose His indignation, the solid Earth itself would melt, and hell would engulf every rebel. Who knows the power of your anger, O Lord? We see the fullness of God's compassion, but we never see all His wrath.

Psalm 78:39 *For he remembered that they were but flesh; a wind that passeth away, and cometh not again.*

EXPOSITION: Verse 39. *For he remembered that they were but flesh.* They were forgetful of God, but He was mindful of them. He knew that they were made of earthy, frail, corruptible material, and therefore He dealt leniently with them. Though in this He saw no excuse for their sin, yet He constrained it into a reason for mercy; the Lord is ever ready to discover some plea or other upon which He may have compassion.

A wind that passeth away, and cometh not again. Man is but a breath, gone never to return. Spirit and wind are in this alike, so far as our humanity is concerned; they pass and cannot be recalled. What a nothing is our life. How gracious on the Lord's part to make man's insignificance an argument for staying His wrath.

> **Psalm 78:40** *How oft did they provoke him in the wilderness, and grieve him in the desert!*

EXPOSITION: Verse 40. *How oft did they provoke him in the wilderness.* Times enough did they rebel: they were as constant in provocation as He was in His patience. In our own case, who can count his errors? In what book could all our perverse rebellions be recorded? The wilderness was a place of manifest dependence, where the tribes were helpless without divine supplies, yet they wounded the hand which fed them while it was in the act of feeding them. Is there no likeness between us and them? Does it bring no tears into our eyes, while as in a glass, we see our own selves?

And grieve him in the desert. Their provocations had an effect; God was not insensible to them, He is said to have been grieved. His holiness could not find pleasure in their sin, His justice in their unjust treatment, or His truth in their falsehood. What must it be to grieve the Lord of love! Yet we also have vexed the Holy Spirit, and He would long ago have withdrawn himself from us, were it not that He is God and not man. We are in the desert. We are in the desert where we need our God; let us not make it a wilderness of sin by grieving Him.

> **Psalm 78:41** *Yea, they turned back and tempted God, and limited the Holy One of Israel.*

EXPOSITION: Verse 41. *Yea, they turned back.* Their hearts sighed for Egypt and its fleshpots. They turned to their old ways again and again, after they had been scourged out of them. Full of twists and turns, they never kept the straight path.

And tempted God. As far as in them lay they tempted Him. His ways were good, and they in desiring to have them altered tempted God. Before they would believe in Him they demanded signs, defying the Lord to do this and that, and acting as if He could be cajoled into being the minion of their lusts. What blasphemy was this! Yet let us not tempt Christ lest we also be destroyed by the destroyer.

And limited the Holy One of Israel. Doubted His power and so limited Him, dictated to His wisdom and so did the same. To chalk out a path for God is arrogant impiety. The Holy One must do right, the covenant God of Israel must be true, and it is profanity itself to say unto Him thou shalt do this or that, or otherwise I will not worship thee. Not in this way is the Eternal God to be led by a string by His impotent creature. He is the Lord and He will do as seems good to Him.

Psalm 78:42 *They remembered not his hand, nor the day when he delivered them from the enemy.*

EXPOSITION: Verse 42. *They remembered not his hand.* Such displays of divine power as those which smote Egypt with astonishment, it must have needed some more than usual effort to blot it from the tablets of memory. It is probably meant that they practically, rather than actually, forgot. He who forgets the natural returns of gratitude may justly be charged with not remembering the obligation.

Nor the days when he delivered them from the enemy. The day itself was erased from their calendar, so far as any due result from it or return for it. Strange is the faculty of memory in its oblivion as well as its records. Sin perverts man's powers, makes them forceful only in wrong directions, and practically dead for righteous ends.

Psalm 78:43 *How he had wrought his signs in Egypt, and his wonders in the field of Zoan.*

EXPOSITION: Verse 43. *How he had wrought his signs in Egypt.* The plagues were ensigns of Jehovah's presence and proofs of His hatred of idols; these instructive acts of power were wrought in the open view of all, as signals are set up to be observed by those far and near.

And his wonders in the field of Zoan. In the whole land were miracles wrought, not in cities alone, but in the broad territory, in the most select and ancient regions of the proud nation. This the Israelites ought not to have forgotten, for they were the favored people for whom these memorable deeds were wrought.

Psalm 78:44 *And had turned their rivers into blood; and their floods, that they could not drink.*

EXPOSITION: Verse 44. *And had turned their rivers into blood.* The waters had been made the means of the destruction of Israel's newborn infants, and now they do as it were betray the crime—they blush for it, they avenge it on the murderers. The Nile was the vitality of Egypt, its true life blood, but at God's command it became a flowing curse; every drop of it was a horror, poison to drink, and terror to gaze on. How soon might the Almighty One do this with the Thames or the Seine. Sometimes He has allowed men, who were His rod, to make rivers crimson with gore, and this is a severe judgment; but the event now before us was more mysterious, more general, more complete, and must, therefore, have been a plague of the first magnitude.

And their floods, that they could not drink. Lesser streams partook in the curse, reservoirs and canals felt the evil; God does nothing by halves. All Egypt boasted of the sweet waters of their river, but they were made to loathe it more than they had ever loved it. Our mercies may soon become our miseries if the Lord shall deal with us in wrath.

Psalm 78:45 *He sent divers sorts of flies among them, which devoured them; and frogs, which destroyed them.*

EXPOSITION: **Verse 45.** *He sent diverse sorts of flies among them, which devoured them.* Small creatures become great tormentors. When they swarm they can sting a man until they threaten to eat him up. In this case, various orders of insects fought under the same banner; lice and beetles, gnats and hornets, wasps and gadflies[163] dashed forward in fierce battalions, and worried the sinners of Egypt without mercy. The tiniest plagues are the greatest. What sword or spear could fight with these innumerable bands? Vain were the monarch's armor and robes of majesty, the little cannibals were no more lenient towards royal flesh than any other; it had the same blood in it, and the same sin upon it. How great is that God who thus by the minute can crush the magnificent.

And frogs, which destroyed them. These creatures swarmed everywhere when they were alive, until the people felt ready to die at the sight; and when the reptiles died, the heaps of their bodies made the land to stink so foully, that a pestilence was imminent. Thus not only did ground and air send forth armies of horrible life, but the water also added its legions of loathsomeness. It seemed as if the Nile was first made nauseous and then caused to leave its bed altogether, crawling and leaping in the form of frogs. Those who contend with the Almighty little know what arrows are in His quiver; surprising sin shall be visited with surprising punishment.

Psalm 78:46 *He gave also their increase unto the caterpiller, and their labour unto the locust.*

---

163. horseflies, for example

EXPOSITION: **Verse 46.** *He gave also their increase unto the caterpillar, and their labour unto the locust.* Different sorts of devourers ate up every green herb and tree. What one would not eat another did. What they expected from the natural fertility of the soil, and what they looked for from their own toil, they saw devoured before their eyes by an insatiable multitude against whose depredation no defense could be found. Observe in the text that the Lord did it all—"he sent," "he gave," "he destroyed," "he gave up," etc.; whatever the second agent may be, the direct hand of the Lord is in every national visitation.

Psalm 78:47 *He destroyed their vines with hail, and their sycomore trees with frost.*

EXPOSITION: **Verse 47.** *He destroyed their vines with hail.* No more shall your butler press the clusters into your cup, O Pharaoh! The young fruit bearing shoots were broken off, the vintage failed.

And their sycomore trees with frost. Frost was not usual, but Jehovah regards no laws of nature when men regard not His moral laws. The sycomore fig[164] was perhaps more the fruit of the many than was the vine, therefore this judgment was meant to smite the poor, while the former fell most heavily upon the rich. Mark how the heavens obey their Lord and yield their stores of hail, and note how the fickle weather is equally subservient to the divine will.

Psalm 78:48 *He gave up their cattle also to the hail, and their flocks to hot thunderbolts.*

EXPOSITION: **Verse 48.** *He gave up their cattle also to the hail.* What hail it must have been to have force

---

164. a large tree that bears large fruit in clusters on the branches

enough to batter down bullocks and other great beasts. God usually protects animals from such destruction, but here He withdraws His safeguards and gave them up: may the Lord never give us up. Some read, "shut up," and the idea of being abandoned to destructive influences is then before us in another shape.

And their flocks to hot thunderbolts. Fire was mingled with the hail; the fire ran along upon the ground, it smote the smaller cattle. What a storm must that have been: its effects were terrible enough upon plants, but to see the poor dumb creatures stricken must have been heartbreaking. Hard indeed was that heart which quailed not under such plagues as these, harder than adamant those hearts which in after years forgot all that the Lord had done, and broke off from their allegiance to Him.

Psalm 78:49 *He cast upon them the fierceness of his anger, wrath, and indignation, and trouble, by sending evil angels among them.*

EXPOSITION: Verse 49. *He cast upon them the fierceness of his anger, wrath, and indignation, and trouble.* His last arrow was the sharpest. He reserved the strong wine of His indignation to the last. Note how the psalmist piles up the words, and well he might; for blow followed blow, each one more staggering than its predecessor, and then the crushing stroke was reserved for the end.

By sending evil angels among them. Messengers of evil entered their houses at midnight, and smote the dearest objects of their love. The angels were evil to them, though good enough in themselves; those who to the heirs of salvation are ministers of grace are to the heirs of wrath executioners of judgment. When God sends angels, they are sure to come, and if He bids them to slay they will not spare. See how sin sets all the powers of Heaven in array against man; he has no friend left in the universe when God is his enemy.

Psalm 78:50 *He made a way to his anger; he spared not their soul from death, but gave their life over to the pestilence;*

EXPOSITION: Verse 50. *He made a way to his anger*, coming to the point with them by slow degrees; assailing their outworks first by destroying their property, and then coming in upon their persons as through an open breach in the walls. He broke down all the comforts of their life, and then advanced against their life itself. Nothing could stand in His way; He cleared a space in which to do execution upon His adversaries.

He spared not their soul from death, but gave their life over to the pestilence. In their soul was the origin of the sin, and He followed it to its source and smote it there. A fierce disease filled the land with countless funerals; Jehovah dealt out myriads of blows, and multitudes of spirits failed before Him.

Psalm 78:51 *And smote all the firstborn in Egypt; the chief of their strength in the tabernacles of Ham:*

EXPOSITION: Verse 51. *And smote all the firstborn in Egypt.* No exceptions were made; the monarch bewailed his heir as did the menial at the mill. They smote the Lord's firstborn, even Israel, and He smites theirs.

The chief of their strength in the tabernacles of Ham. Swinging His scythe over the field, death topped off the highest flowers. The tents of Ham knew each one its own peculiar sorrow, and were made to sympathize with the sorrows which had been ruthlessly inflicted upon the habitations of Israel.

Thus curses come home to roost. Oppressors are repaid in their own coin, without the discount of a penny.

Psalm 78:52 *But made his own people to go forth like sheep, and guided them in the wilderness like a flock.*

EXPOSITION: **Verse 52.** *But made his own people to go forth like sheep.* The contrast is striking, and ought never to have been forgotten by the people. The wolves were slain in heaps; the sheep were carefully gathered, and triumphantly delivered. The tables were turned, and the poor serfs became the honored people, while their oppressors were humbled before them. Israel went out in a compact body like a flock; they were defenseless in themselves as sheep, but they were safe under their Great Shepherd; they left Egypt as easily as a flock leaves one pasture for another.

And guided them in the wilderness like a flock. Knowing nothing of the way by their own understanding or experience, they were, nevertheless, rightly directed, for the All-Wise God knew every spot of the wilderness. To the sea, through the sea, and from the sea, the Lord led His chosen; while their former taskmasters were too cowed in spirit, and broken in power, to dare to molest them.

Psalm 78:53 *And he led them on safely, so that they feared not: but the sea overwhelmed their enemies.*

EXPOSITION: **Verse 53.** *And he led them on safely, so that they feared not.* After the first little alarm, natural enough when they found themselves pursued by their old taskmasters, they plucked up courage and ventured forth boldly into the sea, and afterwards into the desert where no man dwelt.

But the sea overwhelmed their enemies. They were gone, gone forever, never to disturb the fugitives again. That tremendous blow effectually defended the tribes for forty years from any further attempt to drive them back. Egypt found the stone too heavy and was glad to let it alone. Let the Lord be praised who thus effectually freed His elect nation.

What a grand narrative have we been considering. Well might the mightiest master of sacred song select "Israel in Egypt" as a choice theme for His genius; and well may every believing nation live as if unmindful of it all, and yet such is human nature. Alas, poor man! Rather, alas, base heart!

We now, after a pause, follow again the chain of events, the narration of which had been interrupted by a retrospect, and we find Israel entering into the Promised Land, there to repeat her follies and enlarge her crimes.

Psalm 78:54 *And he brought them to the border of his sanctuary, even to this mountain, which his right hand had purchased.*

EXPOSITION: Verse 54. *And he brought them to the border of his sanctuary.* He conducted them to the frontier of the Holy Land, where He intended the tabernacle to become the permanent symbol of His abode among His people. He did not leave them halfway upon their journey to their heritage; His power and wisdom preserved the nation until the palm trees of Jericho were within sight on the other side of the river.

Even to this mountain, which his right hand had purchased. Nor did He leave them then, but still conducted them until they were in the region round about Zion, which was to be the central seat of His worship. This the Lord had purchased in type of old by the sacrifice of Isaac, fit symbol of the greater sacrifice which was in due season to be presented there: that mountain was also redeemed by power, when the Lord's right hand enabled His valiant men to smite the Jebusites, and take the sacred hill from the insulting Canaanite. Thus shall the elect of God enjoy the sure protection of the Lord of hosts, even to the border land of death, and through the river, up to the hill of the Lord in glory. The purchased people shall safely reach the purchased inheritance.

Psalm 78:55 *He cast out the heathen also before them, and divided them an inheritance by line, and made the tribes of Israel to dwell in their tents.*

EXPOSITION: Verse 55. *He cast out the heathen also before them*, or "he drove out the nations." Not only were armies routed, but whole peoples displaced. The iniquity of the Canaanites was full; their vices made them rot above ground; therefore, the land ate up its inhabitants, the hornets vexed them, the pestilence destroyed them, and the sword of the tribes completed the execution to which the justice of long provoked Heaven had at length appointed them. The Lord was the true conqueror of Canaan; He cast out the nations as men cast out filth from their habitations, He uprooted them as noxious weeds are extirpated by the husbandman.

And divided them an inheritance by line. He divided the land of the nations among the tribes by lot and measure, assigning Hivite, Perizzite, and Jebusite territory to Simeon, Judah, or Ephraim, as the case might be. Among those condemned nations were not only giants in stature, but also giants in crime: those monsters of iniquity had too long defiled the Earth; it was time that they should no more indulge the unnatural crimes for which they were infamous; they were, therefore, doomed to forfeit life and lands by the hands of the tribes of Israel. The distribution of the forfeited country was made by divine appointment; it was no scramble, but a judicial appointment of lands which had fallen to the crown by the attainder of the former holders.

And made the tribes of Israel to dwell in their tents. The favored people entered upon a furnished house: they found the larder supplied, for they fed upon the old corn of the land, and the dwellings were already built in which they could dwell. Thus does another race often enter into the lot of a former people, and it is sad indeed when the change which judgment decrees does not turn out to be much for the better, because the incomers inherit the evils as well as the goods of the ejected. Such a case of judicial visitation ought to have had a salutary influence upon the tribes; but, alas, they were incorrigible, and would not learn even from examples so near at home and so terribly suggestive.

Psalm 78:56 *Yet they tempted and provoked the most high God, and kept not his testimonies:*

EXPOSITION: **Verse 56.** *Yet they tempted and provoked the most high God.* Change of condition had not altered their manners. They left their nomadic habits, but not their tendencies to wander from their God. Though every divine promise had been fulfilled to the letter, and the land flowing with milk and honey was actually their own, yet they tried the Lord again with unbelief, and provoked Him with other sins. He is not only high and glorious, but most High, yea, the most High, the only being who deserves to be so highly had in honor; yet, instead of honoring Him, Israel grieved Him with rebellion.

And kept not his testimonies. They were true to nothing but hereditary treachery; steadfast in nothing but in falsehood. They knew His truth and forgot it, His will and disobeyed it, His grace and perverted it to an occasion for greater transgression. Reader, do you need a looking glass? See here is one which suits the present expositor well; does it not also reflect your image?

> **Psalm 78:57** *But turned back, and dealt unfaithfully like their fathers: they were turned aside like a deceitful bow.*

EXPOSITION: Verse 57. *But turned back.* Turned over the old leaf, repeated the same offences, started aside like an ill-made bow, were false and faithless to their best promises.

And dealt unfaithfully like their fathers, proving themselves legitimate by manifesting the treachery of their sires. They were a new generation, but not a new nation—another race yet not another. Evil propensities are transmitted; the birth follows the progenitor; the wild ass breeds wild asses; the children of the raven fly to the carrion. Human nature does not improve, the new editions contain all the errors of the first, and sometimes fresh errors are imported.

They were turned aside like a deceitful bow, which not only fails to send the arrow towards the mark in a direct line, but springs back to the archer's hurt, and perhaps sends the shaft among his friends to their serious jeopardy. Israel boasted of the bow as the national weapon, they sang the song of the bow, and hence a deceitful bow is made to be the type and symbol of their own lack of steadfastness; God can make men's glory the very ensign of their shame, He draws a bar sinister[165] across the escutcheon of traitors.

> **Psalm 78:58** *For they provoked him to anger with their high places, and moved him to jealousy with their graven images.*

---

165. a bar added to a coat of arms from lower left to upper right to indicate illegitimacy in the family line

EXPOSITION: **Verse 58.** *For they provoked him to anger with their high places.* This was their first error—the worship of God, otherwise than according to His command. Many think lightly of this, but it was no small sin; and its tendencies to further offence are very powerful. The Lord would have His holy place remain as the only spot for sacrifice; and Israel, in willful rebellion, (no doubt glossed over by the plea of great devotion,) determined to have many altars upon many hills. If they might have but one God, they insisted upon it that they would not be restricted to one sacred place of sacrifice. How much of the worship of the present day is neither more nor less than sheer will worship! Nobody dares to plead a divine appointment for a tithe of the offices, festivals, ceremonies, and observances of certain churches. Doubtless God, so far from being honored by worship which He has not commanded, is greatly angered at it.

And moved him to jealousy with their graven images. This was but one more step; they manufactured symbols of the invisible God, for they lusted after something tangible and visible to which they could show reverence. This also is the crying sin of modern times. Do we not hear and see superstition abounding? Images, pictures, crucifixes, and a host of visible things are had in religious honor, and worst of all men nowadays worship what they eat, and call that a God which passes into their belly, and thence into baser places still. Surely the Lord is very patient, or He would visit the Earth for this worst and basest of idolatry. He is a jealous God, and abhors to see himself dishonored by any form of representation which can come from man's hands.

Psalm 78:59 *When God heard this, he was wroth, and greatly abhorred Israel:*

EXPOSITION: Verse 59. *When God heard this, he was wroth.* The mere report of it filled Him with indignation; He could not bear it, He was incensed to the uttermost, and most justly so.

And greatly abhorred Israel. He cast His idolatrous people from His favor, and left them to themselves, and their own devices. How could He have fellowship with idols? *"What concord hath Christ with Belial?"* [2 Corinthians 6:15]. Sin is in itself so offensive that it makes the sinner offensive too. Idols of any sort are highly abhorrent to God, and we must see to it that we keep ourselves from them through divine grace, for rest assured idolatry is not consistent with true grace in the heart. If Dagon[166] sits aloft in any soul, the ark of God is not there. Where the Lord dwells no image of jealousy will be tolerated. A visible church will soon become a visible curse if idols are set up in it, and then the pruning knife will remove it as a dead branch from the vine.

Note that God did not utterly cast away His people Israel even when he greatly abhorred them, for He returned in mercy to them, so the subsequent verses tell us: so now the seed of Abraham, though for awhile under a heavy cloud, will be gathered yet again, for the covenant of salt shall not be broken. As for the spiritual seed, the Lord has not despised nor abhorred them; they are His peculiar treasure and lie forever near His heart.

Psalm 78:60 *So that he forsook the tabernacle of Shiloh, the tent which he placed among men;*

EXPOSITION: Verse 60. *So that he forsook the tabernacle of Shiloh, the tent which he placed among men.* His glory would no more reveal itself there; He left Shiloh to

---

166. a false god worshiped by the Amorites

become a complete ruin. At the door of that tent shameless sin had been perpetrated, and all around it idols had been adored, and therefore the glory departed and Ichabod[167] was sounded as a word of dread concerning Shiloh and the tribe of Ephraim. Thus may the candlestick be removed though the candle is not quenched. Erring churches become apostate, but a true Church still remains; if Shiloh is profaned Zion is consecrated. Yet it is ever a solemn caution to all the assemblies of the saints, admonishing them to walk humbly with their God, when we read such words as those of the Prophet Jeremiah in is seventh chapter,

> *Trust ye not in lying words, saying, The temple of the Lord, The temple of the Lord, The temple of the Lord, are these. . . . Go ye now unto my place which was in Shiloh, where I set my name at the first, and see what I did to it for the wickedness of my people Israel.* [Jeremiah 7:4, 12]

Let us take heed, lest as the ark never returned to Shiloh after its capture by the Philistines, so the gospel may be taken from us in judgment, never to be restored to the same church again.

Psalm 78:61 *And delivered his strength into captivity, and his glory into the enemy's hand.*

EXPOSITION: Verse 61. *And delivered his strength into captivity.* It was a black day when the mercy seat was removed, when the cherubim took flight, and Israel's palladium was carried away.

And his glory into the enemy's hand. The ark was the place for the revealed glory of God, and His enemies exulted

---
167. "The glory has departed from Israel" (See 1 Samuel chapters 2 and 4.)

greatly when they bore it away into their own cities. Nothing could more clearly have shown the divine displeasure. It seemed to say that Jehovah would sooner dwell among His avowed adversaries than among so false a people as Israel; He would sooner bear the insults of Philistia than the treacheries of Ephraim. This was a fearful downfall for the favored nation, and it was followed by dire judgments of most appalling nature. When God is gone, all is gone. No calamity can equal the withdrawal of the divine presence from a people. O Israel, how low are you brought! Who shall help you now that your God has left you!

Psalm 78:62 *He gave his people over also unto the sword; and was wroth with his inheritance.*

EXPOSITION: Verse 62. *He gave his people over also unto the sword.* They fell in battle because they were no longer aided by the divine strength. Sharp was the sword, but sharper still the cause of its being unsheathed.

And was wroth with his inheritance. They were His still, and twice in this verse they are called so; yet His regard for them did not prevent His chastening them, even with a rod of steel. Where the love is most fervent, the jealousy is most cruel. Sin cannot be tolerated in those who are a people near unto God.

Psalm 78:63 *The fire consumed their young men; and their maidens were not given to marriage.*

EXPOSITION: Verse 63. *The fire consumed their young men.* As fire slew Nadab and Abihu literally, so the fire of divine wrath fell on the sons of Eli, who defiled the sanctuary of the Lord, and the like fire, in the form of war, consumed the flower of the people.

And their maidens were not given to marriage. No nuptial hymn were sung, the bride lacked her bridegroom, the edge of the sword had cut the bands of their espousals, and left unmarried those who else had been extolled in hymns and congratulations. Thus Israel was brought very low, she could not find husbands for her maids, and therefore her state was not replenished; no young children clustered around parental knees. The nation had failed in its solemn task of instructing the young in the fear of Jehovah, and it was a fitting judgment that the very production of a posterity should be endangered.

> **Psalm 78:64** *Their priests fell by the sword; and their widows made no lamentation.*

EXPOSITION: Verse 64. *Their priests fell by the sword.* Hophni and Phineas were slain; they were among the chief in sin, and, therefore, they perished with the rest. Priesthood is no shelter for transgressors; the jeweled breastplate cannot turn aside the arrows of judgment.

And their widows made no lamentation. Their private griefs were swallowed up in the greater national agony, because the ark of God was taken. As the maidens had no heart for the marriage song, so the widows had no spirit, even to utter the funeral wail. The dead were buried too often and too hurriedly to allow of the usual rites of lamentation. This was the lowest depth; from this point things will take a gracious turn.

> **Psalm 78:65** *Then the* LORD *awaked as one out of sleep, and like a mighty man that shouteth by reason of wine.*

EXPOSITION: Verse 65. *The Lord awaked as one*

out of sleep. Justly inactive, He had suffered the enemy to triumph, His ark to be captured, and His people to be slain; but now He arouses himself, His heart is full of pity for His chosen, and anger against the insulting foe. Woe to you, O Philistia, now you shall feel the weight of His right hand! Waking and putting forth strength like a man who has taken a refreshing draught, the Lord is said to be, *like a mighty man that shouteth by reason of wine.* Strong and full of energy the Lord dashed upon His foes, and made them stagger beneath His blows. His ark from city to city went as an avenger rather than as a trophy, and in every place the false gods fell helplessly before it.

Psalm 78:66 *And he smote his enemies in the hinder parts: he put them to a perpetual reproach.*

EXPOSITION: **Verse 66.** *He smote his enemies in the hinder parts.* The emerods[168] rendered them ridiculous, and their numerous defeats made them yet more so. They fled but were overtaken and wounded in the back, to their eternal disgrace.

He put them to a perpetual reproach. Orientals are not very refined, and we can well believe that the hemorrhoids were the subject of many a taunt against the Philistines, as also were their frequent defeats by Israel until at last they were crushed under, never to exist again as a distinct nation.

Psalm 78:67 *Moreover he refused the tabernacle of Joseph, and chose not the tribe of Ephraim:*

EXPOSITION: **Verse 67.** *Moreover he refused the tabernacle of Joseph.* God had honored Ephraim, for to that tribe belonged Joshua the great conqueror, and Gideon the

---
168. hemorrhoids

great judge, and within its borders was Shiloh the place of the ark and the sanctuary; but now the Lord would change all this and set up other rulers. He would no longer leave matters to the leadership of Ephraim, since that tribe had been tried and found wanting.

And chose not the tribe of Ephraim. Sin had been found in them; folly and instability, and therefore they were set aside as unfit to lead.

Psalm 78:68 *But chose the tribe of Judah, the mount Zion which he loved.*

EXPOSITION: Verse 68. *But chose the tribe of Judah.* To give the nation another trial this tribe was elected to supremacy. This was according to Jacob's dying prophecy. Our Lord sprang out of Judah, and He it is whom His brethren shall praise.

The mount Zion which he loved. The tabernacle and ark were removed to Zion during the reign of David; no honor was left to the wayward Ephraimites. Hard by this mountain the Father of the Faithful had offered up his only son, and there in future days the great gatherings of his chosen seed would be, and therefore Zion is said to be lovely unto God.

Psalm 78:69 *And he built his sanctuary like high palaces, like the earth which he hath established for ever.*

EXPOSITION: Verse 69. *And he built his sanctuary like high palaces.* The tabernacle was placed on high, literally and spiritually it was a mountain of beauty. True religion was exalted in the land. For sanctity it was a temple, for majesty it was a palace.

Like the earth which he hath established for ever. Stability was well as stateliness was seen in the temple, and so also in the Church of God. The prophets saw both in vision.

Psalm 78:70 *He chose David also his servant, and took him from the sheepfolds:*

EXPOSITION: **Verse 70.** *He chose David also his servant.* It was an election of a sovereignly gracious kind, and it operated practically by making the chosen man a willing servant of the Lord. He was not chosen because he was a servant, but in order that he might be so. David always esteemed it to be a high honor that he was both elect of God, and a servant of God.

And took him from the sheepfolds. A shepherd of sheep he had been, and this was a fit school for a shepherd of men. Lowliness of occupation will debar no man from such honors as the Lord's election confers, the Lord sees not as man sees. He delights to bless those who are of low estate.

Psalm 78:71 *From following the ewes great with young he brought him to feed Jacob his people, and Israel his inheritance.*

EXPOSITION: **Verse 71.** *From following the ewes great with young he brought him to feed Jacob his people, and Israel his inheritance.* Exercising the care and art of those who watch for the young lambs, David followed the ewes in their wanderings; the tenderness and patience thus acquired would tend to the development of characteristics most becoming in a king. To the man thus prepared, the office and dignity which God had appointed for him, came in due season, and he was enabled worthily to wear them. It is wonderful how often divine wisdom so arranges the early and obscure portion of a choice life, so as to make it a preparatory school for a more active and noble future.

Psalm 78:72 *So he fed them according to the integrity of his heart; and guided them by the skilfulness of his hands.*

EXPOSITION: **Verse 72.** *So he fed them according to the integrity of his heart.* David was upright before God, and never swerved in heart from the obedient worship of Jehovah. Whatever faults he had, he was unfeignedly sincere in his allegiance to Israel's superior king; he shepherded for God with an honest heart.

And guided them by the skilfulness of his hands. He was a sagacious ruler, and the psalmist magnifies the Lord for having appointed him. Under David, the Jewish kingdom rose to an honorable position among the nations, and exercised an influence over its neighbors. In closing the psalm which has described the varying conditions of the chosen nation, we are glad to end so peacefully; with all noise of tumult or of sinful rites hushed into silence. After a long voyage over a stormy sea, the ark of the Jewish state rested on its Ararat, beneath a wise and gentle reign, to be wafted no more hither and thither by floods and gales. The psalmist had all along intended to make this his last stanza, and we too may be content to finish all our songs of love with the reign of the Lord's anointed. Only we may eagerly enquire, when will it come? When shall we end these desert roamings, these rebellions, the chastenings, and enter into the rest of a settled kingdom, with the Lord Jesus reigning as the Prince of the house of David?

Thus have we ended this lengthy parable, may we in our life parable have less of sin, and as much of grace as are displayed in Israel's history, and may we close it under the safe guidance of *"that great Shepherd of the sheep"* [Hebrews 13:20]. Amen.

Psalm 79
Psalm 79:1–Psalm 79:13

Psalm 79:1 *O god, the heathen are come into thine inheritance; thy holy temple have they defiled; they have laid Jerusalem on heaps.*

EXPOSITION: Verse 1. *O God, the heathen are come into thine inheritance.* It is the cry of amazement at sacrilegious intrusion; as if the poet were struck with horror. The stranger pollutes thine hallowed courts with his tread. All Canaan is your land, but your foes have ravaged it.

Thy holy temple have they defiled. Into the inmost sanctuary they have profanely forced their way, and there behaved themselves arrogantly. Thus, the holy land, the holy house, and the holy city, were all polluted by the uncircumcised. It is an awful thing when wicked men are found in the Church and numbered with her ministry. Then are the tares sown with the wheat, and the poisoned gourds cast into the pot.

They have laid Jerusalem on heaps. After devouring and defiling, they have come to destroying, and have done their work with a cruel completeness. Jerusalem, the beloved city, the joy of the nation, the abode of her God, was totally wrecked. Alas! For Israel! It is sad to see the foe in our own house, but worse to meet him in the house of God; they strike hardest who smite at our religion. The psalmist piles up the agony; he was a suppliant, and he knew how to bring out the strong points of his case. We ought to order our case before the Lord with as much care as if our success depended on our pleading. Men in Earth's courts use all their powers to obtain their ends, and so also should we state our case with earnestness, and bring forth our strong arguments.

> **Psalm 79:2** *The dead bodies of thy servants have they given to be meat unto the fowls of the heaven, the flesh of thy saints unto the beasts of the earth.*

EXPOSITION: Verse 2. *The dead bodies of thy servants have they given to be meat unto the fowls of the heaven, the flesh of thy saints unto the beasts of the earth.* The enemy cared not to bury the dead, and there was not a sufficient number of Israel left alive to perform the funeral rites; therefore, the precious relics of the departed were left to be devoured of vultures and torn by wolves. Beasts on which man could not feed fed on him. The flesh of creation's Lord became meat for carrion crows and hungry dogs. Dire are the calamities of war, yet have they happened to God's saints and servants. This might well move the heart of the poet, and he did well to appeal to the heart of God by reciting the grievous evil. Such might have been the lamentation of an early Christian as he thought of the amphitheatre and all its deeds of blood. Note in the two verses how the plea is made to turn upon God's property in the temple and the people—we read "thine inheritance," "thy temple," "thy servants," and "thy saints." Surely the Lord will defend His own, and will not suffer rampant adversaries to despoil them.

> **Psalm 79:3** *Their blood have they shed like water round about Jerusalem; and there was none to bury them.*

EXPOSITION: Verse 3. *Their blood have they shed like water round about Jerusalem.* The invaders slew men as if their blood was of no more value than so much water; they poured it forth as lavishly as when the floods deluge the plains. The city of holy peace became a field of blood.

And there was none to bury them. The few who survived were afraid to engage in the task. This was a serious trial and grievous horror to the Jews, who evinced much care concerning their burials. Has it come to this, that there are none to bury the dead of your family, O Lord? Can none be found to grant a shovelful of earth with which to cover up the poor bodies of your murdered saints? What woe is here! How glad we should be that we live in so quiet an age, when the blast of the trumpet is no more heard in our streets.

Psalm 79:4 *We are become a reproach to our neighbours, a scorn and derision to them that are round about us.*

EXPOSITION: Verse 4. *We are become a reproach to our neighbours.* Those who have escaped the common foe make a mockery of us; they fling our disasters into our face, and ask us, "Where is your God?" Pity should be shown to the afflicted, but in too many cases it is not so, for a hard logic argues that those who suffer more than ordinary calamities must have been extraordinary sinners. Neighbors especially are often the reverse of neighborly; the nearer they dwell the less they sympathize. It is most pitiable it should be so.

A scorn and a derision to them that are round about us. To find mirth in others' miseries, and to exult over the ills of others, is worthy only of the devil and of those whose father he is. Thus the case is stated before the Lord, and it is a very deplorable one. Asaph was an excellent advocate, for he gave a telling description of calamities which were under his own eyes, and in which he sympathized, but we have a mightier Intercessor above, who never ceases to urge our suit before the eternal throne.

Psalm 79:5 *How long,* LORD? *wilt thou be angry for ever? shall thy jealousy burn like fire?*

EXPOSITION: Verse 5. *How long, Lord?* Will there be no end to these chastisements? They are most sharp and overwhelming; will you continue them much longer?

Wilt thou be angry for ever? Is His mercy gone so that He will forever smite?

Shall thy jealousy burn like fire? There was great cause for the Lord to be jealous, since idols had been set up, and Israel had gone aside from His worship, but the psalmist begs the Lord not to consume His people utterly as with fire, but to abate their woes.

Psalm 79:6 *Pour out thy wrath upon the heathen that have not known thee, and upon the kingdoms that have not called upon thy name.*

EXPOSITION: Verse 6. *Pour out thy wrath upon the heathen that have not known thee.* If you must smite look further afield; spare your children and strike your foes. There are lands where you are in no measure acknowledged; be pleased to visit these first with your judgments, and let your erring Israel have a respite.

And upon the kingdoms that have not called upon thy name. Hear us the prayerful, and avenge yourself upon the prayerless. Sometimes providence appears to deal much more severely with the righteous than with the wicked, and this verse is a bold appeal founded upon such an appearance. It in effect says—Lord, if you must empty out the vials of your wrath, begin with those who have no measure of regard for you, but are openly up in arms against you; and be pleased to spare your people, who are yours despite all their sins.

Psalm 79:7 *For they have devoured Jacob, and laid waste his dwelling place.*

EXPOSITION: Verse 7. *For they have devoured Jacob.* The oppressor would quite eat up the saints if he could. If these lions do not swallow us, it is because the Lord has sent His angel and shut the lions' mouths.

And laid waste his dwelling place, or His pasture. The invader left no food for man or beast, but devoured all as the locust. The tender mercies of the wicked are cruel.

Psalm 79:8 *O remember not against us former iniquities: let thy tender mercies speedily prevent us: for we are brought very low*

EXPOSITION: Verse 8. *O remember not against us former iniquities.* Sins accumulate against nations. Generations lay up stores of transgressions to be visited upon their successors; hence this urgent prayer. In Josiah's days the most earnest repentance was not able to avert the doom that former long years of idolatry had sealed against Judah. Every man has reason to ask for an act of oblivion for his past sins, and every nation should make this a continual prayer.

Let thy tender mercies speedily prevent us: for we are brought very low. Hasten to our rescue, for our nation is hurrying down to destruction; our numbers are diminished and our condition is deplorable. Observe how penitent sorrow seizes upon the sweeter attributes, and draws her pleas from the "tender mercies" of God; see, too, how she pleads her own distress, and not her goodness, as a motive for the display of mercy. Let souls who are brought very low find an argument in their abject condition. What can so powerfully appeal to pity as dire affliction? The quaint prayer book version is touchingly expressive: "O remember not our old sins, but have mercy upon us, and that soon; for we are come to great misery." This supplication fits a sinner's life. We have known seasons when this would have been as good a prayer for our burdened heart as any that human mind could compose.

> **Psalm 79:9** *Help us, O God of our salvation, for the glory of thy name: and deliver us, and purge away our sins, for thy name's sake.*

EXPOSITION: Verse 9. Help us O God of our salvation, for the glory of thy name. This is masterly pleading. No argument has such force as this. God's glory was tarnished in the eyes of the heathen by the defeat of His people, and the desecration of His temple; therefore, His distressed servants implore His aid, that His great name may no more be the scorn of blaspheming enemies.

And deliver us, and purge away our sins, for thy name's sake. Sin—the root of the evil—is seen and confessed; pardon of sin is sought as well as removal of chastisement, and both are asked not as matters of right, but as gifts of grace. God's name is a second time brought into the pleading. Believers will find it their wisdom to very frequently use this noble plea: it is the great gun of the battle, the mightiest weapon in the armory of prayer.

> **Psalm 79:10** *Wherefore should the heathen say, Where is their God? let him be known among the heathen in our sight by the revenging of the blood of thy servants which is shed.*

EXPOSITION: Verse 10. Wherefore should the heathen say, Where is their God? Why should those impious mouths be filled with food so sweet to them, but so bitter to us? When the afflictions of God's people become the derision of sinners, and cause them to ridicule religion, we have good ground for earnest opposition with the Lord.

Let him be known among the heathen in our sight by the revenging of the blood of thy servants which is shed. Justice is desired that God may be vindicated and feared. It is right that those who taunted the people of God because they smarted under the Lord's rod, should themselves be made to smart by the same hand. If any complain of the spirit of this imprecation, we think they do so needlessly; for it is the common feeling of every patriot to desire to see his country's wrongs redressed, and of every Christian to wish a noble vengeance for the Church by the overthrow of error. The destruction of the Antichrist is the recompense of the blood of the martyrs, and by no means is it to be deprecated; it is by far one of the most glorious hopes of the latter days.

Psalm 79:11 *Let the sighing of the prisoner come before thee; according to the greatness of thy power preserve thou those that are appointed to die;*

EXPOSITION: Verse 11. *Let the sighing of the prisoner come before thee.* When your people cannot sing, and dare not shout aloud, then let their silent sigh ascend into your ear, and secure for them deliverance. These words are suitable for the afflicted in a great variety of conditions; men of experience will know how to adapt them to their own position and to use them in reference to others.

According to the greatness of thy power preserve thou those that are appointed to die. Faith grows while it prays; the appeal to the Lord's tender mercy is here supplemented by another addressed to the divine power, and the petitioner rises from a request for those who are brought low, to a prayer for those who are on the verge of death, set apart as victims for the slaughter. How consoling it is to desponding believers to reflect that God can preserve even those who bear the sentence of death in themselves. Men and devils may consign us to perdition, while sickness drags us to the grave, and sorrow sinks us in the dust; but, there is One who can keep our soul alive, aye, and bring it up again from the depths of despair. A lamb shall live between the lion's jaws if the Lord wills it. Even in the charnel,[169] life shall vanquish death if God is near.

Psalm 79:12 *And render unto our neighbours sevenfold into their bosom their reproach, wherewith they have reproached thee, O Lord.*

EXPOSITION: **Verse 12.** *And render unto our neighbours sevenfold into their bosom their reproach, wherewith they have reproached thee, O Lord.* They denied your existence, mocked your power, insulted your worship, and destroyed your house; up, therefore, O Lord, and make them feel to the full that you are not to be mocked with impunity. Pour into their laps a good store of shame because they dared insult the God of Israel. Recompense them fully, until they have received the perfect number of punishments. It will be so. The wish of the text will become matter of fact. The Lord will avenge His own elect though He bears long with them.

Psalm 79:13 *So we thy people and sheep of thy pasture will give thee thanks for ever: we will shew forth thy praise to all generations.*

---

169. cemetery

EXPOSITION: **Verse 13.** *So we thy people and sheep of thy pasture will give thee thanks for ever: we will shew forth thy praise to all generations.* The gratitude of the Church is lasting as well as deep. On her tablets are memorials of great deliverances, and, as long as she shall exist, her sons will rehearse them with delight. We have a history which will survive all other records, and it is bright in every line with the glory of the Lord. From the direst calamities God's glory springs, and the dark days of His people become the prelude to unusual displays of the Lord's love and power.

STUDY GUIDE

1.) In Psalm 51:1 note how King David appeals to three attributes of God. List those attributes and what they mean to you.

_____
_____
_____
_____

2.) David wrote in Psalm 51:4, *Against thee, thee only, have I sinned, and done this evil in thy sight: that thou mightest be justified when thou speakest, and be clear when thou judgest. Against thee, thee only, have I sinned.* Question: David had sinned against other people. Why does he say he has sinned only against God?

_____

3.) Saul persistently sought to persecute and even kill David though David did him no evil but helped him often. David well knew the power that Saul had and his intent to kill him. Yet, what did David say in Psalm 59:11 about God slaying his enemies? Why did he pray this way?

_____
_____
_____

4.) Psalm 63:1—*O God, thou art my God; early will I seek thee: my soul thirsteth for thee, my flesh longeth for thee in a dry and thirsty land, where no water is.*

The God-loved and forgiven King David passionately cries out his allegiance to the only living God; and firm faith enables him to claim Him as his own. David has learned also to seek time with God early in the morning when everything is fresh—the beginning of a brand new day. Note David's eagerness to be in communion with the Lord. He has learned that this is the way to live constantly in His presence. This relationship is for all believers. Have you sought this blessing today? Encourage others to seek Him by telling them how it has helped and blessed you in your spiritual growth. Write out this psalm in your own words and make it your prayer today.

_____
_____
_____
_____

5.) Psalm 68:9—*Thou, O God, didst send a plentiful rain, whereby thou didst confirm thine inheritance, when it was weary.* God supplied the Israelites with everything they needed during their forty years in the wilderness. There are at least fourteen needs He supplied mentioned in Spurgeon's exposition of this verse. Turn to the exposition and list the ones you find there.

_____
_____
_____
_____
_____

6.) Psalm 68:18—Thou hast ascended on high, thou hast led captivity captive: thou hast received gifts for men; yea, for the rebellious also, that the LORD God might dwell among them. In Ephesians 4:8–13, the Apostle Paul lists five gifts that God has bestowed on the Church after Christ's ascension. What are they?
1. _____ 2. _____ 3. _____ 4. _____ 5. _____

STUDY GUIDE

7.) In Psalm 71:22–24 David praises the Lord extravagantly. Name the three distinct ways that David gives praise unto the Lord in these Scriptures.
1. _____
2. _____
3. _____

8.) Psalm 79:13—*So we thy people and sheep of thy pasture will give thee thanks for ever: we will shew forth thy praise to all generations.* Spurgeon writes: "From the direst calamities God's glory springs, and the dark days of His people become the prelude to unusual displays of the Lord's love and power." How have you seen this truth in your own life? How can you show forth praise to God for what He has done for you, even in your greatest difficulties?

Pure Gold Classics
Timeless Truth in a Distinctive, Best-Selling Collection

An Expanding Collection of the Best-Loved Christian Classics of All Time.
AVAILABLE AT FINE BOOKSTORES.
FOR MORE INFORMATION, VISIT WWW.BRIDGELOGOS.COM

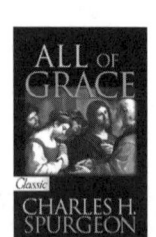

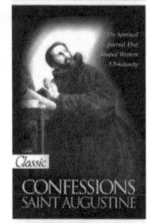

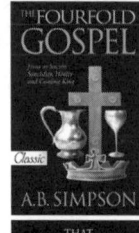

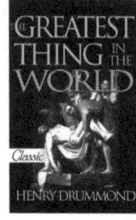

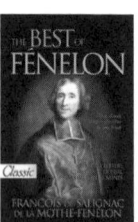

- ABSOLUTE SURRENDER — Andrew Murray
- ALL OF GRACE — Charles H. Spurgeon
- THE AMAZING WORKS OF JOHN NEWTON
- ANSWERS TO PRAYER — George Mueller
- THE BEST OF FENELON — François de Salignac de la Mothe-Fénelon
- THE CHRISTIAN'S SECRET OF A HAPPY LIFE — Hannah Whitall Smith
- CONFESSIONS — Saint Augustine
- DARK NIGHT OF THE SOUL AND OTHER GREAT WORKS — Saint John of the Cross
- E. M. BOUNDS THE CLASSIC COLLECTION ON PRAYER
- EVENING BY EVENING — Charles H. Spurgeon
- FINNEY ON REVIVAL — Charles G. Finney
- THE FOURFOLD GOSPEL — A. B. Simpson
- FOXE'S BOOK OF MARTYRS — John Foxe
- GOD THE CREATOR — John Calvin
- GOD THE REDEEMER — John Calvin
- GOD OF ALL COMFORT — Hannah Whitall Smith
- THAT GOD MAY BE ALL IN ALL — Andrew Murray
- GRACE ABOUNDING TO THE CHIEF OF SINNERS — John Bunyan
- THE GREATEST THING IN THE WORLD — Henry Drummond
- R. A. TORREY: THE HOLY SPIRIT — WHO HE IS AND WHAT HE DOES

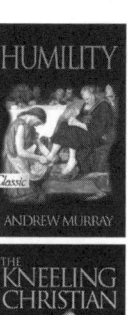

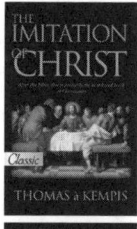

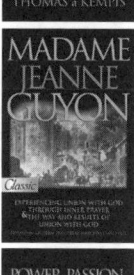

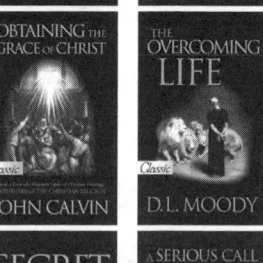

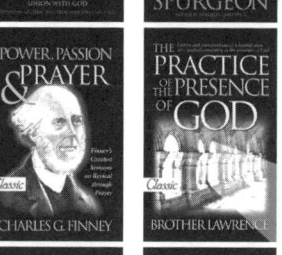

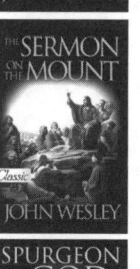

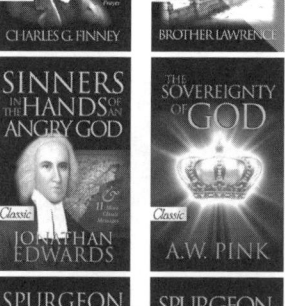

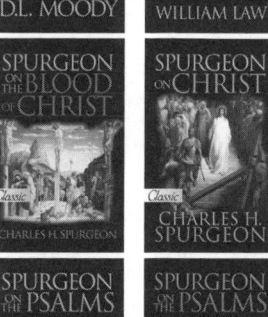

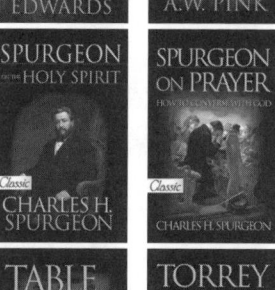

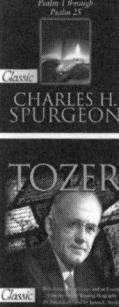

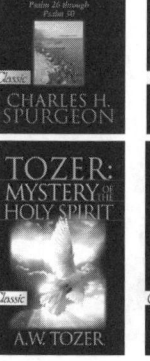

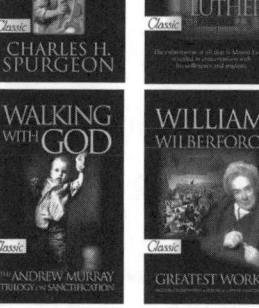

THE HOLY SPIRIT POWER — JOHN WESLEY	THE HOLY CATHOLIC CHURCH — JOHN CALVIN	HUMILITY — ANDREW MURRAY	THE IMITATION OF CHRIST — THOMAS à KEMPIS	IN HIS STEPS — CHARLES M. SHELDON	
INTERIOR CASTLE — TERESA OF AVILA	JEWELS FROM E.M. BOUNDS — E.M. BOUNDS	THE KNEELING CHRISTIAN — AN UNKNOWN CHRISTIAN	MADAME JEANNE GUYON	MORNING BY MORNING — CHARLES H. SPURGEON	
OBTAINING THE GRACE OF CHRIST — JOHN CALVIN	THE OVERCOMING LIFE — D.L. MOODY	THE PILGRIM'S PROGRESS IN MODERN ENGLISH — JOHN BUNYAN	POWER, PASSION & PRAYER — CHARLES G. FINNEY	THE PRACTICE OF THE PRESENCE OF GOD — BROTHER LAWRENCE	
SECRET POWER — D.L. MOODY	A SERIOUS CALL TO A DEVOUT & HOLY LIFE — WILLIAM LAW	THE SERMON ON THE MOUNT — JOHN WESLEY	SINNERS IN THE HANDS OF AN ANGRY GOD — JONATHAN EDWARDS	THE SOVEREIGNTY OF GOD — A.W. PINK	
SPURGEON ON THE BLOOD OF CHRIST — CHARLES H. SPURGEON	SPURGEON ON CHRIST — CHARLES H. SPURGEON	SPURGEON ON GOD — CHARLES H. SPURGEON	SPURGEON ON THE HOLY SPIRIT — CHARLES H. SPURGEON	SPURGEON ON PRAYER — CHARLES H. SPURGEON	
SPURGEON ON THE PSALMS, BOOK ONE (Psalm 1 through Psalm 25) — CHARLES H. SPURGEON	SPURGEON ON THE PSALMS, BOOK TWO (Psalm 26 through Psalm 50) — CHARLES H. SPURGEON	SPURGEON ON THE PSALMS, BOOK THREE (Psalm 51 through Psalm 79) — CHARLES H. SPURGEON	TABLE TALK — MARTIN LUTHER	TORREY ON PRAYER: THE POWER OF PRAYER & THE PRAYER OF POWER	
TOZER: FELLOWSHIP OF THE BURNING HEART	TOZER: MYSTERY OF THE HOLY SPIRIT — A.W. TOZER	WALKING WITH GOD — THE ANDREW MURRAY TRILOGY ON SANCTIFICATION	WILLIAM WILBERFORCE GREATEST WORKS	WITH CHRIST IN THE SCHOOL OF PRAYER — ANDREW MURRAY	